D0220853

The Handbook of International Trade and Finance

THIRD EDITION

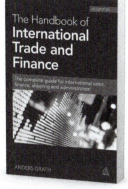

The Handbook of International Trade and Finance

Anders Grath

KoganPage

LONDON   PHILADELPHIA   NEW DELHI

Publisher's note

Every possible effort has been made to ensure that the information contained in this book is accurate at the time of going to press, and the publishers and author cannot accept responsibility for any errors or omissions, however caused. No responsibility for loss or damage occasioned to any person acting, or refraining from action, as a result of the material in this publication can be accepted by the editor, the publisher or the author.

First published in Great Britain in 2005 by Nordia Publishing Ltd for The Institute of Export as *International Trade Finance*
Published in Great Britain and the United States in 2008 by Kogan Page Limited as *The Handbook of International Trade and Finance*
Second edition 2012
Third edition 2014

Apart from any fair dealing for the purposes of research or private study, or criticism or review, as permitted under the Copyright, Designs and Patents Act 1988, this publication may only be reproduced, stored or transmitted, in any form or by any means, with the prior permission in writing of the publishers, or in the case of reprographic reproduction in accordance with the terms and licences issued by the CLA. Enquiries concerning reproduction outside these terms should be sent to the publishers at the undermentioned addresses:

2nd Floor, 45 Gee Street   1518 Walnut Street, Suite 1100   4737/23 Ansari Road
London EC1V 3RS   Philadelphia PA 19102   Daryaganj
United Kingdom   USA   New Delhi 110002
www.koganpage.com   India

© Anders Grath, 2005, 2008, 2012, 2014

The right of Anders Grath to be identified as the author of this work has been asserted by him in accordance with the Copyright, Designs and Patents Act 1988.

ISBN   978 0 7494 6954 2
E-ISBN 978 0 7494 6955 9

British Library Cataloguing-in-Publication Data

A CIP record for this book is available from the British Library.

Library of Congress Cataloging-in-Publication Data

Grath, Anders, 1943-
  The handbook of international trade and finance : the complete guide for international sales, finance, shipping and administration / Anders Grath. – Third edition.
     pages cm
  Includes index.
  ISBN 978-0-7494-6954-2 – ISBN 978-0-7494-6955-9 (ebk)   1. International trade.
2. International finance.   I. Title.
  HF1379.G725 2013
  332'.042–dc23
                                                                         2013027700

Typeset by Graphicraft Limited, Hong Kong
Printed and bound in India by Replika Press Pvt Ltd

CONTENTS

Preface vii
Acknowledgements/Disclaimer ix

Introduction 1

01 Trade risks and risk assessment 9

International trade practices 9
Product risks 15
Commercial risks (purchaser risks) 19
Adverse business risks 21
Political risks 24
Currency risks 27
Financial risks 29

02 Methods of payment 33

Different methods of payment 33
Bank transfer (bank remittance) 36
Cheque payments 45
Documentary collection 47
Letter of credit 54
Counter-trade 74

03 Bonds, guarantees and standby letters of credit 77

The use of bonds and guarantees 77
Common forms of guarantee 85
Demand guarantees 90
Standby letters of credit 92
The structure and design of guarantees 95

04   Currency risk management   99

Currency risk   99
The currency markets   102
The spot trade   102
Currency exposure   106
Hedging currency risks   110
Practical currency management   118

05   Export credit insurance   121

A mutual undertaking   121
The private sector insurance market   124
Export credit agencies (official export credit institutions)   129
Investment insurance   139

06   Trade finance   141

Finance alternatives   141
Pre-shipment finance   143
Supplier credits   146
Refinancing of supplier credits   151
Buyer credits   160
The international money market   165

07   Structured trade finance   169

International leasing   169
Lines of credit and local currency finance   174
Project finance and joint venture   176
Multilateral development banks   180

08   Terms of payment   185

Terms of payment and cash management   185
Contents of the terms of payment   186
Structure of the terms of payment   190
Composite terms of payment   194
The final design of the terms of payment   197

Glossary of terms and abbreviations   199
Index   219

PREFACE

This handbook was originally published more than 30 years ago, and has since been expanded and updated in new editions. Originally it was published as separate country-specific editions in different European countries where it soon become a reference handbook for companies, banks and other institutions involved in international trade, irrespective of their size or the nature of their business.

However, for practical and logistical reasons it was not possible to cover more than a handful of countries in this way, thus the idea for a completely new and country-neutral edition that could be marketed in most countries involved in international trade around the world. The only drawback with this approach is that it is then not feasible to describe the specifics for every country; on the other hand, the basic aspects of international trade, payments and finance are almost the same all over the world, which is also the foundation for this handbook.

Furthermore, there is great advantage in being able to combine this basic description with detailed references where such country-specific information can be found. This information is nowadays readily available from internet sites from a variety of domestic institutions in most countries. It has then been possible to create a situation where this book provides both this foundation but also at the same time giving readers from all over the world the possibility to add whatever detailed and country-specific information they require. There is another big advantage in such an approach: that the basics of this handbook should be relatively stable over time, whereas detailed information from local and domestic institutions will certainly change over time.

All editions published over the years have been based on the same concept, which is their practical nature. They contain no theoretical elements, just information based on the author's 30 years of payment and finance experience gained from managerial positions as head of international departments in a number of European banks. In such positions you are necessarily involved in thousands of trade transactions each year, and the advice and comments given in this book are based on that experience.

I am very pleased with this third international edition now published by Kogan Page, and feel confident that it will continue to be the reference handbook of choice in numerous countries around the world, for many years to come. It will certainly be of significant benefit to international traders in the daily work of expanding their businesses or when entering new global markets, but the book will equally be increasingly used in trade education and as a practical tool within international departments of commercial banks and other trade-related institutions.

ACKNOWLEDGEMENTS/ DISCLAIMER

The author would like to thank the companies, banks and other institutions that have contributed with support, advice and comments when creating this book; however, the author is solely responsible for the views, illustrations and recommendations expressed.

While every care has been taken to ensure the accuracy of this work, no responsibility for loss occasioned to any person or company acting or refraining from action as a result of any statement in it can be accepted by the author or publisher.

Introduction

An international trade transaction, no matter how straightforward it may seem at the start, is not completed until delivery has taken place, any other obligations have been fulfilled and the seller has received payment. This may seem obvious; however, even seemingly simple transactions can, and sometimes do, go wrong.

There are many reasons why these things happen, but behind them all is the basic fact that the risk assessment of the transaction and/or the way these risks were covered went wrong. An example is the risk assessment of the customer, where exporters do not always fully realize that some larger countries are divided into regions or states, often with different cultures, which may affect trade patterns and practices. In some countries, what the seller thought was a signed contract may just be seen as a letter of intent by the buyer until it also has been countersigned by them by a more senior and internally authorizing manager. Or it may be that the seller has agreed to terms that were previously used but are not suitable in a changed environment.

Another reason may be that the parties simply did not use the same terminology or did not focus on the details of the agreed terms of payment. This would inevitably lead to undefined terms, which are potentially subject to future disputes, something that would perhaps not be revealed until delivery has been made – when the seller is in a weaker bargaining position. Even though such errors may not result in non-payment, it is more likely that they will lead to delays in payment, with an increased commercial and/or political risk as a consequence.

Another common consequence of unclear or undefined terms of payment is that the seller may have outstanding claims on the buyer; or that the buyer is of the same opinion with regard to the seller and takes the opportunity to make unilateral payment deductions owing to real or alleged faults or deficiencies in the delivery.

Each area of international trade requires its own knowledge to be used, from the first contact between buyer and seller to final payment. One such area of expertise is therefore how to develop professional and undisputed terms of payment and how to solve currency and trade finance questions in a competitive way. These areas are of vital importance both in the offer and in subsequent contract discussions, not just within difficult countries or markets or in larger, more complicated deals, but also in quite ordinary day-to-day transactions.

The choice of currency could be of great importance, particularly in an increasingly competitive market, and the ability to extend finance has become a major competitive factor in negotiations. In such an environment the terms of such credits are mostly to the advantage of the buyer and, as a consequence, demand for longer periods and more advantageous terms has increased.

Terms of payment, currency and finance alternatives can, in some cases, and/or in similar and repetitive transactions, be developed as standard models but must, in other cases, be adapted to each transaction and its specific preconditions. This is even more obvious if one looks at Table 0.1 and evaluates the basic structure of international trade. There are also more than 150 other countries, including many developing and emerging markets, which are not even listed in this table, and in many of these markets, the structuring of the terms of payment is the key to more frequent and profitable business.

Every transaction contains many different preconditions, apart from aspects such as the buyer, the country, the nature of the goods, size, extent and complexity. This requires the seller to carry out an individual risk assessment and make decisions that ensure a profitable and secure deal, with a level of risk that is both defined and accepted at the outset.

It is therefore of great importance for both buyer and seller to know how to structure practical terms of payment. In practice this often means that during negotiations the seller must be willing and able to compromise – even when it comes to specific questions related to guarantees, payments, currency and finance. In these situations, and often together with other difficult negotiations, it is important to understand the connections between these parts, what is essential to hold on to and what can be waived.

Any successful negotiation must take reasonable and equal consideration of the demands from both commercial parties in order to find a compromise and avoid unnecessary discussions or misunderstandings. The experienced seller will always try to avoid such situations, thereby strengthening also the potential for future business deals, provided that fundamental demands have been met to safeguard the transaction.

This handbook should be used as a reference manual in the practical day-to-day business of the international trading company within the sales,

TABLE 0.1 Leading exporters and importers in world merchandise trade, 2011 (billion US$)

Exporters			Importers		
1	China	1898	1	United States	2266
2	United States	1480	2	China	1743
3	Germany	1472	3	Germany	1254
4	Japan	823	4	Japan	855
5	Netherlands	661	5	France	714
6	France	596	6	United Kingdom	638
7	Korea, Republic of	555	7	Netherlands	599
8	Italy	523	8	Italy	557
9	Russian Federation	522	9	Korea, Republic of	524
10	Belgium	477	10	Hong Kong, China	511
				– retained imports	130
11	United Kingdom	473	11	Canada	463
12	Hong Kong, China	456	12	India	463
	– domestic exports	17			
	– re-exports	439			
13	Canada	452	13	Belgium	461
14	Singapore	410	14	Spain	374
	– domestic exports	224			
	– re-exports	186			
15	Saudi Arabia	365	15	Singapore	366
				– retained imports	180
16	Mexico	350	16	Mexico	361
17	Spain	309	17	Russian Federation	324
18	Taipei, Chinese	308	18	Taipei, Chinese	281
19	India	305	19	Australia	244
20	United Arab Emirates	285	20	Turkey	241
21	Australia	270	21	Brazil	237
22	Brazil	256	22	Thailand	228
23	Switzerland	234	23	Switzerland	208
24	Thailand	229	24	Poland	208
25	Malaysia	227	25	United Arab Emirates	205
26	Indonesia	201	26	Austria	191
27	Poland	187	27	Malaysia	188
28	Sweden	187	28	Indonesia	177
29	Austria	178	29	Sweden	176
30	Czech Republic	162	30	Czech Republic	152
31	Norway	159	31	Saudi Arabia	132
32	Turkey	135	32	South Africa	122
33	Iran	132	33	Viet Nam	107
	World	**18255***		**World**	**18438***

* Includes significant re-exports or imports for re-export.

SOURCE: WTO, World Trade Statistics 2011
(**www.wto.org/english/res_e/statis_e/its2012_e/its2012_e.pdf**)

FIGURE 0.1 World commodity profiles 2011

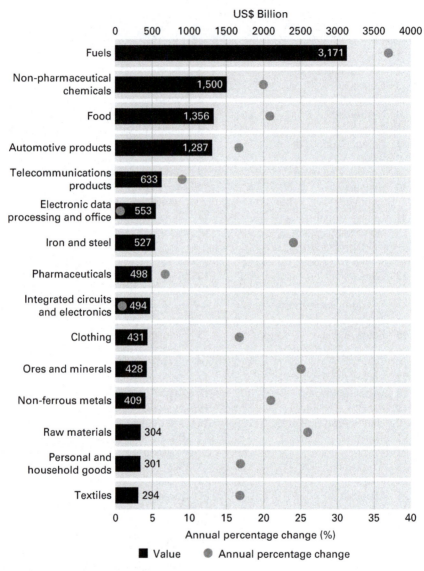

SOURCE: WTO, World Trade Statistics 2011
(**http://www.wto.org/english/res_e/statis_e/its2012_e/its2012_e.pdf**)

shipping, administrative and back-office departments. For small- and medium-sized companies that do not always have the specialist finance functions in-house this is obvious, but this will also be the case even within the largest companies, where specialization often means that many employees have detailed knowledge in some, but not all, of these financial areas.

This goes not only for the exporting company, but also within importing companies buying goods or services from abroad. Many comments and references will also be made in this book about the interactive negotiating process between the commercial parties in an international trade transaction; useful knowledge for both the seller and the buyer.

That is exactly the way these handbooks have been used over the years.

Cash management

One important development over recent years has been the demand for capital rationalization, or 'cash management'. This has affected all aspects of business, not least the sections covered in this handbook.

It is especially obvious within the areas of payment, currency and finance where every decision has direct consequences on the capital required during all phases of the transaction, until payment is received.

This handbook demonstrates primarily how the seller can act, within the framework of a defined risk level and with their competitive edge maintained, to optimize the profitability of international trade transactions. They can then also determine, with a high degree of accuracy, when, where and how payments will be made and therefore how to minimize the capital required. The concept of risk is directly connected to the probability of timely payment, the choice of currency related to the exchange rate when paid and the financing connected to the cost of the outstanding credit. The importer will use the same knowledge, but from their own perspective.

The expression 'cash management' is seldom explicitly used in the text, but most sections contain comments or advice that, directly or indirectly, has a bearing on the use and the latent risk of the amounts involved. With this in mind, this handbook could also be read as a manual for improved cash management in connection with international trade (more on this is in the final chapter concerning the practical structure and design of the terms of payment).

The main composition of this handbook

This handbook is intended to be a practical reference guide to help in the daily work – mainly seen from the perspective of the seller – within sales, shipping and administration. The contents have, therefore, been structured as follows:

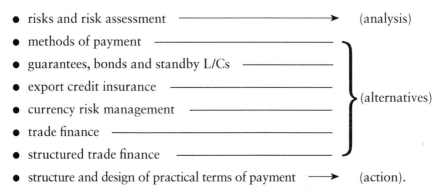

- risks and risk assessment ⟶ (analysis)
- methods of payment
- guarantees, bonds and standby L/Cs
- export credit insurance
- currency risk management   } (alternatives)
- trade finance
- structured trade finance
- structure and design of practical terms of payment ⟶ (action).

To get a clearer picture of the focus of this handbook, please consider the following questions and answers:

1 Why are some companies doing more frequent and successful export deals than others?

It is because they manage to cover even the most difficult export risks – only then are they in the best position to enter totally new markets.

Sell more – win market shares – enter new markets.

Who doesn't want that? But the problem is often not making the sale but ensuring that you get paid.

Why do things sometimes go wrong in the export chain, from quotation to payment – or in the worst case, non-payment? The answer is that the seller often underestimates, or simply does not fully understand, the risks involved in the transaction. Or the seller does not get the terms of payment originally anticipated and, at that stage, does not manage to cover the transaction in some other way, or even abstains from the deal altogether. Basically it is a matter of learning how to cover the trade risks in a professional way, allowing the seller to manage transactions even in the more difficult parts of the world.

However, the follow-up must also be done professionally at home.

2   What is needed is effective handling of the transaction until shipment occurs and, thereafter, effective debt supervision.

Time is money – look at the time arrow below.

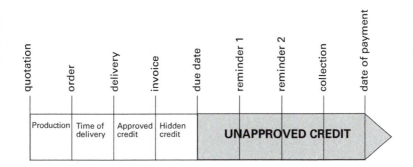

The follow-up starts immediately after the contract is signed. It can be a forward currency hedge, the issuing of guarantees, communication with the insurance company about an export credit risk policy or follow-up of the obligations of the buyer, for example the correct issue of a letter of credit. To end up in the grey area of the time arrow is always risky; there the seller is more exposed – the goods have been shipped but without payment being received in time.

Worst of all, if pre-shipment control is not in place, even the most secure letter of credit may be worthless if the seller is not able to comply fully with its terms later on. It is often in sales negotiations in foreign countries far away from the home organization that the details for a profitable transaction have to be decided. And once the deal is signed, it may be difficult to get changes to the advantage of the seller – not least regarding the terms of payment.

The follow-up is crucial and will ultimately decide the profitability of the transaction.

Trade risks and risk assessment

International trade practices

All forms of business contain elements of risk, but when it comes to international trade, the risk profile enters a new dimension. Internationally, you seldom have common laws that can support the transaction, as would be the case within one country. Instead, established trade practices and conventions are used to settle the undertakings made by the parties. The main sources for international trade practices are publications issued by the International Chamber of Commerce (ICC), which will be referred to many times throughout this book.

Successful trade transactions, therefore, depend on a knowledge of these established practices and ensuring that the undertakings in the individual contract are in line with such practices. This is why it is crucial for the seller to have started with a correct risk assessment before entering into the transaction. Sometimes, however, the circumstances in a particular case are so obvious that one hardly thinks of it as a risk assessment, whereas in other situations a thorough risk assessment needs to be done.

In every new transaction one has to take it for granted that, from the outset, the parties will have at least somewhat different views about various aspects of the terms of payment. This is quite logical since the most important function of these terms for both seller and buyer is to minimize not only the risks involved, but also the cost of payment and of the financing of the transaction.

The negotiation process

The seller will always try to get terms that will maximize the outcome and minimize the risk. However, they must also be prepared to accommodate reasonable demands from the buyer in order to match other competitors and reach a deal that is acceptable to both parties, thereby also developing a good long-term business relationship.

Should the seller be inflexible on this point, it could result in an adverse competitive situation with the potential risk of losing the deal. On the other hand, demands from the buyer that are too stringent can have the same result, or be resolved by means of a higher price or some other adjustment to the final agreement.

The outcome of these negotiations will depend on past knowledge and experience, which is even more important if the buyer bases their request for tender on simplified or standardized terms of payment, usually to their own advantage. In many cases, such terms are adapted to conditions that are not optimal for the seller, compared with what the seller could have reached if they were individually negotiated. In such a case it is important to be able to argue and convince the buyer that there might be other solutions that can satisfy any reasonable demands, in order to find the optimal result for both parties.

There is, however, another – and in many countries very common – way to bridge the gap between the parties, if the seller has to abstain from some demands in negotiations with the buyer. The seller could instead approach a third party, often a credit insurance company, to reduce the commercial risk that could not be covered through the agreed terms of payment.

Finally, it should be noted that the business practices that have been established over time in different countries or regions also create at least a common ground for both parties when starting their payment negotiations, ie choice of currency, form of payment and terms of financing. Local banks, trade councils and the chambers of commerce in both the seller's and the buyer's country can draw on their experience and give impartial advice on local business practice regarding both the form of payment and the more specific terms of payment, while also taking the size, commodity and other aspects of the potential transaction into account. Such considerations can then be the starting point for negotiations between the parties.

Different forms of trade risk

There are always potential drawbacks in trying to categorize such a general concept as trade risks which could have so many different forms and shapes, but it also has great illustrational advantages, particularly when they also coincide with commonly used business expressions. Figure 1.1 shows the main risk structure in international trade, which will affect both the seller's and the buyer's view of the terms of payment.

Obviously, all these risks combined do not often occur in one and the same transaction. For example, a sale to a Norwegian customer in USD may

FIGURE 1.1 Different form of risk in international trade

be just a matter of a straight commercial risk on the buyer, whereas delivery of a tailor-made machine to Indonesia has to be risk assessed in quite another way.

In quite general terms, the risk structure is directly linked to the obligations undertaken by the seller. This assessment can often be made relatively simple as a commercial risk only, but, in other cases, for example if the transaction also involves assembly, installation, testing or a maintenance responsibility, the assessment has to involve many other aspects as well.

The question of risk is to a large degree a subjective evaluation, but it is still important for both parties to have a good knowledge of these matters in order to carry out a proper and meaningful risk assessment. Only thereafter does the question arise about how to cover these risks through the terms of payment together with other limitations in the contract, if applicable, and together with separate credit risk insurance or guarantees, as the case may be.

It should also be noted that most export credit insurance, taken by the seller as additional security, could be impaired or even invalid should the seller themselves not have fulfilled – or been able to fulfil – their obligations according to the contract. This is another reason why it is so important that the obligations of the seller, according to the contract, are always directly related to those of the buyer. Otherwise the seller may end up in a risk situation that is worse than anticipated at the time of entering into the contract.

When all the necessary evaluations have been done, the final decision as to whether the deal is secure enough to be entered into has to be taken. The worst that can happen is finding, after the contract has been signed, that it contains risks that the seller was unaware of at that time. It is then often too late to make changes on equal terms.

Terms of delivery and terms of payment

This handbook describes in detail the structure and design of the terms of payment as an integral part of the contract. However, the terms of delivery also have to be defined in order to determine when and where the seller has fulfilled the obligations to deliver according to the contract and what is needed to do so. There is a clear connection between these two sets of terms insofar as payment is mostly related to the point at which the risk passes from the seller to the buyer as specified by the terms of delivery; it is to be made either at that particular time or at a specific time thereafter. This connection makes it necessary to outline some basic facts about the different terms of delivery.

The standard rules of reference for the interpretation of the most commonly used trade terms in international trade are Incoterms® (International Commercial Terms), issued by the International Chamber of Commerce (ICC). These rules are now generally recognized throughout the world, so any other unspecified trading terms, which may often have different meanings for companies in different countries, should be avoided.

Due to a number of changes in both global and domestic trade during recent years, a new version of Incoterms came into effect on 1 January 2011, referred to as Incoterms® 2010 (ICC publication 715), which are now also officially endorsed by the United Nations Trade Law Commission, confirming their position as the global standard for international business transactions. However, all contracts made under the former Incoterms 2000 remain valid even after 2011, and it is therefore important always to clearly specify the chosen version.

The basic purpose of the rules is to define how each Incoterm, as agreed in the sales contract, should be dealt with in terms of delivery, risks and costs, and specify the responsibility of the buyer and seller. For example, who should arrange and pay freight, other transport charges, insurance, duties and taxes? These aspects are often referred to as the critical points in international trade, detailing at what point the risk is transferred from the seller to the buyer and how the costs involved should be split between the parties.

The new Incoterms 2010 consists of 11 terms, separated into two groups, namely:

1 *Those applicable to all modes of transport:*

EXW: EX WORKS (... named place of delivery)
FCA: FREE CARRIER (... named place of delivery)
CPT: CARRIAGE PAID TO (... named place of destination)
CIP: CARRIAGE AND INSURANCE PAID TO (... named place of destination)
DAT: DELIVERED AT TERMINAL (... named terminal at port or place of destination)
DAP: DELIVERED AT PLACE (... named place of destination)
DDP: DELIVERED DUTY PAID (... named place)

2 *Those only applicable to sea and inland waterway transport:*

FAS: FREE ALONGSIDE SHIP (... named port of shipment)
FOB: FREE ON BOARD (... named port of shipment)
CFR: COST AND FREIGHT (... named port of destination)
CIF: COST, INSURANCE AND FREIGHT (... named port of destination)

Complete details are available in the ICC publication 715, but considerable information can also be obtained via the internet.

When choosing the appropriate terms of delivery, deciding factors (here seen from the seller's perspective) include:

- the mode of transport and the transportation route, the buyer and the nature of the goods;
- standard practice, if any, in the buyer's country or any regulation set by the authorities of that country to benefit their own transport or insurance industry;
- procedures, where the seller should avoid terms of delivery, which are dependent on obtaining import licences or clearance of goods to countries they cannot properly judge;
- the competitive situation, where the buyer often suggests their preferred terms of delivery and the seller has to evaluate these terms in relation to the risks involved.

The International Chamber of Commerce (ICC)

The ICC is the world's only truly global business organization and is recognized as the voice of international business. Based in Paris, its core services/activities include:

- practical services to business;
- working against commercial crime;
- being an advocate for international business;
- spreading business expertise;
- promoting growth and prosperity;
- setting rules and standards;
- promoting the multilateral trading system.

ICC membership groups thousands of companies of every size in over 130 countries worldwide, mainly through its national committees. They represent a broad cross-section of business activity, including manufacturing, trade, services and the professions.

Through membership of the ICC, companies shape rules and policies that stimulate international trade and investment. These companies in turn count on the prestige and expertise of the ICC to get business views across to governments and intergovernmental organizations, whose decisions affect corporate finances and operations worldwide.

The ICC makes policy and rules in a number of areas related to the contents of this book. This includes terms of delivery as described in this chapter and banking techniques and practices for documentary payments and guarantees as described in Chapters 2 and 3, but also areas such as anti-corruption, arbitration and commercial law and practice. The ICC runs a comprehensive bookshop specializing in these areas, where the complete texts can be found.

Further information about the ICC and the ICC Business Bookshop can be found at **www.iccwbo.org** and **www.iccbooks.com**.

For a standard delivery between established trade partners, neighbouring countries or countries belonging to a common trading area, these terms are often easily agreed upon as a matter of standard practice with only an adjustment related to the actual freight and insurance charges, often in connection with open account trading. In these cases, the buyer often takes the main responsibility for transport and risk of the purchased goods. However, in other cases the seller wants to have better control of the delivery process and to be able to select transport and/or insurance, and consequently chooses delivery terms where these aspects are better protected.

Product risks

Product risks are risks that the seller automatically has to accept as an integral part of their commitment. First, it is a matter of the product itself, or the agreed delivery; for example, specified performance warranties or agreed maintenance or service obligations.

There are many examples of how new and unexpected working conditions in the buyer's country have led to reduced performance of the delivered goods. It could be negligence concerning operating procedures or restrictions, careless treatment or lack of current maintenance, but also damage due to the climate or for environmental reasons.

Commercial documentation and official requirements

The preceding pages give a description of the relation between the terms of delivery and the terms of payment, including the consequential insurance aspects. These areas have to be integral parts of the sales contract, detailed in such a way that it leaves no doubt about the responsibility involved for both parties.

The sales contract should therefore include information about, or reference to, commercial documentation and official requirements. This is most easily dealt with in standard and recurring trade, but in other cases it may be a major issue that must be worded in detail in order to avoid disputes later.

The standard shipping documentation for ordinary deliveries is described in Chapter 2. It is important to remember that many importing countries have specific requirements regarding not only layout and contents but also verification or legalization of these documents, often by assigned authorities or chosen parties. Most exporting countries have trade councils or other similar bodies to assist in such matters (the forwarding agent may also have a similar role). The exporter should never underestimate the time needed for such a task, which could substantially delay the period between shipment and due preparation of the documentation.

There are often other official requirements to deal with, such as export declarations for customs and value added tax (VAT) purposes in the exporting country. Import licences or certificates related to import permission, duty, VAT or import sales tax in the importing country also need to be considered. However, when such requirements or uncertainties arise in the buyer's country, the established trade practice has mostly been adjusted accordingly, including the use of terms of payment that automatically reduce or eliminate such risks. This is described in detail in 'Documentary collection' and 'Letter of Credit' in Chapter 2.

Matters of this nature may well lead to disputes between the parties after the contract has been signed and to increased cost for the delivery as a whole. It is important for the seller to have the contract, and specifically the terms of payment, worded in such a way that any such changes, which are directly or indirectly due to the actions of the buyer or originating within their country, will automatically include compensation or corresponding changes in the seller's commitments. This can be in economic terms, in originally agreed time limits, or both.

It goes without saying that these risks become even more complicated when it comes to whole projects or larger and more complex contracts. These are often completed over longer periods and involve many more possible combinations of interrelated commitments between the commercial parties, not only between the seller and the buyer, but also often involving other parties in the buyer's country, both commercial and political.

Manufacturing risks

The concept of product risk could also include some elements of the manufacturing process itself (although in principle that subject falls beyond the scope of this handbook). This risk appears all too frequently when the product is tailor-made or has unique specifications. In these cases there is often no other readily available buyer if the transaction cannot be completed, in which case the seller has to carry the cost of any necessary readjustment, if that is even an option.

Risks of this nature occur as early as the product planning phase but may often be difficult to cover from that time owing to the special nature of these products. But they also involve specific risks for the buyer, who often has to enter into payment obligations at an early stage but without the security of the product itself until it has been delivered and installed. To safeguard the interests of both parties, the terms of payment are often divided into part-payments related to the production and delivery phases, in combination with separate guarantees, to cover the risks as they occur in different phases of the transaction.

Transport risks and cargo insurance

From a general risk perspective it is not only the product but also the physical movement of the goods from the seller to the buyer that has to be evaluated, based on aspects such as the nature of the product, size of delivery, the buyer and their country, and the actual transportation route. Most goods in international trade, apart from smaller and non-expensive deliveries, are covered by cargo insurance, providing cover against physical loss or damage while in transit, by land, sea or air, or by a combination of these modes of transport.

The cover under a cargo insurance (which is a sub-branch of marine insurance) is almost always defined by standard policy wordings issued by the Institute of London Underwriters (or the American Institute of Marine Underwriters). These are called Institute Cargo Clauses. While there are numerous clauses that will apply to different cargos, the widest cover is provided under Institute Cargo Clauses A (Institute Cargo Clauses [Air] for transport by air), or with more restrictive cover under Institute Cargo Clauses B and Institute Cargo Clauses C. (The new A-clauses are intended to replace the previous Institute Cargo Clauses All Risks.) Cargo insurance is therefore normally provided through one of these Institute Cargo Clauses A, B or C, plus separate war clauses and strike clauses. This is shown in the example of a letter of credit in Chapter 2.

The question of who should arrange the insurance is determined by the agreed terms of delivery, as defined by the relevant Incoterms as described earlier. These terms also define the critical point during transport, where the risk is transferred from the seller to the buyer. That can be any given point between a named place at the seller's location (Ex Works) and a named place at the buyer's location (Delivered Duty Paid, DDP). That specified critical point determines the seller's and the buyer's responsibility to arrange insurance, as required.

However, there is another aspect of risk coverage that the seller has to be particularly aware of, and that is the potential risk of the buyer arranging insurance according to some of the terms of delivery. If such a term of delivery is chosen, for example FOB (... named port of shipment), and the buyer fails to insure in a proper and agreed way, the goods may arrive at the destination in a damaged condition and without adequate insurance cover. If, at the same time, the terms of payment allow for payment after delivery, this risk de facto becomes a risk for the seller, who may end up with unpaid for, uninsured and damaged goods at the point of destination. Such a situation is obviously a consequence of the seller agreeing to terms of payment that did not cover the actual commercial risk, but the insurance risk involved could, in most cases, have been eliminated by separate seller's interest contingency insurance, as described below.

From the seller's perspective, there are basically three different ways to insure the cargo, either with an open insurance policy covering most or all shipments within the seller's basic trade as agreed in advance with the insurer, or with a specific insurance policy, covering specific shipments on an ad hoc basis or those which are outside the set criteria of the open policy. The open policy is by far the most common in international trade, normally reviewed on an annual basis, and with a 30–60-day cancellation clause should conditions deteriorate substantially. The open cover is the most cost-effective alternative, but it also has obvious administrative advantages and will automatically secure the actual coverage of all individual shipments under the policy.

The third basic form of cargo insurance is seller's interest contingency insurance, normally only offered as a complement to the open policy or as an integral part of a specific policy, and on an undisclosed basis as far as the buyer is concerned. This insurance covers the risk that the goods may arrive at their destination in a damaged condition, resulting in the buyer's refusal to accept them (even if the risk was on their part according to the terms of delivery), or they may simply be unable or unwilling to pay for commercial or political reasons, including failure to produce a valid import licence. In such cases the insurance covers the physical loss of, or damage to, the goods but it does not cover the credit risk (commercial or political) on the buyer, which has to be covered through the terms of payment in conjunction with any other arrangements.

The seller should bear in mind that cargo insurance is a specialized business, where cover and conditions may vary according to the commodity or goods to be shipped, the transportation route and the mode of transport, which is a major reason why open policy cover is the most common in international trade. But normal risk management procedures will always apply: new and adverse conditions and/or additional risks must be reported or approved by the insurer, and the policy normally excludes loss or damage due to wilful misconduct or insufficient, unsuitable or inadequate packing or container stowage by the assured party.

Cargo insurance can be obtained directly from an insurance company or, very often today, directly through the transporting company or the forwarding agent handling the goods. In some countries it is also quite common to use independent cargo insurance brokers, who may be more able to select the most cost-efficient insurance package, based on specific conditions or the trade structure in each individual case.

However, the seller should always ensure that the selected insurer has or is part of an established international network for dealing with claims and settlement procedures. This is often also a requisite of the buyer, and if not explicitly agreed in the sales contract, such conditions may appear later on, for example in the insurance specifications in a letter of credit, as shown in the 'Letter of Credit' example in Chapter 2.

More information about cargo clauses and their coverage can be obtained through any broker, insurance or transportation company involved in international trade.

Commercial risks (purchaser risks)

Commercial risk, also called purchaser risk, is often defined as the risk of the buyer going into bankruptcy or being in any other way incapable of fulfilling their contractual obligations. One might first think of the buyer's payment obligations but, as seen above, it also covers all other obligations of the buyer, according to the contract, necessary for the seller to fulfil their obligations.

How does the seller, therefore, evaluate the buyer's ability to fulfil their obligations? In most industrialized countries within the Organization for Economic Cooperation and Development (OECD) area, it is relatively easy to obtain a fair picture of potential buyers, either to study their published accounts or to ask for an independent business credit report, which is a more reliable way of dealing with customer risks. This will often also give much broader information about the buyer and their business, and not simply some selected economic figures from which the seller often cannot draw any decisive conclusions.

Credit information

Export trade may be an important factor in the potential growth of business; however, the risks involved in carrying out international business can also be high. In little more than a decade, the world of commerce has changed dramatically. In this commercial environment, the global suppliers of credit information have become a vital source of knowledge and expertise, based on the great wealth of information that they maintain about consumers and how they behave, about businesses and how they perform, and about different markets and how they are changing.

The more the seller understands their customers, the more they are able to respond to their individual needs and circumstances. Credit information suppliers help the seller use information to reach new customers and to build, nurture and maximize lasting customer relationships. Credit information thus forms a vital part of establishing the structure of a potential export transaction and, in particular, the terms of payment to be used. In some cases the information can be provided instantly, inexpensively and in a standardized manner over the internet, but in other cases a more researched profile is required.

Each seller must have a policy for obtaining up-to-date information about the commercial risk structure in connection with any new potential buyer or business and with outstanding export receivables. How this is done may differ depending on the volume and structure of the exports, but it is recommended at least to review the business information systems offered by the larger providers and to choose an alternative that is optimal for the individual seller as to the services and costs involved.

The seller should, however, be aware that the contents and accuracy of the business information may vary, depending on the registered information available about the company. The contents can sometimes also be difficult to evaluate and questions always arise about how up to date it really is, particularly when dealing with customers outside the most advanced industrialized countries.

With buyers from non-OECD countries, the matter becomes more complicated. The information, if available, will be much more difficult to evaluate and it will be harder to assess how it has been produced and how it should be analysed. In these cases, the information probably has limited value anyway, because other risk factors, such as the political risk, may be greater – and terms of payment that reflect this combined risk have to be chosen.

The seller may also be able to get assistance abroad through the export or trade council or similar institutions in their country, and/or from the commercial sections of embassies abroad, which may assist with market surveys and other studies in that country. Banks can participate by issuing introductory letters to their branches or correspondents, enabling the seller to obtain more up-to-date information about the local business conditions and form an opinion about the buyer and their business in connection with the contract negotiations.

Providers of international credit reports

Information about potential foreign counterparts can be obtained from a number of independent providers of business information that either have their own offices in different countries or operate through correspondents or affiliated companies around the world. Such credit reports can be provided on a case-by-case basis or be part of a broader risk management solution, offered by domestic or multinational business information companies that keep huge databases of customers from all over the world.

The information required could be on an ad hoc basis or as an ongoing process of monitoring actual and potential customers. It could be of a general or more specific nature depending on what other information is already available, and delivered through various media and within different time frames, which will be reflected in the cost structure. Since domestic banks also make use of such credit information, they could in most cases give the exporter valuable advice on which provider to turn to, based on their individual needs.

Some of the global providers of credit information are listed in alphabetical order below, covering the most important trade markets with millions of companies in their databases:

- *Atradius* – a global credit information and management group of companies, providing both credit and market information through their own or partners' international network; **www.atradius.com**.

- *Coface* – one of the world's largest export insurance groups. Apart from insurance, Coface also specializes in providing global credit information on companies worldwide; **www.coface.com**.

- *D&B* (formerly Dun & Bradstreet) – one of the largest providers of business information for credit, marketing and purchasing decisions worldwide; **www.dnb.com**.

- *Experian* – a global provider of credit information and related consulting services; **www.experian.com**.

Adverse business risks

Adverse business risks include all business practices of a negative nature, which are not only common but also almost endemic in some parts of the world. This could have serious consequences for the individual transaction, but also for the general business and financial standing of the seller, as well as their moral reputation.

We are, of course, referring to all sorts of corrupt practices that flourish in many countries, particularly in connection with larger contracts or projects: bribery, money laundering and a variety of facilitation payments:

> Bribery in general can broadly be defined as the receiving or offering of an undue reward by or to any holder of public office or a private employee designed to influence them in the exercise of their duty, and thus to incline them to act contrary to the known rules of honesty and integrity.

This quotation is taken from a UK government body, and even if it is not a legal definition, it gives an accurate description of the problem.

If bribery is generally a technique to press the seller for undue rewards, money laundering often has the opposite purpose, which is to invite the seller to do a deal that may on the face of it seem very advantageous, but where the true intention is to disguise or conceal the actual origin of the money involved. It covers criminal activities, corruption and breaches of financial sanctions. It includes the handling, or aiding the handling, of assets, knowing that they are the result of crime, terrorism or illegal drug activities.

Criminal and terrorist organizations generate large sums of cash, which they need to channel into the banking, corporate and trade financial systems, and both banks and traders can innocently fall victim to such activity if not exercising due diligence. A frequently used technique is over-invoicing or inflated transactions, with or without payment to a third party, where the seller may be completely unaware that they could be part of a ruse to launder money. The seller should be particularly observant in the case of cash payments and be aware that new anti-money laundering regulations must be complied with for such payments in most countries.

A reputable business adds respectability to any organization being used for laundering operations, and money launderers will try to use any business, directly through ownership or indirectly by deceit. Developing nations are particularly vulnerable to money launderers because they usually have poorly regulated financial systems. These provide the greatest opportunities to criminals.

In general terms, a suspicious transaction is one that is outside the normal range of transactions from the seller's point of view, in particular in relation to new customers or where an old customer changes transaction structure in an unusual way. It can include:

- unusual payment settlements;
- unusual transfer instructions;
- secretiveness;

- rapid movements in and out of accounts;
- numerous transfers;
- complicated accounts structures.

Any of the above should be considered suspicious.

Bribery, money laundering and any other form of corrupt behaviour is bad for business; it distorts the normal trade patterns and gives unfair advantages to those involved in it. It is also extremely harmful for the countries themselves, owing to the damage it causes to the often fragile social fabric; it destroys the economy and is strongly counterproductive for trade and all forms of foreign investments into the country.

In the long run, such practices also prevent social and economic stability and development, and it has an especially negative impact on the most disadvantaged parts of the population. Even within the countries where these practices are frequent among individual public and private employees, it is almost always illegal, even if these countries often lack the means and the resources to tackle these problems effectively.

The need for a strong policy

The World Bank and the OECD have put a great deal of resources into combating corruption worldwide, and in most countries corruption is now illegal even when committed overseas. The companies also have full responsibility for the wrongdoings of their employees abroad when acting for the company.

As a consequence of the inclusion of anti-corruption laws, which are in place in most countries today, it is also incorporated in the procedures of their government departments, for example in the rules of the respective export credit agency (which will be described at length later in this book). Any violation of the anti-corruption statement that the seller has to give when applying for such insurance could have serious implications for its validity.

It is often not just the threat of prosecution that should most worry the seller. There have been a number of cases in which companies were allegedly involved in corrupt behaviour, but where the true circumstances were not fully disclosed. The allegation could be damaging enough, sometimes based only on rumours emanating from economic groups or political factions within the society (a frequently used method), to stop or postpone a project or to favour another bidder. Such rumours, true or false, or involving either smaller facilitation payments or large-scale bribery to senior private or public officials, can drag on for years, with economic and detrimental consequences for the company, both overseas and at home.

Every company involved in overseas trade or investments should have a clear anti-corruption policy that is implemented and clearly understood by all its employees, and supervised by the management in an appropriate way. Such a policy is also supported by local laws, which give both the company and its employees a much stronger moral and legal defence against every attempt to extort bribes from them or to induce them into any other form of corrupt practice.

Political risks

Political risk or country risk is often defined as:

> the risk of a separate commercial transaction not being realized in a contractual way due to measures emanating from the government or authority of the buyer's own or any other foreign country.

No matter how reliable the buyer may be in fulfilling their obligations and paying in local currency, their obligations to the seller (according to the contract) are nevertheless dependent on the current situation in their own country – or along the route of transport to that country.

However, in practice, it may be difficult to separate commercial and political risk because political decisions, or other similar acts by local authorities, also affect the local company and its capabilities of honouring the contract. For example, some countries may change taxes, import duties or currency regulations, often with immediate effect, which could undermine the basis for contracts already signed.

Other common measures include import restrictions or other regulations intended to promote local industry and to save foreign currency. Even with just the risks of such actions, they all have the same negative implications for the transaction and the buyer's possibility of fulfilling their part of the contract.

Seen from a broader perspective, political risk could be divided into different underlying causes, such as:

- political stability;
- social stability;
- economic stability.

Political stability (ie local political structures and ideology combined with external relations with other countries) is often seen as an important criterion of the real political risk. This stability indicates, in general terms, the likelihood or the probability of a country's involvement in, or being affected by, acts of terror, war or internal violence from groupings within the country or sanctions or blockades from other nations.

The constant risk of rapid and unexpected change in economic policy or in the form of nationalization or similar measures as a consequence of political instability will have the same effect: they are all extremely damaging for any private commercial economic activity in the country. Unfortunately, there are presently numerous examples of this political instability in many parts of the world.

Detailed country information

Before deciding the detailed terms of payment that should be proposed in each particular case, the seller should try to obtain the best background information possible about the buyer, and about the economic and political structure in the importing country. Particularly in emerging economies or developing countries, the main risk is often both political and commercial, and the terms of payment have to be structured accordingly.

Country information can be bought from specialized credit report companies, but is also often available through the domestic export council or similar institution. If that is not available, other sources that can be used, mostly free of charge, are websites from the main exporting countries, for example UK Trade & Investment, **www.ukti.gov.uk**. These sites contain information, country by country, on more general aspects that are important to exporters in most countries, such as:

- country and market profiles and key facts;

- customs and regulations;

- selling and communications;

- main export opportunities and the public procurement market;

- connections to other trade-related websites.

More detailed country information can also be obtained from the larger export insurance companies, for example Coface, through their country rating, which can be found on **www.trading-safely.com**. These sites contain more financially oriented information such as country risk assessment, insolvency trends and payment methods.

The above sources of information, together with the additional practical banking and financial experience that can be obtained from larger commercial banks, could form a good background when deciding on the terms of payment in an individual transaction.

The *social stability* of a country is also of great importance, mainly on a long-term basis. However, the developments in many countries, not only developing countries, show all too well how social instability (uneven income distribution and ethnic or religious antagonism) can turn into violence or terrorist activity that can paralyse the country or its economy, often at very short notice.

Economic stability is equally important to maintain the confidence of a country and its economy. A weak infrastructure, dependence on single export or import commodities, a high debt burden and lack of raw materials are critical factors that, together with other developments, can easily change economic stability in a short time. Even currency restrictions and other more indirect currency regulations such as introducing or abolishing different forms of 'pegging' against other currencies, often USD, could have serious economic consequences. The turbulent situation in many developing countries is a constant reminder of the fragility of economic stability in many parts of the world.

Other forms of political or similar risk

Apart from the real political risks already discussed, there are other measures taken by authorities in the buyer's home country that can affect the buyer and their ability or willingness to fulfil the transaction; for example, demands for product standards, new or changed energy or environmental requirements – measures that could have a genuine purpose or be put in place partly to act as trade barriers to promote sectors or important industries within the country. Irrespective of the purpose, such actions, often called 'non-tariff barriers', could have a negative impact on already agreed business transactions, since such measures are often introduced with immediate effect. Other, more open measures are sometimes also implemented, also often at short notice, as has been seen within the European Union (EU), for example, where the objective has been to prevent a rapid increase in imports from some emerging market countries, in order to protect the EU's own industry or allow more time to adapt to new trade patterns.

Countries involved in the transit of goods have to be considered as well as countries related to subcontractors or suppliers of crucial components. In these cases, perhaps it is not the political risk as defined, but other measures that are more important; for example, the risk of labour market conflicts in the form of strikes or lockouts that could interrupt delivery of components needed for the timely execution of the agreed sales contract.

Finally, the risk involved in ordinary force majeure clauses should be mentioned, even if the background is not political but caused by other factors outside the control of the commercial parties themselves. When used by other parties, such clauses could, for example, release a subcontractor from their delivery obligations during the periods they are applicable, with corresponding effects for the seller. Even bank guarantees and other obligations in favour of the seller could be of limited value during such periods if, as is normally the case, they only cover commitments according to a contract, which may refer to such clauses. The same goes for presentation of documents under a letter of credit, where the bank will not accept documents that have expired during such interruption.

However, when used by the seller, such clauses could protect them against actions for breach of contract, where performance of their contractual obligations is prevented by incidents outside their control. This is often referred to as 'frustration of contract' and a typical clause might say:

> The Company shall have no liability in respect of any failure or delay in fulfilling any of the Company's obligations to the extent that fulfilment thereof is prevented, frustrated, impeded and/or delayed or rendered uneconomic as a consequence of any fire, flood, earthquake, other natural disaster or Act of God, industrial dispute or other circumstances or event beyond the Company's reasonable control ('force majeure conditions').

Currency risks

If payment is going to be made in a currency other than that in which the seller incurs their costs, a new currency risk will arise. In most cases, the seller's main costs will be in their own local currency, which automatically creates such a risk if invoicing in another currency. The size of that risk will depend on the currency and the outstanding period until payment.

Since the introduction of the euro, invoicing in that currency has become increasingly common in European trade and also with sellers outside the euro zone. Even with the problems currently affecting this particular currency, the development is likely to accelerate with additional countries joining the euro zone.

Traditionally, however, the USD has been the preferred third-party currency. This applies both to international trade in general, but particularly to raw materials and certain commodities, and for many other services such as freight and insurance. It is also commonly used in countries where the United States maintains or historically has had a strong economic or political influence.

Available statistics do not always show currency distribution for international trade of goods and services, but it can generally be expected that exports invoiced in smaller trade currencies are diminishing in favour of the larger ones, and will probably continue to do so. Most exporters will therefore have to become accustomed to invoicing in foreign currency and to the management of currency risk exposure.

Assessment of currencies

Traditionally, currencies have been divided into 'strong' and 'weak', and this view has affected the general conception of preferred trade currencies, even though the highest preference is normally for the currency of the home country. The yen (JPY), the Swiss franc (CHF) and maybe some others would probably be regarded as strong currencies, while most other currencies would be seen as neutral, weak, unstable or volatile.

However, a division into strong or weak currencies may have its justification in a longer perspective where the home countries have (or have not) maintained economic and political stability over the years, together with a strong economy, low inflation and stable confidence in the future maintenance of this policy. But the development of increased trade imbalances and country indebtedness together with subsequent competitive currency devaluations aiming to strengthen a country's own exports have made currency exchange rates much more volatile in recent years.

Currency abbreviations

The International Organization for Standardization (ISO) has established official abbreviations for all currencies, which are now commonly used.

The abbreviations for some of the most common trade currencies are as follows:

US dollar	USD	Japanese yen	JPY
Euro	EUR	Chinese yuan*	CNY
Pound sterling	GBP	Swedish krona	SEK
Swiss franc	CHF	Hong Kong dollar	HKD
Canadian dollar	CAD		

* The yuan is the base unit of account while Renminbi is the name of the actual currency.

The abbreviations of currencies for most other countries can easily be found on the web; see, for example, **www.wikipedia.org**>currency codes.

Furthermore, for most parties involved in international trade it is not the long-term currency development that is most interesting, but rather the shorter perspective, limited to the time-span during which current deals are made up and finally paid. Then the situation can be reversed, for in that shorter perspective a currency can have a development in complete contrast to its long-term trend. In this shorter perspective, other factors, real or expected, may be more important, such as interest rate changes, political news and larger price movements in base commodities, central bank currency interventions, statements and statistics. All these factors, combined with subjective evaluations by millions of participants in the currency markets, will together constantly create new short-term trends.

For those who want to follow short-term currency development, most banks and many other financial or currency institutions publicize information via the internet or e-mail on a regular basis – both retrospectively and actual, together with analysis and evaluations of future trends, but one should always be reminded that these are only more or less accurate predictions, nothing else.

Financial risks

In practice, every international trade transaction contains an element of financial risk. Purchasing, production and shipment all place a financial burden on the transaction that forces the seller to determine how alternative terms of payment would affect liquidity during its different phases until payment – and how this should be financed. And, if the deal is not settled as intended, an additional financial risk occurs. In the case of subcontractors, who do not share the risks of the transaction and are paid according to separate agreements, the risk increases accordingly and even more so should the seller have to offer a supplier credit for a shorter or longer period. When it comes to larger and more complex transactions, this financial risk aspect is even more obvious. One of the major problems for the seller could be to obtain bankable collateral for the increased need for finance and guarantees. Even after production and delivery, the seller could still be financially exposed in the case of unforeseen events and delays until final payment.

Sometimes the interaction between the seller and the buyer can make it difficult to establish the exact cause of the delay in payment and there are then fewer chances for the seller to refer to a specific breach of contract on the part of the buyer. On the other hand, if the seller has paid enough attention when drafting the sales contract, including the terms of payment, then it is more likely that any reason for delays will be possible to determine according to the clauses of the contract. There could be numerous reasons for such delays, for example issuing a letter of credit too late, late changes in specification of the goods, late arrival of the vessel, congestion in port and changes in the transport route, to name a few.

The real risk also tends to increase with longer and consequently more costly transport distances. Bureaucratic delays in many countries, as well as delays in the banking system, will have the same result – the final payment to the seller will not be made as anticipated according to the contract.

Apart from ordinary overdrafts during production and delivery, the need for finance is also determined by the amount of credit that the seller may have to offer as part of the deal. If so, the financial risk is increased in line with the prolonged commercial and/or political risk.

Financial risk and cash management

Other forms of financial risk are more obvious but have to be underlined in this context; for example, if the seller misjudges the risks involved in the transaction and becomes exposed through terms of payment that do not cover the real risk situation, or mistakenly enters into the deal without proper risk protection. It goes without saying that such miscalculations can have serious financial consequences, from delays in payment to loss of capital.

The financial risks are generally intimately connected to the structure of the terms of payment. The safer they can be made, the more the financial risk will automatically be reduced, the timing of the payments will be more accurate and the liquidity aspect of the transaction better assessed – in fact, the very essence of cash management.

The safer the terms of payment the parties have agreed upon, the more costly they will normally be. And, if they contain bank security, such as a letter of credit or a bank guarantee, that may also reduce available credit limits within the buyer's own bank.

However, the buyer is often not prepared to accept higher costs and the use of their own credit limits to satisfy what might be seen as excessive demands from the seller, involving methods of payments which, in their opinion, are not normal practice in their country or normally accepted by the company. It is then up to the seller to evaluate the transaction, including potential competition from other suppliers. Eventually, the seller may have to accept the terms of payment offered and try to cover the remaining risks in some other way, for example through a separate export credit insurance, or to find a compromise by offering compensation to the buyer for the additional costs incurred.

FIGURE 1.2 Risk assessment – a summary

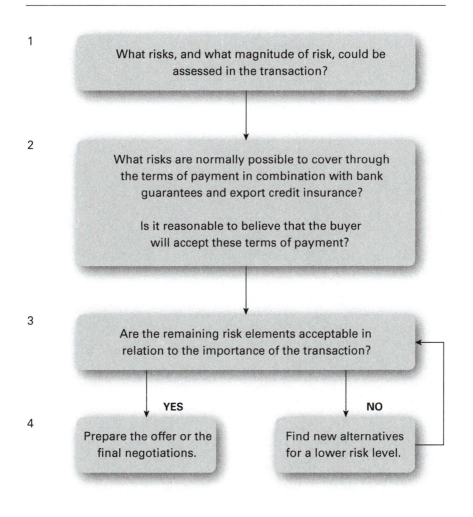

1   What risks, and what magnitude of risk, could be assessed in the transaction?

2   What risks are normally possible to cover through the terms of payment in combination with bank guarantees and export credit insurance?

Is it reasonable to believe that the buyer will accept these terms of payment?

3   Are the remaining risk elements acceptable in relation to the importance of the transaction?

YES   **NO**

4   Prepare the offer or the final negotiations.   Find new alternatives for a lower risk level.

Methods of payment

Different methods of payment

The method of payment determines how payment is going to be made, ie the obligations that rest with both buyer and seller in relation to monetary settlement. However, the method of payment also determines – directly or indirectly – the role the banks will have in that settlement.

Methods of payment and terms of payment

These two expressions are sometimes used synonymously, but in this book they have been kept separate.

'Methods of payment' represents the defined form of how the payment shall be made, ie on open account payment terms through a bank transfer, or through documentary collection or letter of credit.

'Terms of payment' defines the detailed obligations of both commercial parties in relation to the payment, not only the form of payment and when and where this payment shall be made by the buyer, but also the obligations of the seller: to deliver according to the contract and, for example, to arrange stipulated guarantees or other undertakings prior to or after delivery.

As this chapter mainly deals with the different methods of payment, this distinction should be kept in mind – terms of payment will be discussed in Chapter 8.

Methods of payment can be categorized in different ways, depending on the purpose. This is often based on the commercial aspect seen from the exporter's perspective in terms of security. In security order, the basic methods of payment could then be listed as follows:

- cash in advance before delivery;
- documentary letter of credit (L/C);

- documentary collection;
- bank transfer (based on open account trading terms);
- other payment or settlement procedures, such as barter or counter-trade.

However, as can be seen in the following text, the security aspect is usually not that simple to define in advance. In reality, there are many different variations and alternatives that will affect the order of such a listing; for example, if the open account is supported by a guarantee, a standby L/C or separate credit insurance, or how a barter or counter-trade is structured. Even the nature and wording of the letter of credit will eventually determine what level of security it offers the seller.

Seen from a more practical point of view of how the payment is actually made and the role of the commercial parties and the banks, there are, in principle, only four basic methods of payment that are used today in connection with monetary settlement of international trade (apart from e-commerce and barter and counter-trade transactions, which are described later on in this chapter). One of these methods is always the basis for the terms of payment:

1 bank transfer (also often called bank remittance);

2 cheque payment;

3 documentary collection (also called bank collection);

4 letter of credit (also called documentary credit).

Table 2.1 illustrates the most important aspects of the obligations that the buyer and seller have to fulfil in each case. In reality things are often a bit more complex, particularly when it comes to the documentary methods of payment, which have many alternatives. For example, there is complexity in handling, speed in execution and level of costs and fees, but the most important factor is the difference in security they offer. This aspect is thoroughly dealt with in this chapter.

Bank charges and other costs

The costs of the different alternatives are mainly governed by what function the banks will have in connection with the execution of payment. Other forms of fees, which can have an indirect connection to the payment, do sometimes arise, such as different charges related to the creation of the underlying documents, for example consular fees and stamp duties. However, such fees

TABLE 2.1 Summary of the different payment methods

Method of payment	Seller's obligations	Buyer's obligations	Money transfer	Document handling	Payment guarantee
	The role of commercial parties		The role of banks		
Bank transfer[1]	Sending an invoice to the buyer after delivery	Arranging for payment according to the invoice	X		
Payment by cheque[1]	Same as above	Arranging for a cheque to be sent to the seller	X		
Documentary collection	After delivery, having the agreed documents sent to the buyer's bank	Pay/accept at the bank against the documents presented	X	X	
Letter of credit	After delivery, presenting conforming documents to the bank	To have the letter of credit issued according to contract	X	X	X

[1] Bank transfers and bank cheques are often referred to as 'clean payments', in comparison with documentary payments (collections and letters of credit).

are related more to the delivery than to the payment and are normally borne by the party that has to produce these documents according to the terms of delivery. Other costs, such as payment of duties and taxes, are also governed by the agreed terms of delivery.

Bank charges will arise not only in the seller's but also in the buyer's country; they can vary hugely between different countries, both in size and, more importantly, in structure. In some cases they are charged at a fixed rate, in others as a percentage of the transferred amount. Sometimes they are negotiable, sometimes not, and these differences occur not only between countries but also between banks.

The best solution for both parties is often to agree to pay the bank charges in their respective country, but whatever the agreement, it should be included in the sales contract. Such a deal would probably minimize the total costs of the transaction since each party would have a direct interest in negotiating these costs with their local bank. Bank charges in one's own country are more easily calculated and, even if the difference between banks in the same country is relatively small, they are often negotiable for larger amounts.

Bank charges are often divided into the following groups:

- standard fees for specified services – normally charged at a flat rate;
- payment charges – normally charged at a flat fee or in some cases as a percentage of the amount paid;
- handling charges, ie for checking of documents – normally charged as a percentage on the underlying value of the transaction;
- risk commissions, ie the issuing of guarantees and confirmation of letters of credit – normally charged as a percentage of the amount at a rate according to the estimated risk and the period of time.

Detailed fee schedules, applicable in each country and for each major bank, can easily be obtained directly from the banks or found on their websites, but as pointed out earlier, for larger transactions, fees, charges and commissions are often negotiable.

Bank transfer (bank remittance)

Most trade transactions, particularly in regional international trade, are based on so-called 'open account' payment terms. This means that the seller delivers goods or services to the buyer without receiving cash, a bill of exchange or any other legally binding and enforceable undertaking at the time of delivery, and the buyer is expected to pay according to the terms of the sales contract and the seller's later invoice. Therefore the open account involves a form of short, but agreed, credit extended to the buyer, in most cases verified only by the invoice and the specified date of payment therein, together with copies of the relevant shipping or delivery document, verifying shipment and shipment date.

When the terms of payment are based on open account terms and the seller receives no additional security for the buyer's payment obligations, the normal bank transfer is by far the simplest and most common form of payment. The buyer, having received the seller's invoice, simply instructs their bank to transfer the amount, a few days before the due date, to a bank chosen by the seller. This can be done either directly to the seller's account at a bank in their country (which is the most common case) or to a separate collection account that the seller may have at a bank in the buyer's country (see Figure 2.1.)

FIGURE 2.1

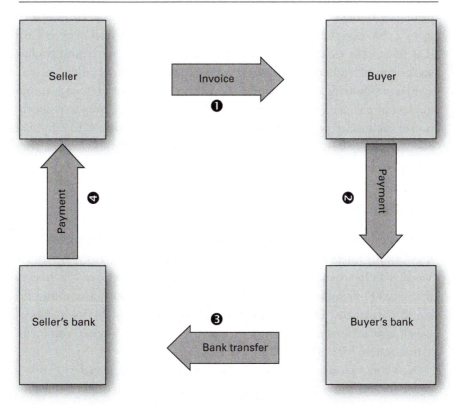

1. Invoice sent upon delivery.
2. Invoice payment in the bank, normally in local currency.
3. Bank transfer through the SWIFT system.
4. Payment in local or foreign currency, according to invoice and/or seller's instructions.

(The seller may prefer not to exchange foreign into local currency, but have it credited to a currency account; see 'Currency steering' in Chapter 4)

Payment structure follows the trade pattern

Bank transfers are a method of 'clean payments' (as compared with documentary payments, to be described later), which predominate both in size and in number: more than 80 per cent of all commercial international payments are estimated to be in this form. The main reason is not only that it is a simple method of payment, cheap and flexible for both buyer and seller, but that it is also an indication of the underlying general trade pattern.

The majority of all international trade is regional, where the commercial risk is generally regarded as low and open account terms traditionally used. Such trade has the advantage of short shipping distances and often regular business patterns between well-known companies, even between companies belonging to the same group, or companies that can be properly evaluated from a risk assessment point of view. In these cases it is also quite normal that there exist established market practices, where open account trading settled through a bank transfer is the most common form of payment.

Even in individual cases where the seller would have preferred a safer method of payment, this can often be difficult to achieve owing to competition or established practice. Instead, many sellers use export credit insurance covering the risk on different customers or even their whole export; with this cover, bank transfer may be the best payment alternative.

The SWIFT system

Nowadays, most bank transfers are processed through an internal bank network for international payments and messages, the SWIFT (Society for Worldwide Interbank Financial Telecommunication) system, in which more than 10,000 financial institutions in more than 200 countries around the world participate. This network is cooperatively owned by its members, which have created a low-cost, secure and very effective internal communication system for both payments and messages.

As a consequence of the introduction of SWIFT, bank transfers between countries and banks are now completed much faster than before. When the instructions are fed into the system by the buyer's bank they are normally available at the seller's chosen bank two banking days later and usually available for the seller the next day or according to local practice. Urgent SWIFT messages (express payments) are processed even faster, but at a higher fee.

However, it should be stressed that even if the speed of processing has increased through SWIFT, this happens only when the payment instruction has been communicated to the network. The seller is, as before, dependent on the buyer giving correct instructions in time to their bank and it is still up to the seller to maintain a high standard in their own systems and routines for close monitoring of outstanding payments.

It is also of great importance to use the correct address code system developed by ISO, the Business Identifier Code (BIC), which is a unique identification code for both financial and non-financial institutions. This code is a unique address which, in telecommunication messages, identifies the financial institutions to be involved in the transaction. The BIC code consists of eight characters (11 if it also includes a separate branch code), identifying the bank, the country and the location (for example, Bank of China in Beijing = BKCHCNBJ). This code, often called the SWIFTBIC, must therefore be correctly included in the terms of payment and later in invoices and other correspondence with the buyer. (The BIC code for any relevant institution can best be obtained from the local bank or on the internet.)

Irrespective of where the payment originated, or where it is to be sent, it is up to the seller to provide the buyer with the correct and necessary information to pass on to their bank, information which must also appear in the terms of payment and in the invoice. Many receiving banks now process these payments automatically, but they have to do it manually if incorrect or incomplete information is given, and will in such cases charge a higher fee.

SWIFT messaging services

To enable banks and other financial institutions to offer risk management and information services appropriate to today's corporate supply chain, SWIFT has developed different new messaging services over a standard platform called SWIFTNet. This is basically a central trade data information-matching database, which will provide both banks and their customers with a tool for monitoring the chain of individual transactions, thereby increasing transparency and reducing the uncertainty of the transaction. The introduction of SWIFTnet has been made in phases as a basis for developing new financial services, not least in the area of trade finance.

This development is also in line with an increase over the last years in corporate demand for a direct SWIFT connectivity. This requirement has typically been driven by strategic initiatives among larger corporates within areas such as treasury centralisation, payment centres and a centralised liquidity management. In fact, this corporate access to SWIFT is a significant development since it provides these corporations with a single channel to communicate with all of their banking partners. For more information, see **www.swift.com**.

Advance payments

Receiving payment in advance before or in direct connection with the actual shipment is the ideal situation for the seller, in terms of both liquidity and commercial risk. However, such agreement is less advantageous for the buyer and would, in most cases, put the seller in an uncompetitive situation compared to other suppliers offering more favourable terms.

Payment before delivery is therefore not frequently used in day-to-day transactions in international trade, but there are some exceptions to this rule:

- *Smaller individual transactions:* where the liquidity and commercial risk aspect is of minor importance to the buyer and/or where this form of payment has become standard practice owing to the simple handling process and low transaction costs. Ordering of spare parts, trial orders, bookings and subscriptions are typical examples, often with a cheque enclosed with the order.

- *E-commerce:* where the order and payment are made simultaneously, with the payment mostly being arranged as a card transaction.

- *Larger, tailor-made transactions:* where payment before delivery is part of an overall payment structure, usually involving payment before delivery, at delivery and often with a part payment after delivery, installation or acceptance. Such a payment scheme should reflect the structure of the transaction and cover the inherent risk and liquidity risks involved for both seller and buyer.

Payment before delivery as part of a composite terms of payment package is described in detail in Chapter 8, together with some practical examples. These payments are almost always carried out as bank transfers, sometimes combined with a corresponding payment guarantee in favour of the buyer, should the seller not fulfil their contractual obligations.

Collection accounts abroad

The bank transfer has, so far, been described as a payment involving two countries, arriving directly from the buyer's bank to that of the seller, and that is usually the case. However, it is increasingly common for the seller to choose to open an account in local currency in the larger OECD countries, where they already have, or can expect, larger flows of payments within one and the same country. The buyer will then make a domestic, not an international, payment to this account, which is both easier and usually cheaper – and the seller will have direct access to the payment when it has reached that account.

These accounts are often established with branches of the seller's bank abroad or in cooperation with one of their banking partners. The structure can vary depending on if and how these accounts are integrated in the seller's cash management system and the cost will depend on the set-up and the service level required.

The use of collection accounts has also been accelerated by other developments within the banking systems in some countries, such as a quicker or online reporting of transactions and balances on these accounts, whereby the seller can monitor individual transactions on a daily basis, through their own terminal connected to the bank. The balance can then also be used for local payments within that country, for intra-company transfers or for direct transfer back to the seller's head-office account.

Payment delays in connection with bank transfers

Since the main role of the banks in connection with bank transfers is to provide an intermediary function, the responsibility for correct and timely payment rests with the commercial parties. It is the buyer who has to give correct payment instructions to their bank, but this obligation does not normally arise until the seller has fulfilled their delivery obligations according to the contract.

EU payments

In order to achieve uniformity in the handling of bank transfers between the European Economic Space (EES) countries, the EU has established a maximum limit of three banking days from the time the buyer gives instructions to the bank to the time when the payment is available to the receiving bank, which then must make the amount available to the seller's account according to local practice, normally one day later. These rules also stipulate that banks, under certain conditions, must charge payments within the EU in the same way as domestic payments, as long as they are in a currency of the remitting or receiving country: so-called 'EU payments'.

There are certain restrictions for a transfer to classify as an EU payment. The maximum amount is EUR 50,000 or the counter-value thereof, and the receiver's account must be stated in the European IBAN standard (International Bank Account Number), containing account number, country and bank code according to a standardized structure. The receiving bank must also be identified with the correct SWIFTBIC code.

Delays in payment are common, not only with different countries but also with individual buyers. Sometimes the reason may be non-acceptance of delivery or other related claims, but in these cases an ongoing dialogue should already have been established between the parties, and the seller can be expected to be fully aware of the situation and the reason for the delay in payment. However, in some cases the seller may not be aware of any such payment disputes with the buyer, and will not have received payment in time – this may be for many different reasons:

- In some countries or companies it may be established practice to delay local payments, and international payments are then treated in the same way.

- Bank credit limits or other restrictions could make it advantageous or necessary for the buyer to delay all payments, including payments to foreign suppliers.

- Supplier payments are often based on open account payment terms, ie without a bill of exchange or similar instrument. Such payments could have a low priority among other debts.

- The buyer may want a self-liquidated deal in order to improve liquidity, and may prefer to delay the payment until they have been paid by their customer.

- The buyer may see currency advantages in delaying the exchange from local currency into the currency to be transferred to the seller.

- Larger corporations often have internal payment systems with batch payments made at certain intervals during the month.

- In the worst case, the delay may be due to liquidity or solvency problems on the part of the buyer, or if applicable, the buyer's country.

Reducing payment delays

Even if it is not possible to establish the exact cause of the delay in payment, there are always some steps the seller can take to reduce such delays.

First, the seller must have an agreement or a sales contract with clear terms of payment. This should include detailed instructions on how to pay and the invoice to be issued after delivery should specify the same information, a fixed due date, full bank name and address, account number and SWIFTBIC references.

It could also prove advantageous to stress the right, according to the contract, for a late payment interest charge and to specify the applicable rate. Even if it may be difficult to collect interest afterwards, the mere indication of it could have a positive effect on the speed of payment.

Supervision and follow-up

All companies should have strict but sensitive credit controls to enable the buyer to understand that whatever has been agreed should be honoured. However, many sellers are reluctant to fulfil the direct or indirect threat of further action for fear that it will undermine the prospects for future businesses. This fear is often unfounded; if the terms of payment are clearly defined from the beginning and the invoice correctly issued, then further reminders or actions may not be appreciated but they will be respected as part of the agreement.

Experience has shown that if no early agreement can be made with the buyer as to how to settle overdue payments, it is important for the seller to involve a reputable collection company early in the process. Such a company can help the seller with a clearer understanding of the cause of the delay and can also act swiftly in consultation with the seller.

Tight supervision after delivery is a key element of the transaction – and an integrated part of efficient cash management.

The most important and effective way to speed up payments related to open account payment terms thus lies in the structure and efficiency of the internal system implemented within the company to treat outstanding and overdue payments. The seller must have clear internal rules and guidelines with a limit for amounts, timing and frequency of individual overdue payments, together with instructions on reporting and how to deal with such matters.

It is equally important to have functional communication between the sales and administrative departments within the company so that the salesperson responsible for that particular buyer becomes aware of any late payments. This person might have additional information and can contact and get support from their opposite number at the buyer, who is not normally the person responsible for payments and may be totally unaware of the delay.

Above all, the seller should not let the matter linger too long. If the buyer has financial problems, the seller will often learn about it once it has become common knowledge among local business partners, who will then be the first to press for payment. The buyer might also be more dependent on them than on a foreign supplier for ongoing business, and might act accordingly in their payment priorities.

E-commerce

The rapid pace of technology and the explosive growth of the internet are having a profound effect on many markets, and there are huge opportunities for companies in most countries to develop new products and services in the area of international trade. To support this development and to strengthen their e-commerce industry, governments in many countries have established policies for creating a stable regulatory environment that supports and underpins competition in both the network and service sectors.

This development is also supported on the supranational level by guidelines set by the OECD for business-to-consumer (B2C) e-commerce. These guidelines were developed to set a level playing field for businesses and to protect customers, for example in matters relating to transparency, fair business and marketing practices, online disclosures, information obligations and payment practices, and are incorporated into rules in most countries involved in e-commerce.

The problem with e-commerce in general has always been the security aspect and the risk of unauthorized use of customer and account information, spread over an open system – not least for international payments. Many e-commerce transactions are still made on open account terms with payment after delivery, either by ordinary bank transfers or by cheque, even if cheque payments could be proportionately expensive for small payments. When it comes to international payments, most e-commerce businesses want to see the actual money being transferred before shipping the goods.

However, new technology and the creation of separate worldwide e-commerce payment systems that are both secure and reliable have created the background for a rapid increase in e-commerce transactions in international trade. These are based on payments through debit/credit cards, particularly in areas such as leisure, travel and most segments of the retail market where card payments have been the norm for many years.

When it comes to business-to-business (B2B) transactions, the picture is somewhat different. Customer relations are often more established, the amounts involved are normally larger and the payment terms are often based on open account or documentary payment terms. Even when marketing and sales are based on e-commerce as an alternative or complement to other sales channels, actual trade payments between companies are generally done through the banks, based on established SWIFT or SWIFTNet systems as described earlier.

Cheque payments

Paying by cheque was once common, but following the introduction of more cost-effective and faster ways of processing international bank transfers, this is no longer the case. Perhaps not more than a few per cent of all international payments are now processed by cheque. In countries where this form of payment is still commonly used in domestic trade, for example in the UK and the United States, the situation may be different, and cheques may for that reason be more frequently used for payment also in international trade.

Sometimes the buyer prefers to pay with their own cheques for cash management purposes, as opposed to through a 'bank cheque' (banker's draft). The corporate cheque (usually post-dated and mailed at due date by the buyer) will not be paid to the seller until it is received and presented to the seller's bank, usually with a considerably delayed value date. This will delay the receipt of liquidity for the seller and often incur additional fees, but the payment will also be subject to the cheque being honoured later on by the buyer's bank when sent back to them for reimbursement. Only at that late stage will the cheque be charged to the buyer's own account – with a profit for the buyer of a long interest-free period.

In some countries it may take weeks to get a corporate cheque from abroad cleared between the banks, during which time the cheque has to be sent to the account holding bank for collection. In such cases, both banks involved may charge collection commissions with high minimum charges, which could add up to large amounts for the exporter, not to mention the liquidity disadvantages. These procedures vary between countries and the seller should always check in advance with their bank before agreeing to accept a corporate cheque as payment in international trade.

The seller should also be aware that if payment by cheque is agreed, and no other stipulation is made, then it is likely that they will receive a corporate cheque, with the liquidity and cost disadvantages mentioned above. However, larger companies may have this payment procedure as a policy, which the seller then may have to accept but, in such cases, this may be of minor importance compared to other aspects of the transaction.

Figure 2.2 shows how the handling of cheques is different from bank transfers. However, as a form of clean payment with no direct connection to the underlying trade documents, the level of security for the seller is almost identical to that of the bank transfer and with the same disadvantages as described earlier.

FIGURE 2.2 Cheque payment (corporate cheque)

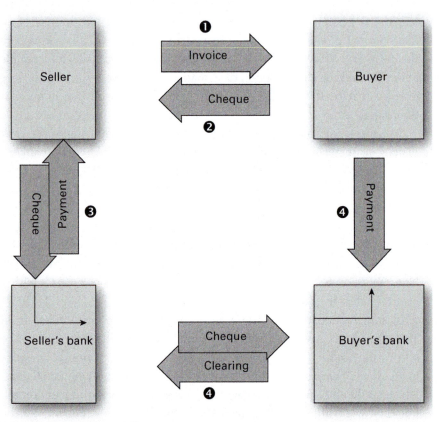

1. Invoice sent upon delivery.
2. The cheque is sent as payment to the seller.
3. The seller receives payment from their bank, either with a longer deferred value date or, in many cases, only at the later stage when the cheque has been received by the buyer's bank.
4. The cheque is 'cleared' between the banks, and the cheque is debited to the buyer's account.

Should a bank cheque [banker's draft] be used, the procedure will be slightly different; the buyer will first have to buy the cheque from their bank; the seller will then receive payment when the cheque is presented to their bank.

There is, however, one further risk aspect relating to cheques in general, which is the postal risk. If lost in transit to the seller, or delayed because of strikes or any other reason, the buyer can claim that they have paid by sending the cheque, but the seller has not received payment. The terms of payment should decide which of the parties has to carry this risk but this is often not the case. If the terms clearly state that payment should be made through a bank transfer, that risk is normally eliminated.

The conclusion is that if payment is to be made by cheque, the terms must clearly state if this should be a bank cheque or if a corporate cheque is acceptable. Then both parties will know what has been agreed and the exporter is aware of the risks involved.

As shown in Figure 2.3, the front of the bank cheque is crossed. This is often done as a safety precaution; such a cheque will not be paid in cash but will only be credited to an account of the payee, in this case the seller, in the bank where it is cashed.

FIGURE 2.3 Sample bank cheque

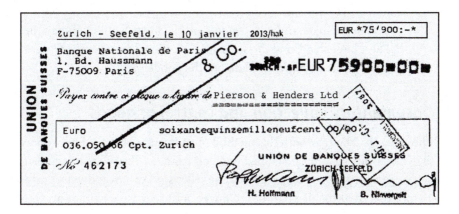

Documentary collection

Documentary collection, also sometimes referred to as bank collection, is a method of payment where the seller's and buyer's banks assist by forwarding documents to the buyer against payment or some other obligation, often acceptance of an enclosed draft or bill of exchange. (Normally the term 'draft' is used before, and 'bill of exchange' after, it has been accepted by the drawee, at which point it becomes a legal debt instrument.) The basis for this form of payment is that the buyer should either pay or accept the draft before they gain control over the documents that represent the goods.

The role of the banks in documentary collection is purely to present the documents to the buyer, but without the responsibility that they will be honoured by them. The collection contains no guarantee on behalf of the banks, which act only upon the instruction of the seller, but it is nevertheless a demand against the buyer, performed by a collection bank at their domicile, often their own bank. It is, in most cases, a more secure alternative for the seller, compared to trading on open account payment terms.

The collections are often divided into two main groups:

- *Documents against payment (D/P)* – when the bank notifies the buyer that the documents have arrived and requests them to pay the amount as instructed by the seller's bank.

- *Documents against acceptance (D/A)* – when the buyer is requested to accept a term draft (bill of exchange) that accompanies the documents instead of payment. The seller's risk deteriorates by handing over the documents against a bill of exchange instead of receiving payment and is dependent on the buyer's ability to pay the bill at a later stage, and the seller has lost the advantage of having control of the documents related to the goods.

Documentary collection and control of goods

The general advantage with this method of payment is that the buyer knows that the goods have been shipped and can examine the related documents before payment or acceptance. From the seller's perspective, the documents are not placed at the disposal of the buyer until they have paid or accepted the enclosed draft (bill of exchange); see Figure 2.4.

However, the practical value for the seller of this control of the documents depends on the documents involved (in most cases the transport documents). For example, compare the two scenarios below.

Scenario 1

The goods are being sent by air to the buyer, who will be able to get hold of them on arrival, without presentation of the relevant air waybill. The goods will generally have arrived at the buyer's destination long before the documents have arrived at the bank.

FIGURE 2.4 Documentary collection (bank collection)

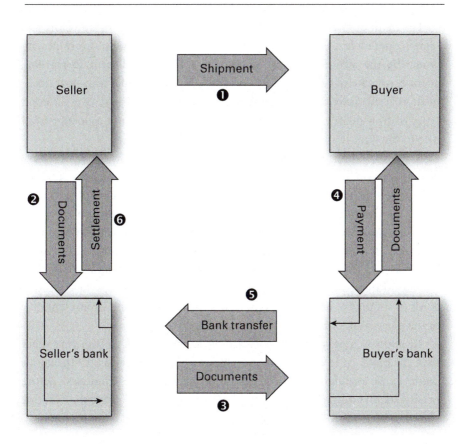

(1–2)   The first step in the collection procedure normally comes after shipment, when the seller is preparing the documents which, together with their instructions, are sent to their bank.

(3)   The bank checks the seller's instructions and that they conform with the enclosed documents. They are then sent to the collection bank chosen by the buyer, together with instructions.

(4)   The buyer is advised about the collection. Before payment/acceptance, they have the right to inspect the document – that they are all included as agreed with the seller and that they appear to conform to the agreed terms. If so, the buyer is expected to pay or accept the enclosed draft and receives the documents.

(5–6)   Payment is transferred to the seller's bank and thereafter to the seller as per instructions. In the case of acceptance, the bill of exchange (the accepted draft) is generally kept at the collection bank until maturity and is then presented for payment as a 'clean collection', that is, without other documents.

Scenario 2

The goods are sent by sea to the same buyer who, in this case, cannot get hold of them until the corresponding shipping documents, ie the bill of lading, can be presented; the bill of lading is among the documents under collection at the bank.

The main difference between the two cases is the mode of transport and related documents. The air waybill is simply a receipt of goods for shipment, issued by the airline company, similar to a rail waybill or a forwarding agent certificate of receipt (FCR). Sometimes a multimodal transport document is used, providing for combined transport by at least two different types of transport, which is also a receipt of goods but not a document of title to the goods.

A bill of lading is not only an acknowledgement that the goods have been loaded on board the ship, but also a separate contract with the shipping company, which includes the title to the goods. The buyer cannot get access to the goods under a bill of lading without possession of this document. If other transport documents are used and the seller is anxious to have control of the goods until the buyer honours the presented documents at the bank, then this has to be arranged in some other way. For example, the goods may be addressed to a consignee other than the buyer, perhaps the collecting bank (if it agrees), or alternatively to the forwarding agent's representative at the place of destination.

To address freight bills or forwarding agent receipts to someone other than the buyer or to insert restriction clauses about the release of the goods could cause problems, or even be prohibited in some countries. Before taking such action, the seller should get prior approval from the bank or shipping agent.

Inspection of the goods

So far our description has mainly been given from the seller's viewpoint; however, the use of documentary collection could have certain disadvantages for the buyer. Perhaps the most important of these is that there are no opportunities to examine the goods before payment: the buyer has to rely solely on what can be seen from the documents presented. There are, however, some actions that the buyer can take to help deal with this drawback. The buyer or the buyer's agent may have the opportunity to inspect the goods before shipment or may use a company specializing in such inspections to do so, as part of the agreement. Such a certificate could then be included in the set of documents sent for collection. This procedure is described in connection with letters of credit later in this chapter.

Other ways for the buyer to increase security in connection with documentary collections could be to have the contractual right to postpone payment/acceptance until the goods have arrived and then to have the right to inspect them or to take samples. Measures like this have to be approved by the seller but there might be considerable practical and logistical problems with such procedures.

Another solution could be to avoid collection altogether and instead agree on a bank guarantee or a standby letter of credit (both terms described in Chapter 3) in favour of the seller, thus covering the buyer's payment obligations. The parties can then agree on open account payment terms and use bank transfer instead of collection as the method of payment and the buyer can inspect the goods upon arrival before payment, knowing that the guarantee can only be drawn upon by the seller if and when they have fulfilled their delivery obligations. The buyer is then obliged to pay anyway under the terms of the contract. The disadvantages for the buyer are of course the costs involved and that such a guarantee has to be issued under available credit limits with their bank.

If the buyer does not accept documentary collection but only open account terms without any guarantee, one alternative for the seller could be to agree to such terms, but in combination with separate credit risk insurance covering the payment obligations of the buyer. However, if no such insurance can be obtained, the seller should probably anyway opt for a safer method than documentary collection, ie a letter of credit.

Documentary collection documents

It is important that the documents required under a collection are specified in the terms of payment in order to avoid disputes with the buyer later on, which will only delay the collection procedure. Documents often used include:

- draft/bill of exchange, issued at sight or as a term bill (usance bill) (see Figure 2.5);
- invoice, sometimes also separate consular invoices;
- specifications and separate packing or weight lists;
- relevant transport documents;
- certificate of origin;
- other certificates, such as health test or performance certificates;
- inspection certificates, verifying quality or quantity of the goods;
- insurance documents.

FIGURE 2.5 Example of a trade-related bill of exchange

Drawer's reference number:	Date of issue	Maturity
EA 2891-83	12/02/13	At sight

Payable at:	Pay against this Bill of Exchange to:
Overseas Chinese Banking Corp Ltd, 261 High Street, Singapore	Pierson & Henders Ltd

Amounts in words and currency:	Currency and amount in figures:
Five thousand and three hundred US dollars only	USD 5,300.00

For:
Value received in goods as per invoice no. 2891-83 of February 12th, 2013

Accepted by Drawee:	Drawer's Signature: Pierson & Henders Ltd
[Signature of Drawee along with full name and address]	**[Drawer's signature along with full name and address]**

1. The bill of exchange, often also called a documentary draft, is similar to a cheque when signed by the buyer, constituting a legal undertaking in accordance with the terms of the bill. The wording varies between countries; often the term 'draft' or 'term draft' is used when issued by the exporter, but 'bill' or 'bill of exchange' only after it has been accepted by the buyer.

   Documents to distant countries are sometimes sent as duplicates in two different mails, one bill marked 'First Bill of Exchange (second not paid)' and the other marked 'Second Bill of Exchange (first not paid)'. But otherwise only one bill of exchange is issued, as in this case.

2. The date of issue should normally be the same as the invoice date, shipment date or any other specified date related to the underlying contract or agreement.

3. The example is due at sight, which means that this draft is not supposed to be accepted but paid by the buyer at first presentation. If it is to be accepted as a term bill, the maturity date could be a fixed future date or at a certain date after presentation to the buyer, for example 90 days' sight, or from the date of issue (ie 90 days' date).

4. The draft is normally payable to the drawer, as in this case, but, as a term bill of exchange, it could also be endorsed (countersigned by the drawer) on the back in order to have its title and its rights transferred, either in blank (to the bearer) or to a specific order, the collecting bank or a refinancing institution.

5. The place of payment specifies the obligations of the drawee (see Chapter 8, 'Place of payment'). If not specified in some other way, a bill should be presented at sight or at maturity either at the debtor's bank or to the debtor personally, which is normally executed as a part of the original instructions in the documentary collection.

6. Commercial trade bills should have the statement that value has been received, referring to the invoice and/or the underlying contract, in order to specify its origin as a trade instrument.

International rules for documentary collection

The International Chamber of Commerce (ICC) has issued a set of standardized rules and guidelines, Uniform Rules for Collection (URC 522), along with a separate commentary (No 550) to minimize the difficulties that banks and their customers may face in connection with documentary collections through banks. They contain common standards and definitions, rules for the banks, obligations and responsibilities, guidelines for presentation of documents and for payment or acceptance. They also contain guidelines for protesting bills of exchange and the banks' responsibilities after payment/acceptance.

These rules have successively been updated and are now used by practically all international and most local banks around the world, and should always be referred to. They can be obtained from the banks or directly from the ICC (**www.iccbooks.com**).

If import or currency licences are required in connection with a documentary collection, this must always be part of the contract, together with a statement of the buyer's responsibility to produce these documents prior to shipment. However, if this is the case, that is in itself a sign of a considerable political risk involved in the transaction and the seller should then consider if collection really is the most suitable form of payment, or if a letter of credit would not be more appropriate.

If the documents are to be released against acceptance, a term draft/bill of exchange issued by the seller should also be included. (At a later stage this bill will be presented for payment under a so-called 'clean collection', where no other documents are included.) Even if the documents are to be released against payment it is still common that an 'at sight' or 'on demand' draft is included for the following reasons:

- it will show the total amount due for collection, which will avoid misunderstandings where several invoices and credit notes are included;

- it will show the name of the company to whom presentation should be made, which is not always the same as in the documents;

- it is in itself a request for payment, with a reference to the underlying contractual obligation of the buyer as shown in the enclosed documents.

Letter of credit

The letter of credit (L/C) is a combination of a bank guarantee issued by a bank upon the request of the buyer in favour of the seller (normally through an advising bank) and a payment at sight or at a later stage against presentation of documents which conform to specified terms and conditions. This is more strictly defined in the 2007 revision of ICC Uniform Customs and Practice for Documentary Credits (UCP 600), under which rules practically every L/C is issued.

According to these rules, the documentary credit/letter of credit (or just credit) means any arrangement, however named or described, that is irrevocable and thereby constitutes a definite undertaking by the issuing bank to honour a complying presentation. This sentence involves two major expressions that will be described in detail later in this chapter, namely:

- the expression 'complying presentation', which means that the documents presented should be in accordance with the terms and conditions of the L/C, but also in accordance with the UCP 600 rules and with international standard banking practice;

- the expression 'honour', which allows three different possibilities for payment to be made upon presentation of compliant documents: at sight, by deferred payment or by acceptance of a bill of exchange ('draft').

Terminology

'Documentary credit' is the formal name used by the ICC, often abbreviated as DC or simply credit, but in this book we will use the expression 'letter of credit' and its abbreviated form L/C, terms that are well recognized and still widely used throughout the world.

The correct terms used in connection with an L/C are 'applicant', 'issuing bank', 'advising bank' and 'beneficiary'. However, when dealing with commercial trade only, and for the sake of simplicity, this book sometimes uses the term 'buyer' instead of 'applicant' and 'seller' instead of 'beneficiary'. 'Issuing bank' is also known as 'opening bank', but only the former expression is used here.

The L/C is normally advised to the seller through another bank (the advising bank) but without engagement for that bank, unless instructed otherwise. The advising bank is usually located in the seller's country and its role is to take reasonable care to check the authenticity of the L/C and to advise the seller according to its instructions. This authentication fulfils a very important role, as can be seen from the extract in the 'Fraud warning' box below.

Fraud warning

The importance of knowing your customer cannot be overemphasized; it is the best protection against fraud. Unfortunately, there have been instances where forged documents or documents relating to non-existent goods have been presented to banks under documentary credits (letters of credit).

Since the documents appeared prima facie to comply with the terms and conditions of the documentary credit, banks have been obliged to pay and debit the importer's account. This arises because all parties, including banks, deal with documents – not with the underlying goods. Exporters should be extremely cautious about shipping goods against the receipt of an unsolicited documentary credit. From time to time, forgeries of documentary credits come to light and there have been instances where exporters have shipped and presented documents against a completely false instrument. If in any doubt, check its authenticity with your bank.

Importers and exporters should be particularly careful about proposals to transact international trade business which is markedly different from their normal line of business or for unusually large amounts. There have been cases where fraudsters have obtained advance payments from foreign traders in the expectation of the award of a contract, which never really existed.

Extract from *Understanding International Trade: an information guide for importers and exporters*, published by HSBC.

The L/C has many advantages for the seller. Payment is guaranteed and there are fewer concerns about the buyer's ability to pay or about other restrictions or difficulties that may exist or arise in the buyer's country – but only if the seller can meet all the terms and conditions stipulated in the L/C.

There are also advantages for the buyer when using an L/C. While it is considerably more expensive than other forms of payment and has to be issued under existing credit limits with the buyer's own bank, the buyer is assured that the stipulated documents will not be paid unless they conform to the terms of the L/C. This may be very important for the buyer in some cases, particularly in connection with goods where fulfilment of special shipping arrangements is essential or in the case of deliveries where timing may be the crucial factor. With regard to cost, an L/C is sometimes of such importance to the seller that the buyer may be able to obtain fair compensation or even a better deal overall if able to offer a form of payment that, in principle, eliminates the seller's commercial and political risks.

The L/C can be issued in many ways, depending on how it is going to be used, and the design will vary in each case. However, an L/C has certain general features that must be included in each case, particularly with regard to:

- period of validity;
- time for payment;
- place of presentation of documents;
- level of security; and
- documents to be presented.

These areas are covered below.

Period of validity

According to the old ICC rules, an L/C could be either irrevocable or revocable, but under the present rules in force since July 2007, L/Cs are always irrevocable, which means that they are without exception binding undertakings on behalf of the issuing bank to honour complying documents presented to either the issuing bank or any nominated bank within the stipulated period of validity. It is therefore no longer necessary to specify that the L/C is irrevocable, but on the other hand there is no harm in doing so.

The nominated bank where the documents must be presented within the validity of the L/C can be any bank specified as such in the L/C. In most cases it is the advising bank, but that does not mean that this bank is under an obligation to pay. Only the issuing bank is under such obligation, unless this undertaking is also confirmed (guaranteed) by some other bank, which will be described later.

Time for payment

An L/C must stipulate when payment is to be made to the seller. It can be payable at sight or at a specified time thereafter, by deferred payment or by acceptance.

An L/C at sight will be paid on presentation of documents at the issuing bank, at the advising bank or at any other nominated bank. If payment is to be effected at a later stage, normally a specified time after shipment or after presentation of documents as specified in the L/C, this can be done either through presentation of a bill of exchange (to be accepted not by the buyer but by one of the banks) or by a stipulated deferred payment in the terms of the L/C, which allows that bank to effect payment at the later specified date.

In the case of both acceptance and deferred payment, the issuing bank is guaranteeing payment on the due date. Based on that guarantee, the seller may generate instant liquidity through discounting or through advance payment from their bank and indirectly finance is thereby provided to the buyer during the same period. Apart from the extended period of risk on the issuing bank (if that is at all an issue), the difference for the seller between an L/C at sight and a term L/C is then mainly a question of interest for the credit period and related bank charges and commissions.

Place of presentation of documents

When referring to the place of presentation of documents under an L/C, this is a question of the place where the documents are to be payable (the expressions 'to be honoured' or 'to be available' are also often used). Unless the L/C is payable only with the issuing bank (in which case it is payable in that country only), this bank must otherwise authorize another bank (the nominating bank, which is often the same as the advising bank) to pay, incur a deferred payment or accept drafts – if all terms and conditions have been complied with. In the case of a freely negotiable L/C, any bank is the nominated bank and presentation of the documents can then be at any place. But seen from the seller's perspective, the best place to present the documents for payment is at the advising bank in their country, for reasons explained below.

As pointed out above, unless it has also confirmed the L/C, the advising or nominated bank is under no obligation to take up the documents when presented by the seller, if at that time this bank – at its own discretion – is uncertain whether the issuing bank will be able to fulfil its obligations to reimburse them for such payment. On the other hand, if the L/C is only payable with the issuing bank, usually but not always domiciled in the country of the buyer, only that bank will make payment or accept the term bill of exchange if the terms and conditions are complied with. But, even in this case, the advising bank or any nominated bank where the documents are presented before they are forwarded to the issuing bank, may still negotiate the documents at presentation and advance funds to the seller, but such negotiation is then made with recourse to the seller until the issuing bank has approved the documents and reimbursed the negotiating bank.

There are thus many reasons why it is more advantageous for the seller to have the documents under the L/C payable with the advising bank at their domicile:

- the payment/acceptance will take place at the earlier stage when the documents are delivered to and approved by the advising bank;
- in case of discrepancies or other faults in the documentation, it may be much easier and quicker to remedy these directly with the advising bank before the documents are forwarded to the issuing bank;
- the seller avoids any postal risk and other delays by the issuing bank until payment is made and effectively transferred to the seller.

However, what is an advantage for the seller could also be a disadvantage for the buyer, who normally, for the same reasons as above, often prefers the L/C to be payable with the issuing bank only. This question has to be decided in each case but, in many countries, local practice will influence this outcome. In some countries this matter may be subject to specific rules or established practice, mostly working in the buyer's favour.

If it is agreed in the terms of payment that the L/C should be payable at the advising bank, that should also be openly stated in its terms and appear in its reimbursement instructions to the advising bank, to enable this bank to make it payable at its counters. But, if nothing is stated to that effect, the L/C might be deemed payable at the issuing bank only. The seller's own bank will know what local practices, if any, are applicable in different countries.

Level of security

The issuing bank always guarantees an L/C for the entire period of its validity without exception. However, many countries have such economic and/or political problems that the seller may be uncertain if the issuing bank can fulfil its obligations and/or is able to transfer the amount out of the country in a freely convertible currency. New and deteriorating events may also take place in the country during the validity of the L/C and, in such cases, the advising bank may refuse to take up the documents until reimbursement is first received from the issuing bank.

To cover the payment obligations of the issuing bank, the seller can also have the L/C confirmed (that is, guaranteed) by the advising bank. This is usually made upon request from the issuing bank based upon instructions from the buyer, according to the agreed terms of payment in the sales contract. Such confirmation may occasionally, although more often as an exception, also be made directly by the advising bank upon request by the seller, without the issuing bank being aware of it. This so-called 'silent confirmation' is also sometimes given by separate forfeiting or other financial institutions in the form of a payment guarantee, if the advising bank for some reason is not willing to do so themselves.

The request for confirmation involves a potential risk on the issuing bank or their country, which the seller's bank may or may not be prepared to enter into without additional cover. The reason may be that the risk on the buyer's bank or the country is not acceptable, or that the seller's bank already has such a high level of exposure on that bank or country that their internal limits are fully used. In such cases, the seller's bank may sometimes be able to apply for a bank letter of credit cover from either a private insurance company or more likely from the domestic export credit agency, which is established by governments in the larger trade countries (see Chapter 5). Such guarantees are based on the assessment made by the insurer of the commercial/political risk on the issuing bank and the risk period involved (usually up to 12 months). The guarantee normally provides cover to the confirming bank of between 50 and 100 per cent depending on risk assessment and risk sharing.

In some countries L/Cs are more or less always confirmed in principle, whereas in other countries that is not normally the case. However, between these two categories there are also many other countries where both alternatives are used. The cost for a confirmation is normally calculated per quarter and varies depending on the assessed risk involved and the length of such confirmation.

The buyer and seller have to agree whether the advising bank should confirm the L/C or not. In some cases, agreeing on a more internationally recognized bank as the issuing bank might provide enough additional security for the seller without the need for a confirmation. In some cases an international bank may also be necessary in order for the advising bank to be willing to add its confirmation. Regarding more 'problematic' countries, this is something the seller should discuss with their bank prior to negotiations with the buyer and, if needed, obtain commitment from this bank to confirm any L/C that may be the outcome of the negotiations. Such commitments are often issued by the banks against a commitment fee.

FIGURE 2.6 Key aspects of a letter of credit

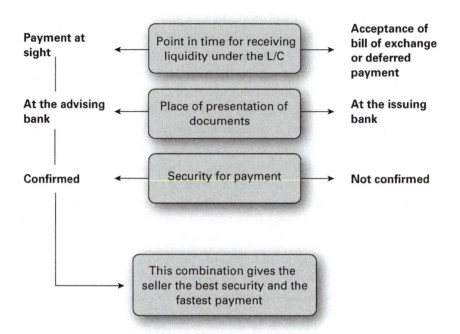

NOTE Since all L/Cs are now irrevocable according to the latest ICC rules (UCP 600), this matter is no longer included in key aspects of a letter of credit as shown above.

Other common forms of letters of credit

It is relatively common that someone other than the seller makes the actual delivery, for example when they are acting as agent, using independent suppliers or having an intermediary function in the transaction. In these cases it can be advantageous to have the L/C expressly stated as being 'transferable', which permits the seller to transfer the rights and obligations under the L/C to another beneficiary, a business partner or some other supplier who will make the actual delivery. (If the master L/C allows partial shipment, parts of this credit can be transferred to different beneficiaries.)

The transferable L/C can be transferred only when it relates to identical goods and with the same terms and conditions as in the master L/C, with the exception of amount, unit price, shipping period and expiry date – or any earlier date of presentation – which may be reduced or curtailed. When later presenting the documents under the master L/C, the seller is also allowed to exchange the suppliers' invoices for their own.

FIGURE 2.7 Letter of credit

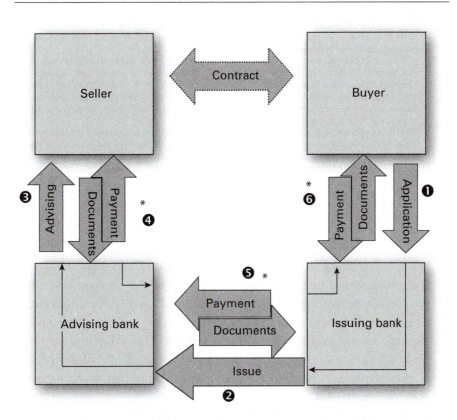

* Payment could also alternatively be acceptance or deferred payment, depending on the stipulations in the L/C.

1. After signing the contract, it is up to the buyer to take the first step by applying to their bank (the bank referred to as the issuing bank in the terms of payment) to issue the agreed L/C.
2. The issuing bank must process a formal credit approval of the application and check that local permissions, import licences or currency approvals, if needed, have been granted. When all formalities and procedures have been dealt with (this may take time), the L/C is issued, hopefully as stipulated in the terms of payment, and forwarded to the selected advising bank.
3. Upon arrival of the L/C from the issuing bank – by letter, fax or mostly nowadays as a SWIFT message – the advising bank will assess its contents and determine where it should be made payable (honoured). If the advising bank is instructed to add its confirmation, this involves a separate credit decision in this bank, after which the seller is notified of the L/C and its details, including information about where it is to be honoured for payment acceptance or deferred payment, and whether it has been confirmed by the advising bank.

   At this point, it is vital that the seller checks the terms of the L/C against the agreed terms of payment to make sure that all the details and instructions can be met at a later stage when the documents are to be produced and delivered. If not, the seller must immediately communicate directly with the buyer so that the necessary amendments are made and confirmed to the seller through the banks. Only then does the seller have the security on which the whole transaction is based.

FIGURE 2.7 *continued*

4. After shipment the seller receives the transport documents and prepares the other documents required. Checks are also made to ensure that they conform to the terms of the L/C, but equally important, that the contents of the documents presented are consistent between themselves.

   The documents are then forwarded to the advising bank, which checks their conformity with the terms of the L/C. The seller is contacted about any discrepancies. Discrepancies that cannot be corrected at this late stage, for example wrong shipping details or late presentation, will be subject to later approval by the buyer, and any payment made by the advising bank will then be with recourse, subject to this approval.
5. The issuing bank will also check the documents and the buyer has to consider any discrepancies. When approved, or if the documents are compliant, the buyer has to pay. If not approved, the documents will be held at the disposal of the advising bank, pending any new negotiation between the buyer and the seller of the terms for such an approval, or ultimately returned to the advising bank (and the seller) against repayment of any earlier payment made with recourse to the seller.
6. The documents are released to the buyer against payment at sight or at any later date as stipulated in the L/C.

However, if the goods to be delivered by other suppliers need to be changed, upgraded or altered before delivery to the ultimate buyer, then the goods may no longer be identical and the L/C may not be used as transferable. In such cases it can nevertheless often be used as supplementary security against which one or more new L/Cs, so-called 'back-to-back credits', can be issued by the advising bank on the seller's behalf in favour of their suppliers and with payment out of documents to be presented under the master L/C.

Sometimes the expression 'red clause letter of credit' is used in international trade, referring to a special clause that can be inserted in the L/C (previously written in red ink, the reason for its name). Through such a clause the seller can receive an advance payment for part of the value of the L/C before presentation of shipping documents (against a written confirmation of a later delivery), enabling them to purchase raw material or to meet other costs prior to receiving full payment upon presentation of conforming documents. However, such a clause creates an additional risk for the buyer who cannot be sure that final documents will be presented under the L/C, and a red clause arrangement is now seldom used other than as part of the overall agreement between the parties when forming the sales contract.

If the L/C is to be used for repeat shipments under a long-term contract or for similar shipments to the same buyer over longer periods, it could be practical to have it issued as a 'revolving letter of credit', which is automatically reinstated to its original value after each presentation of documents or when reaching a certain lower level. However, this L/C must have a final due date and/or limits for the number of times it can be revolved.

Issuing and advising letters of credit electronically

Nowadays it is common practice in most countries for L/Cs to be issued as SWIFT messages in a standardized format. This procedure facilitates both the issue of the L/C and authentication at the advising bank, which will then be able to advise it immediately to the seller. Figure 2.8B shows a freely negotiable L/C in such SWIFT-format, available at sight with the issuing bank, and advised to the seller without the advising bank's confirmation.

Many major banks also advise L/Cs to the seller through their in-house internet-based advising services, which means that the seller can expect to receive the L/C almost immediately after the bank receives it. In this form the L/C can then easily be distributed in a standardized electronic format to and within the company, thus increasing its effectiveness and reducing possible errors in transmission.

The next phase in the chain, the presentation of documents, can also be completed electronically in some cases, but only if the L/C indicates that it is subject to the eUCP (ICC guidelines for electronic presentation of documents under L/Cs), which form a supplement to the new UCP 600 rules. The eUCP should be seen both as a guide to how such electronic presentation should take place and how some often-used documents should be structured to conform to these rules. However, presentation of all documents in electronic format still seems to be very small, the main limitation apparently being the transport documents, which can seldom be presented in an electronic format.

Presentation of documents

The characteristic feature of the L/C in international trade is that the undertaking of the issuing bank is only valid if the specified terms and conditions are fully complied with within the period of its validity. If this is not the case then the issuing bank and the buyer have the right to refuse payment. From the seller's perspective, not complying with all the terms of the L/C could reduce what was originally a bank guaranteed payment to a documentary collection without any such guarantee. This is the main reason why due fulfilment of all terms and conditions specified in the L/C is so important, and why this subject is discussed in such detail below.

As stated earlier, when the seller receives the L/C it is up to them to decide if it is in accordance with the contract and its terms of payment. However, the seller must then also ensure that all details specified in the L/C can be

FIGURE 2.8A Summary example of a letter of credit

Overseas Chinese Banking Corporation Ltd

Date 14 September 2012   Documentary Credit No. 53368
Beneficiary   Applicant
ABC Exporters Ltd   Tan Chee Eng Ltd
Advising bank   Amount
UK Commercial Bank   UK£50,000

Available by your draft(s) in duplicate **at sight** drawn on the advising bank for the full invoice value, accompanied by the following documents:

1. Full set of clean-on-board bills of lading made out to our order showing the applicant as notify party marked 'Freight Paid'.

2. Signed commercial invoices in triplicate.

3. Insurance policy/certificate in assignable form for 10% above the invoice value with claims payable in Singapore covering Institute Cargo Clauses 'A', including war and strikes.

4. Certificate of origin showing goods of UK origin.

Evidence shipment of Diesel Engine Spare Parts CIF Singapore
Partial shipments ~~permitted~~/prohibited   **Transhipment** ~~permitted~~/prohibited
Shipment from UK Port to Singapore no later than 24 Oct. 2012
All documents must be presented within 10 days from date of shipment
This credit is valid until 4 November 2012

This credit is subject to the Uniform Customs & Practice for Documentary Credits, International Chamber of Commerce Publication UCP 600.

Authorized signatures

FIGURE 2.8B Example of an L/C issued through SWIFT

Today, most L/Cs are issued in a standardized SWIFT format, as shown below.

ITD-REF ASNA1415744 0090 DMO 0 MSG-REF 490DM95140300042
OVERSEAS CHINESE BANKING CORPORATION LTD.
RECEIVED BY BB AT 09.59 HRS ON 14TH

DOC CR ISSUE RECEIVED	14 SEPTEMBER 2012
VIA SWIFT	
S700 09/03 GROUP REF	
LCUK53368	
INPUT TIME 1559	INPUT REF 04BEIIIDJAA003093813
OUTPUT TIME 0950	OUTPUT REF 04BBKGB2LBXX313753

MESSAGE AUTHENTICATED

20	DO CR NO.	LCUK53368
31C	DATE OF ISSUE	120914
31D	EXPIRY ON/AT	121104 ENGLAND
50	APPLICANT	TAN CHEE ENG LTD. 1 EAST COAST AVENUE, SINGAPORE
59	BENEFICIARY	ABC EXPORTERS LTD. SHADY LANE, BOLTON, ENGLAND
32B	AMOUNT	UK POUNDS (£) 50,000.00
41D	AVAIL WITH/BY	ANY BANK BY NEGOTIATION
42C	DRAFTS AT	SIGHT (IN DUPLICATE)
42D	DRAWEE	UK COMMERCIAL BANK, MANCHESTER
43P	PART SHIPMENT	NOT ALLOWED
43T	TRANSHIPMENT	NOT ALLOWED
44A	LOAD/DISP/TID	SEAPORT ENGLAND
44B	FOR TRANSP. TO	SINGAPORE
44D	LAST DAY SHIP.	121024
45B	SHPMT OF GOODS	DIESEL ENGINE SPARE PARTS
46A	DOCUMENTS REQD	1. SIGNED COMM INVOICE IN TRIPLICATE
		2. FULL SET OF CLEAN ON BOARD B/L MADE OUT OF ORDER, MARKED FREIGHT PAID AND NOTIFY THE APPLICANT
		3. INSURANCE POLICY/CERTIFICATE (INSTITUTE CARGO CLAUSES 'A' INCLUDING WAR AND STRIKES) IN ASSIGNABLE FORM FOR 10% ABOVE THE INVOICE VALUE WITH CLAIMS PAYABLE IN SINGAPORE.
		4. CERTIFICATE OF ORIGIN SHOWING GOODS OF UK ORIGIN.
47B	ADDNL CONDITIONS	1. ALL DOCS MUST BE PRESENTED WITHIN 10 DAYS FROM DATE OF SHIPMENT.
		2. CONTRACT MATERIALS MUST BE PACKED IN GOOD SEA/AIR WORTHY EXPORT PACKING.
		3. INVOICED FREIGHT NOT TO EXCEED AMOUNT OF FREIGHT DUE ACCORDING TO B/L.
71B	CHARGES	ALL BANKING CHARGES OUTSIDE SINGAPORE INCLUDING REIMBURSEMENT CHARGES ARE FOR BENEF'S ACCOUNT.
79	NARRATIVE	BOTH PARTIES ALREADY UNDERSTAND WITH THE L/C SO THAT YOU COULD JUST ADV IT TO BEN WITHOUT YR RESPONSIBILITY AS PER UCP600 UPON RECEIPT OF CONFORM DOCS WE WILL EFFECT PYT SOONEST.
49	CONF. INSTRCTS	WITHOUT

complied with when the documents later on are to be prepared for presentation at the bank. This requires both experience and caution for, if not accurately scrutinized and, if necessary, amended when the L/C is first received, it may be difficult to get corrections later.

On the other hand, having an uncomplicated L/C and including only the essential documents and specifications, together with a reference to the underlying contract, is normally advantageous for both parties. The documents most commonly used in connection with L/Cs are basically the same as were mentioned earlier in connection with documentary collections, even if the stipulations in the L/C are usually more detailed as to how, and by whom, they should be issued.

Dealing in documents and not in goods

As pointed out earlier in this chapter, documentary payment through banks is a matter of dealing in documents and not in goods or services.

This is particularly important to bear in mind when using L/Cs, where the approval of the documents will be made by the banks, as stated in the new ICC rules: 'Banks must examine a presentation to determine on the basis of the documents alone, whether or not the documents appear on their face to constitute a complying presentation.'

This documentary aspect may be seen as a risk mainly for the buyer, but it is equally important for the seller to be careful with even the smallest detail in the documents, so they in all aspects are, and appear to be, in compliance with the terms of the L/C.

See also the box 'Fraud warning' in the earlier pages where the same message is presented, but from another perspective.

As can be seen in the examples in Chapter 8, wording may also be inserted in the terms of payment to the effect that the L/C should be issued 'in form and substance acceptable to the seller according to contract'. This wording is suggested in order for the seller to have a stronger case when arguing for amendments, should the L/C technically be issued according to the contract but, at the same time, contain additional details or stipulations that will restrict or potentially prevent the seller from fulfilling all conditions at a later stage when the documents are to be presented to the bank.

Third-party documents

One general aspect that must be commented on at this stage is the importance of the seller being particularly observant with regard to documents that are to be produced, verified, stamped or signed by a third party, and also other terms and conditions in the L/C over which the seller may not have full control.

When it comes to the documents, some of them, often the invoice, may have to be certified or legalized by a third party, often a chamber of commerce and/or the embassy of the importing country. If so, the seller has to make certain not only that such a procedure can take place, but that it can be done in time to comply with the dates of the L/C, primarily with regard to the due date of shipment or presentation of documents. The same check has to be made for any other third-party documentation, such as test certificates and inspection records.

The seller should also be aware of the interaction between the terms of delivery and the documents related to the L/C (see Chapter 1). Some terms of delivery stipulate that it is up to the buyer to arrange transportation, after which the transportation documents, for example, the bill of lading, can be released.

Some buyers often try to arrange transportation themselves, in some cases with ships from their own country, perhaps because they have established contacts with the local shipping company, because import regulations need to be followed in order to support the country's shipping industry, or simply because it is cheaper and payment may be made in local currency. For these reasons, the buyer might prefer FOB as their choice of terms of delivery; however, the seller does not in these circumstances have control of the shipping schedules, which might change, or the designated ship may not arrive or be re-routed at short notice.

Should this happen, the seller would not be able to load as planned and will consequently not be able to produce the bill of lading stipulated in the L/C – or will receive it too late to comply with the stipulated time frames. However, there are ways the seller can eliminate even such risks if the parties cannot agree on more suitable terms of delivery, but they have to be agreed beforehand as part of the terms of payment and thereafter form part of the L/C. For example, the seller might stipulate an alternative to the bill of lading, such as a warehouse or other certificate, which they know can be arranged.

International rules covering L/Cs

To reduce the difficulties that users of L/Cs may face through differences in bank terminology and practice, the ICC has issued a number of uniform rules as guidance (Uniform Customs and Practice for Documentary Credits, UCP 600, revised and effective from 1 July 2007). These include different forms of credit, the obligations and responsibility of the participating banks, documents, presentation and validity. Both parties using L/Cs must be familiar with these rules and some general aspects should be stressed:

- all L/Cs must clearly indicate how they are to be honoured (payable) and where documents are to be presented; however, the rules also specify what will be applicable should these aspects not be shown in the L/C;

- all L/Cs must stipulate an expiry date; however, the rules also specify situations when both limitations and extensions to such an expiry date may apply;

- the rules contain a number of articles about ambiguity as to the issuers of documents as well as their contents, particularly regarding the freight and insurance documents, including detailed interpretations;

- the rules also contain articles about definitions of specific words, dates, expressions, terminology and tolerances;

- the rules specify the detailed definition of transferable L/Cs, what rules apply to them and what obligations apply to the banks;

- the rules also deal with the responsibility and the liability of the banks in dealing with L/Cs, including force majeure.

The ICC has also published a new and updated document, International Standard Banking Practice (ISBP), establishing an international standard for examination of documents presented, revised to be in line with the UCP 600 rules. The above rules and other documents, including a special commentary and a users' handbook related to L/Cs, can be obtained directly from ICC (**www.iccbooks.com**).

Inspection of the goods in conjunction with documentary payments

With regard to both documentary collections and L/Cs, the buyer has to honour the documents as presented, but normally without having seen the actual delivery. The documents may be scrutinized by the buyer when presented for collection and by the banks when they check their correctness under the L/C, but the banks have no responsibility for the genuineness or correctness of the information contained therein.

In many cases this may not be important: the parties may know each other through earlier transactions, the goods delivered can be standardized or well known to the buyer, and they can always claim compensation after delivery, whatever value that may have. But in other cases this question may be of great importance to the buyer. The seller must then find other ways to satisfy the buyer for them to agree to an L/C. This can, for example, be done through the inclusion of a separate certificate of inspection in the documentation, issued by an independent surveyor who verifies the goods before delivery through samples or production surveys. Such arrangements must form part of the contract and the certificate should be included in the required documents in the terms of payment.

Frequent discrepancies in documentation

Apart from genuine mistakes in preparing the documentation, some of the more frequent discrepancies include:

- the expiry date of the L/C has passed;
- late presentation, ie the specified period of time after the date of shipment during which presentation should be made, has expired;
- late shipment, ie the shipping document is signed too late or indicates shipment after the stipulated time of shipment;
- a document has not been presented or, if presented, has not been issued by a correct company or authority;
- stipulated tolerances in credit amount, quantity, unit price or other variables have not been met;
- the shipping documents are not in accordance with the terms, for example loading/unloading in the wrong port or not on the specified ship, issued to the wrong order or wrongly endorsed;
- the insurance documents are incorrect, for example not covering the risks required or showing an incorrect insurance value – incorrectly endorsed or not indicating explicit statements as required in the L/C;
- shipping details are incorrect, for example showing part shipments or transhipment, if not allowed, or the packing/marking is not in accordance with the terms.

Finally, not only must each document be issued as stipulated, but they must be consistent between themselves with regard to description of the goods, markings, etc. In practice, however, it is relatively common that this is not the case, owing to carelessness, last-minute changes or lack of documentary knowledge, but it should in principle always be possible to avoid this form of potential discrepancies.

How to avoid discrepancies in the letter of credit

L/Cs that do not in all aspects comply with the terms of the credit are dependent on the approval of the buyer and will, therefore, contain an additional risk that the seller did not anticipate when entering into the deal – if this risk had been known beforehand, the seller might not even have entered into the transaction at all.

As pointed out earlier, the bank guarantee incorporated in the L/C will then disappear and the L/C will, in practice, be transformed into a documentary collection (dependent on the willingness of the buyer to pay). In particular in smaller trading companies with high volumes of export sales with small margins, such an added risk is unacceptable and one such default could lead to bankruptcy. It is also among these trading companies that you often see real professionalism in dealing with L/Cs and the banks very seldom find discrepancies in their documents.

Based on that experience, which can be achieved by all companies, there are at least some measures that can be taken to avoid such discrepancies:

- Many banks have letter of credit checklists, which contain valuable information on how to check the L/C and its required terms and conditions, both when the L/C is received and later on when the documents are presented.

- The ICC rules (UCP 600) contain detailed information about the more commonly used documents in international trade and what they generally should contain to be approved under the L/C, but should be read in connection with the new International Standard Banking Practices (ISBP, No 681), describing in detail the procedures for examining L/C documents.

- It is at the time of receipt of the L/C by the seller that it can be amended (if not issued correctly). Someone in the company must have direct responsibility for such internal approval so as to ensure that there are no problems now or in the future that might prevent the seller from delivering documents without discrepancies.

- The L/C should be payable at the advising bank if possible and the documents should be sent to that bank directly after shipment. This bank will then advise on any discrepancies and the seller will have time to amend the documents if and when it is possible to do so. Should that not be the case, it is usually an indication that the seller's own approval of the L/C when it was issued was incorrect; it should have been amended at that earlier stage.

- Timing is essential: always allow a longer period than expected for issuing the L/C and for shipment, presentation and expiry dates. Deliver the documents in good time before expiry so as to be able to make amendments or deliver completely new documents, if necessary.

- Finally, the banks not only offer practical help on an ad hoc basis but some also offer additional services that could help the seller avoid discrepancies in the documents altogether, for example freight management and even export document preparation.

The letter of credit as a tool in the business process

The advantage of using an L/C is not only the security it gives to the seller, but also its flexibility and adaptability in helping to solve complicated business matters and thereby creating the base for additional business. This enables the seller to offer reasonable advantages to the buyer in return for acceptance of an L/C, for example extended credit on favourable terms, or sharing/absorbing the costs involved.

It is true that once a contract has been signed and the L/C issued, any later amendments will demand corresponding amendments in the L/C as well, and that may take time and involve additional costs for the transaction as a whole. But before that time, almost any transaction can be structured in a way that allows the L/C to function as the glue that holds the deal together and protects the interests of both parties. When the L/C is thereafter correctly issued, both the seller and the buyer know in advance that they are safeguarded in a way that can be controlled by one and the same payment instrument and guaranteed by at least one of the participating banks. Some examples of how the L/C can be used as part of a more complicated business transaction are as follows:

- clauses can be included whereby the seller can arrange necessary start-up preparations for the forthcoming delivery, either at home or in the buyer's country;

- separate procedures can be arranged to secure the fulfilment of the obligations of the buyer in connection with installation and other necessary arrangements prior to delivery;

- if required by the buyer, both tests and samples as well as the process of production and final delivery of the goods can be monitored or verified by using independent inspection certificates under the L/C;

- the transferability of an L/C makes it possible for the seller to arrange for multiple or combined deliveries without added security or liquidity;

- arrangements for different types of barter-trade transactions can also be connected to the underlying contract and covered by a combination of L/Cs (see below);

- arrangements for different supplier or buyer credits with repayment with or without coverage under the L/C can be arranged, at the same time giving credit to the buyer and cash payment to the seller (see example in Chapter 8);

- increased business opportunities are generally available to the seller when using the L/C as supplementary security for pre-financing during the period of purchase, production and delivery (see below).

The letter of credit as a pre-delivery finance instrument

As a guaranteed payment, subject to fixed and known terms and conditions in the individual case, the L/C can also be used as part of the pre-financing needed to produce and deliver the goods. This may be particularly important in cases of longer production and delivery periods or in single large transactions, when the pre-delivery period often is the most difficult to finance, a period before a clear claim on the buyer normally can be obtained. Many such transactions may require pre-financing on a scale that could exceed the seller's ordinary credit limits, even when ignoring any supplier credit given to the buyer, and the L/C may be the tool to close this gap.

The financial consequences of each transaction are directly connected to its size, structure and time of payment, combined with additional demands on the seller for credits and guarantees, perhaps starting several months before delivery and payment, for example:

- demand for performance and/or advance payment guarantees;
- acquisition of raw material or additional/changed production facilities;

- additional contracts with suppliers or subcontractors with a payment structure independent of the underlying contract;
- additional bonds or guarantees covering shipment obligations or insurance;
- additional production modification and/or running costs covering production and delivery.

These additional expenditures, including the costs for insurance cover and necessary reserves for unforeseen events, have to be taken out of the seller's own resources and existing credit limits, but often the financial advantages that the L/C in itself can generate may be needed as well. In these circumstances it is particularly important to get the buyer to accept the L/C as the method of payment so that the seller is able to arrange the supplementary financing that the transaction will require – even if the seller has to compensate the buyer by taking part of the bank charges involved or giving concessions in other areas of the contract.

With this in mind, the advantage of having the L/C transferable is obvious: the possibility of transferring it on to other suppliers will relieve cash-flow pressures from the seller and these suppliers will get the same pre-delivery advantages of knowing what terms and conditions will apply in order to receive payment. Even if the L/C is not made transferable, it could be used as a master L/C and supplementary security for new back-to-back L/Cs in favour of the suppliers, with basically the same advantage to them as a transferable L/C would have had. Even without such an arrangement, or if it is already used for additional finance elsewhere, its mere existence may indirectly help the seller in obtaining new or extended credit either from their bank or from the suppliers involved in the transaction.

Many banks, acting as advising banks, offer special export loans or similar facilities, with a percentage of the value of the L/C as additional working capital, to be repaid from the proceeds upon presentation of documents. Such loans are often backed by a pledge on the underlying L/C.

The L/C may also be used as an important tool in arranging different forms of pre-delivery finance, not least when combined with pre-shipment credit insurance policies (see Chapter 5). Such policies cover the commercial and/or political risks of the transaction from the time when the sales agreement is signed, but may be dependent on the seller having received some form of additional security, for example an L/C, covering at least part of the buyer's obligations. These policies, covering the entire transaction, would strongly facilitate the seller's pre-delivery financial requirements.

Counter-trade

So far the assumption has been that goods are delivered against payment, at sight or at a later date. But there are other forms of transactions, where payment or settlement, wholly or partially, is made in some other way.

The word 'counter-trade' is in itself a general term representing various types of connected transactions or reciprocal arrangements that are linked to each other in a larger structure, necessary for the completion of the individual transactions. The terms may vary, but the following are often used to describe the most common forms of alternative trade transactions:

- *barter trades* – with payment in other goods;
- *compensation trades* – with payment partly in money but also in other goods or services to balance the transaction, agreed between the parties;
- *repurchase agreements* – in which payment is made through products generated by the equipment or goods delivered by the seller;
- *offset counter-trades* – mostly with settlement in money, but with the transaction being dependent on corresponding sales/purchase transactions to balance the payment flow.

There are many reasons why these alternative trade transactions are used, but at least four main reasons are often referred to, namely:

1 To enable trade to take place in markets that are unable to pay for imports. This can occur as a result of a non-convertible currency, a lack of commercial credit or a shortage of foreign exchange.

2 To protect or stimulate the output of domestic industries from a country and to help find new export markets.

3 As a reflection of political and economic policies within a country to plan and balance overseas trade.

4 To gain a competitive advantage over other suppliers.

Pure barter trade or other forms of counter-trade are the oldest forms of trade, today often associated with countries with a state-regulated economy, but also commonly used in many other countries. Some estimates indicate that up to a quarter of all world trade is in this form, although no one knows the exact figures.

Apart from extremely large or complex transactions, particularly within the areas of defence, nuclear installations and complete production plants, large aircraft deals or similar transactions, most other counter-trade transactions are made with or between developing countries – or other countries with a non-competitive or regulated trade system or a non-convertible currency. But sometimes it is the character of the deal itself, its size and complexity, rather than the countries involved, that necessitate these transactions. They are therefore often structured through specialized trading houses that have the overall knowledge and expertise for creating new trading combinations that would otherwise probably not have made the export part of the combined deal possible.

The terms of payment in these transactions depend on the structure of the deal, and the participation of the banks may be totally different compared to ordinary transactions with payment in currency. In real barter-trade situations, only a designated clearing account may be needed to register the value of the transactions and the net balance of the flow of goods. When it comes to other forms of counter-trade, the banks often have a more central role, often through the use of L/Cs, all of them being structured to come into force simultaneously when all other arrangements are in place and approved by the individual trading partners. But thereafter they could either be handled as one deal with separate payment flows or as completely individual transactions, with each L/C being settled separately.

Example of a simple counter-trade transaction

As an example of how the mechanism of a simple counter-trade could work, a US seller of machine equipment has made a deal with a buyer in Honduras. To finance the deal, a US trading house has arranged with a Hong Kong company to buy raw sugar from another company in Honduras for the equivalent amount, which the Hong Kong company plans to sell to an African buyer.

In this example, the Hong Kong company has to take the first step by instructing their bank to issue an L/C in favour of their seller in Honduras, but its validity has to be conditional upon a second L/C being issued by a bank in Honduras in favour of the US seller. Such a clause could have the following wording in the first L/C to be issued, to create the security for the combination of transactions that form the counter-trade:

This letter of credit is not operational until:

1 Banco Central, Honduras, has issued through US Commercial Bank, New York, as advising bank, a letter of credit for the amount of USD 1,000,000, covering shipment of coffee-grinding equipment, in favour of US Grinding

Machinery Inc., Boston. The letter of credit should be payable at sight with the advising bank and contain instructions to this bank to add its confirmation.

2 The advising bank has confirmed that US Grinding Machinery has approved the terms and conditions of the letter of credit above.

When both L/Cs are issued they will become operative at the same time but can thereafter be settled as separate transactions, or alternatively be structured in such a way that payments received under one L/C can be used as outgoing payments under the other in order for the transactions to be liquidity- and currency-neutral. It is then advantageous, but not necessary, if both L/Cs are payable at the same bank which, in this case, will use the payments from the Hong Kong buyer to pay the US seller upon due fulfilment of the terms and conditions under the L/C. In the same way, the payments between the companies in Honduras are settled between their banks, often in local currency.

Counter-trade arrangements – a summary

Counter-trade transactions are by definition a complex area of trade. This is largely due to the fact that one and the same seller often lacks the overall knowledge of potential goods or products suitable or available to arrange the total deal and also because they often do not have direct contact with other potential commercial parties. The structure becomes more complicated in these combined transactions and the risk involved more difficult to assess and to cover.

Counter-trade transactions also often involve countries with a potentially high-risk profile, including both convertible and non-convertible foreign currencies. Such transactions demand longer arrangement periods and incur higher transactional costs. The risk of outside pressure for illegal practices, such as bribery or facilitation payments, may also be higher compared to more standard trade transactions. Equally, the reward could be high to compensate for all these real or potential risks.

The seller therefore seldom acts alone in this type of trade, but normally through or in cooperation with specialized trading houses or international banks that have this expertise. There are also a number of domestic or regional counter-trade associations offering the same services, but the trading parties are generally advised to check with their bank or their trade council or export organization to find a partner that has the relevant knowledge and reputation.

Bonds, guarantees and standby letters of credit

The use of bonds and guarantees

In international trade it has become increasingly common for either or both parties to demand separate undertakings, usually in the form of bonds, guarantees or standby letters of credit, covering the obligations assumed by the other party.

It could be the seller's delivery obligations that have to be secured by a guarantee issued by their bank, or the seller receiving a guarantee covering the payment obligations of the buyer. In any case, this undertaking is often 'the glue' that holds a deal together, a deal that might not otherwise materialize owing to the inherent latent risks involved. This is most common for transactions that, apart from delivery, also cover installation, future performance, warranty periods or similar undertakings, when the parties are mutually dependent on each other, often for a long period.

In certain cases, particularly with more straightforward deals or in combination with a simple service and/or performance, it is often enough that the seller, or the parent or group/company, issues these bonds/guarantees – particularly if the seller is part of a larger or well-known group. However, in most cases, they have to be issued by a separate party, normally in the form of a bank guarantee or an insurance bond (from an insurance company) or as a standby L/C (issued by a bank).

Bank guarantees or standby letters of credit are the most commonly used instruments in connection with ordinary transactions in international trade and will therefore be the focus of this chapter. They could generally be defined as: 'any arrangement by which a bank, upon the request of the principal, irrevocably commits itself to pay a sum of money to the benefi-ciary in accordance with the terms of the guarantee.'

As shown above, and regardless of the obligations covered by it, a bank guarantee or a standby L/C is always a commitment to pay (wholly or partly) a sum of money, but does not guarantee fulfilment of the actual delivery or any other obligation that the principal may have towards the beneficiary. The same goes in most cases, but not always, for a bond issued by an insurance company guaranteeing the obligations of a supplier of goods and services under a contract. Internationally, so-called 'surety bonds' may be issued by insurance or surety companies, with the alternative obligation to fulfil or arrange for the completion of the underlying contract. This could be to appoint another supplier to complete the project if, for any reason, the principal is not capable of doing so. Such surety bonds are mainly designed for building and engineering firms and suppliers of large industrial equipment; banks do not normally involve themselves in any form of surety bond.

Standby letters of credit

In some countries, standby L/Cs are often issued by banks instead of guarantees. In some countries, as in the United States for example, banks may be restricted by law or common practice from issuing guarantees to third parties, so they issue standby L/Cs as the alternative. But they are also commonly used in other parts of the world, one reason being that they can be governed by well-known and generally accepted ICC rules.

In most countries, however, bank guarantees are the more commonly used alternative when issuing separate bank undertakings related to normal international trade transactions. But should a standby L/C be asked for, it can be issued on behalf of the principal with the same wording and the same undertaking as a guarantee.

Most of the text in this chapter is valid also for standby L/Cs even if only the term 'bank guarantee' is used, but the particulars of standby L/Cs will be specifically commented on later in this chapter.

Bank guarantees are generally related to an underlying commercial con-tract between the buyer and the seller. In such cases, and if and when dis-agreement occurs between the commercial parties as to whether the claim is justified or not, payment is normally suspended until such a dispute is settled by later agreement, by arbitration or through the courts.

The risk of disputed claims is also one of the main reasons behind the introduction, in recent years, of 'demand guarantees', with an unlimited right for the beneficiary to claim under the guarantee, irrespective of any objections from the principal or the issuing bank.

Terminology

Bonds, surety bonds, guarantees, standby L/Cs, indemnity or similar expressions are all used to describe undertakings by a third party but, regardless of the title, it is the wording of the written undertaking that is important.

Unless otherwise dictated by the context or by common practice, this book will use the term 'guarantee' and/or 'standby L/C' in accordance with ICC terminology, particularly when dealing with undertakings from banks. Sometimes the word 'obligation' or 'undertaking' is used when referring to all these expressions in general terms.

The text will not deal with the more complex subject of the legal nature of the guarantee, which may not be the same in different countries, but simply describe the main differences between: a) a primary and independent obligation separated from the contractual obligations of the principal; and b) a secondary and accessory obligation, connected to the underlying trade contract. The following expressions will therefore be used in the text in order to separate the following main categories:

- demand guarantees (primary and independent undertakings);
- conditional guarantees (secondary and accessory undertakings);
- standby letters of credit (often used as an alternative to both demand and conditional guarantees, depending on their wording).

Furthermore, the expressions 'principal' and 'beneficiary' are the correct terms in connection with guarantees, but in this book the words 'seller' and 'buyer' are also used in order to focus on the trade aspect and facilitate reading.

Parties involved in the guarantee/standby L/C

The question of who should issue the guarantee/standby L/C is usually determined by the beneficiary, but could also depend on rules or local conditions in that country. In industrialized countries it is often issued directly to the beneficiary by the principal themselves or some head office department, or more frequently by an issuing bank.

Guarantees and standby L/Cs can also be forwarded through an advising bank at the beneficiary's location, but without any responsibility for that bank under the guarantee. The role of the advising bank is then only to forward them to the beneficiary, verifying the authenticity of the issuing bank.

There are also situations when a local bank in the country of the beneficiary has to issue the guarantee (which is the standard procedure in many Islamic and/or developing countries) particularly if the beneficiary is a local authority or similar body. In some countries it may even be stipulated by law that they should be issued by a local bank. In these cases the principal's bank (the instructing bank) will issue a counter-guarantee as an indemnity to the local bank, which will then become the issuing bank. This counter-guarantee would be accompanied by instructions about the wording of the guarantee to be issued – either in a specified form (if that is at all possible) or it will be issued according to local law and practice.

Example of a performance guarantee, related to the underlying contract (conditional guarantee)

Messrs ATV Radiocommunications Spa
18 Vie Rosle, Cassina di Spati
1081 PADOVA, Italy

Guarantee No. G-32768/34

Between you as 'buyer' and Cyber Communication Ltd, 103 Queen's Road, Central Hong Kong, as 'supplier', an agreement has been signed according to contract GHTY 376 dated 25.02.13, regarding the supply of 1075 Satellite Adaptors, model A-346, for a total contract amount of EUR 47,437.00.

At the request of the 'supplier', we, the undersigned bank, hereby guarantee as for our own debt, the due fulfilment of the obligations assumed by the 'supplier' under the above-mentioned contract.

However, we shall not by reason of this undertaking be liable to disburse more than €4,743.00 in total (four thousand, seven hundred and forty-three euros).

This guarantee, issued under Hong Kong law and jurisdiction and to be governed by the ICC rules URCG, ICC 325, is valid until 25 November 2013 by which date (at the latest) all claims must have reached us in writing in order to be taken into consideration. After expiry, this guarantee shall be returned to us for cancellation.

Hong Kong, 15 March 2013

China Commercial Bank

Signature   Signature

FIGURE 3.1 Different structures of bank guarantees

Direct guarantees (Alt A) or guarantees forwarded via an advising bank (Alt B)

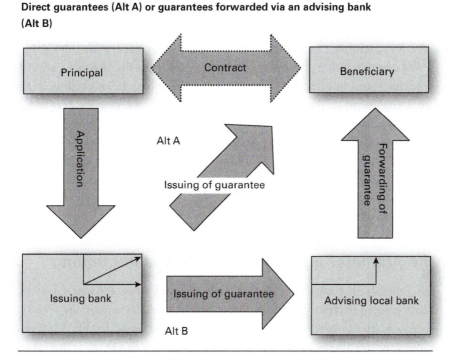

Indirect guarantees (issued by local banks)

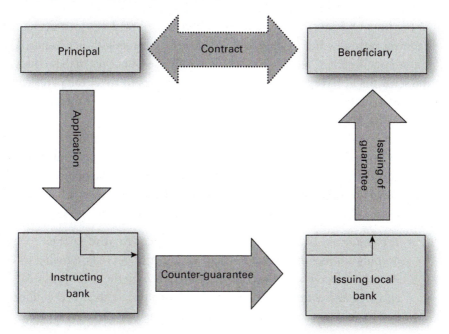

Today, the instructions between the banks involved in the guarantee are often processed in a structured format through the SWIFT system, with the same speed and accuracy as for international payments.

When a guarantee is issued by a local bank in the country of the beneficiary, it is important for the principal to know in advance what rules apply in that country and, if possible, to have the wording of the guarantee agreed in advance and inserted as an appendix to the contract. This will help to avoid any surprises that may appear later on when the guarantee is to be issued, for example if the guarantee is issued without a fixed expiry date or subject to other rules according to local customs and practices. Moreover, it is up to the local issuing bank, and not to the instructing bank, to decide whether a later demand for payment is correct and if payment should be made under the guarantee in accordance with the issuing bank's interpretation of the terms and conditions.

The guarantee underpinning open account trading

The general advantage to both parties from using open account payment terms based on clean payments (bank transfers and cheques) instead of documentary payments is that they are cheaper and more flexible. Changes in delivery can also be made at short notice and they are used, or are often preferred, in trading on an ongoing basis – as long as the credit risk involved is acceptable to both parties, primarily the seller's credit risk on the buyer.

In terms of frequency, overseas trade is largely based on open account payment terms, owing to their widespread use in trade with neighbouring countries where these terms are most commonly used. But even in these cases, the seller might have taken supplementary measures to cover the perceived risk, often in the form of export credit insurance, covering their total exports or just single transactions.

Open account payment terms could also be used in other situations when the risk is greater and/or separate insurance is not available, but must then be supported by some form of bank guarantee, covering the obligations of the buyer. However, some forms of guarantees are more frequently used than others in combination with open account trading, as shown below:

- *A commercial L/C.* This is mainly used as an alternative to open account trading (described in Chapter 2, 'Letter of credit'), owing to its strict adherence to the principle of payment to the seller against specified and correct documents representing the goods. It is therefore less frequently used as a guarantee supporting open account trading.

FIGURE 3.2 Summary of the use of contract bonds/guarantees/ standby L/Cs*

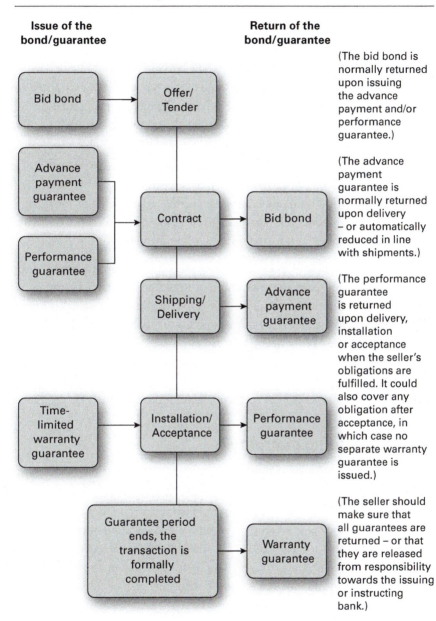

* Only the term guarantee is used in the text to facilitate reading.

- *A conditional payment guarantee*, issued by a bank. This is the most commonly used form of bank support in conjunction with open account terms. Its potential drawback, seen from the seller's perspective, is that it covers the buyer's obligations to pay, but not their willingness to do so, if not accepting the claim owing to alleged deficiencies in the delivery or some other reason.

- *A demand payment guarantee*, issued by a bank. Such a guarantee is seldom used when covering the buyer's commercial payment obligations, since a standby L/C fulfils the same purpose without the additional risks normally involved in a demand guarantee.

- *A commercial standby L/C*. This instrument has many similarities with an ordinary L/C, and is often used instead of a bank guarantee in conjunction with open account trading, either owing to local law or market practices. It may also give the seller a better risk cover than the guarantee, similar to an ordinary commercial L/C.

The decision on whether to use open account trading terms in combination with a conditional payment guarantee or standby L/C has to be made in each case, and depends not only on external legal factors, but also on the goods, value and frequency of the transactions involved as well as the importance of the flexibility needed for short-term changes in the contract or the delivery. But when the transaction involves a high degree of commercial and particularly political risk, open account trading is normally not used at all, and the commercial L/C is then the more secure option.

Costs for issuing guarantees

A guarantee or a standby L/C is normally charged with a flat fee covering handling costs plus a commission fee, usually ranging from 0.5 to 2 per cent per annum on the outstanding amount. The actual cost is determined by factors such as the creditworthiness and financial standing of the customer; customer relations; commercial background; form of guarantee (demand or conditional); guarantee amount; the competitive situation; and the potential for additional business for the issuing institution, such as advising L/Cs or the possibility of arranging finance.

The costs of other banks involved also have to be taken into account if the guarantee is to be either issued by a local bank (based on a counter-guarantee) or forwarded by an advising bank at the beneficiary's location. When more than one bank is involved in the guarantee, in an issuing, counter-guaranteeing or advising capacity, the costs could vary considerably, which is one good reason for not accepting guarantee costs outside one's own country, if possible. This is particularly the case with 'demand guarantees' since these can be prolonged for a considerable time at the sole discretion of the beneficiary (extend or pay). Whatever is finally agreed regarding guarantee charges and other conditions should be included in the sales contract.

Common forms of guarantee

The different forms of guarantee described below under 'Contract guarantees' are often grouped together in this way owing to their direct link with the course of events in a commercial contract consisting of offer, contract, shipment, acceptance of delivery, warranty period and final payment.

However, in practice, some of them are not issued separately but are often incorporated in one and the same guarantee document. This is also reflected in the ICC rules for contract guarantees, where only the three most important and commonly used contract guarantees are formally identified in the rules, namely the tender guarantee (bid bond), the performance guarantee and the repayment guarantee. The remaining guarantees described below are less used nowadays as separate guarantees, but instead are mostly incorporated in one of these three basic contract guarantees, for example in a more comprehensive performance guarantee.

Most guarantees could also, in principle, alternatively be issued as bonds by an insurance company or in the form of a standby L/C issued by a bank, for example as a performance or repayment standby L/C.

Contract guarantees

Tender guarantee or bid bond

This guarantee is delivered in conjunction with the offer or tender for contract, and guarantees the obligation of the seller to stand by the undertaking and that the party submitting it will sign the contract, including the issue of additional guarantees, should the bid be successful. The guarantee amount is commonly between 2 and 5 per cent of the contract.

The guarantee is sometimes replaced by an undertaking to provide a guarantee, often issued by the seller or its parent or group company covering the obligation of the seller to sign the contract if awarded, and to deliver the promised guarantees.

Repayment guarantee (advance payment guarantee)

This guarantee has to be in place before or along with the payment that is to be guaranteed and should cover the obligation on behalf of the principal, normally the seller, to repay the amount (wholly or in part) should the delivery and/or some other contractual undertaking not be fulfilled.

Advance payments normally range between 10 and 25 per cent of the contract value depending on size, complexity and time span of the contract until completion. The guarantees should also be issued with such a wording that it only becomes effective upon receipt by the seller of the agreed advance payment into a specified bank account.

Performance guarantee

This guarantee is perhaps the most commonly used contract guarantee. It should be issued and delivered on behalf of the seller at the signing of the contract or before the start of delivery – guaranteeing the seller's obligations to deliver and perform according to the contract. For ordinary commercial transactions, the amount of a performance guarantee normally ranges between 5 and 10 per cent of the contract value, but could be even higher depending on the risk or consequences for the buyer in the case of non-delivery/performance.

Progress payment guarantee (often issued in the name of or as part of a repayment guarantee)

This form of guarantee is issued when the buyer cannot effectively make use of the seller's delivery or other obligations until these are finally completed but, nevertheless, has agreed to pay in connection with the progress of such work or delivery.

Retention money guarantee (often also issued in the name of or as part of a repayment guarantee)

The purpose of this guarantee is to safeguard the final installation or start-up phase of machinery, equipment or other delivered goods, and to allow the buyer to recover payments already made under the contract should the seller not fulfil these obligations.

Such guarantees are mainly used as an alternative to terms of payment where the buyer would otherwise withhold part of the contract payment, often 10–15 per cent, until completion. The seller will instead receive this part payment against this guarantee at an earlier stage.

Warranty guarantee (often issued in the name of or as part of a performance guarantee)

Many contracts include maintenance or performance obligations of the delivered goods for a certain period of time after delivery or installation. Instead of retaining part of the payment until such period has expired, the buyer will release it at the time of delivery but against this guarantee. The amount could be 10–15 per cent depending on the warranty commitments.

Other common guarantees in international trade or finance

Payment guarantee

Payment guarantees are issued on the instruction of the buyer in favour of the seller, to cover the buyer's payment obligations for goods or services to be delivered according to the contract. This form of guarantee is often used to cover either single or recurring deliveries under a long-term contract, with a total amount covering outstanding and anticipated deliveries. The guarantee covers the buyer's solvency and ability to pay, but not their will to do so if the claim is contested, unless the guarantee is 'on demand'.

The terms of payment used in connection with payment guarantees are often on an 'open account' basis (see earlier pages). The handling of delivery and documentation could then be made more flexible compared to an L/C, but security for the seller depends on the nature and wording of the guarantee.

Guaranteed acceptance (Aval)

Sometimes the acceptance by the buyer of a bill of exchange is not adequate security for the seller to cover the credit risk, in particular over longer periods when this risk may be even more difficult to evaluate. In such cases a bank may strengthen security by adding its guarantee directly to the bill of exchange, by adding and signing the statement 'good per aval' or 'per aval for the account of the drawee', thereby guaranteeing the due payment obligations of the drawee (the buyer).

In many developing countries, where guaranteed acceptances are most common, such a guarantee, if issued by a larger domestic bank, could also automatically include approval of transferring foreign currency out of the country. In other cases such approvals have to be executed separately in the form of a *transfer guarantee*, normally issued by the central bank.

Credit guarantee

This guarantee covers the contractual obligations of the borrower towards a lender. In many countries the seller may have local subsidiaries or affiliates without credit capacity of their own, and the credit guarantee will then support credits from local banks to finance general activities or a specific transaction.

International rules for guarantees/standby L/Cs

The ICC has, for some time, tried to create a recognized and accepted standard for trade-related guarantees in international trade, and has issued common rules for contract guarantees, on-demand guarantees and standby L/Cs.

The rules for contract guarantees (Uniform Rules for Contract Guarantees, URCG, ICC 325) were published in 1978 to curtail unfair or bad faith demands by requiring, as a condition to payment, the presentation of a judgement or arbitral-award or the written acknowledgment of the claim and its amount by the defaulting party. Due to this disadvantage to the beneficiary, the URCG has not been as successful as had been hoped, but these rules are still relevant in the world trade practice.

The rules for on-demand guarantees (Uniform Rules for Demand Guarantees, URDG, ICC 758, updated 2010) were originally introduced in 1991 as a consequence of the increased use of this form of guarantee. These rules are adapted to the prevailing practice with the main purpose of strengthening the rules and guidelines for these guarantees and reducing the risk of unfair calling, through stipulations that claims should be made in writing and supported by documentation showing the circumstances motivating the claim. The revised 2010 rules contain significant practical changes and new definitions and interpretation for greater clarity and precision on how the rules are to be applied.

One of the main advantages of using a standby L/C is that it is supported by an internationally recognized and more commonly known set of rules issued by the ICC (International Standby Practices, ISP 98, in force from 1999) with strong similarities to the universally known Uniform Customs and Practice for Documentary Credits (now in their latest revision, UCP 600).

It is generally recommended that all bank guarantees and standby L/Cs should be governed by one of these sets of rules, whenever possible, as shown in the examples in this chapter. The rules can be obtained from banks or directly from the ICC, **www.iccbooks.com.**

The credit guarantee could also apply to other facilities from local banks, such as overdrafts or credit lines for issuing of guarantees or L/Cs. The support could also cover business obligations against parties other than banks, for example the obligations of subsidiaries towards local main contractors or insurance companies.

The guarantee could, in fact, give cover to any third party in that country, for example in connection with a request to a court to issue an injunction. In all these cases, the guarantee will cover the obligations that the subsidiary cannot cope with on its own merits.

In some cases the credit guarantee may be replaced with more indirect support towards the lender or any third party, in the form of a *letter of support, letter of comfort* or *letter of awareness*. These documents do not impose any formal or legal obligations; rather they are forms of assurance on behalf of the issuer (often a parent or group company), declaring its knowledge of the undertaking and that it will monitor the borrower in order for them to be able to repay the loan or fulfil other obligations. Such letters are often worded as follows:

> Please be informed that we are aware of the business transaction/loan/
> commitment ... entered into by our subsidiary/affiliated company/joint venture ...
> We will assist/monitor the performance of the company/maintain our
> shareholding/appoint members of the board during ... in order for ... to continue
> their operations/to be able to meet their obligations/to honour their obligations.

To be on the safe side, in particular many larger companies insert an explicit statement that such a document is not, and should not be regarded as, a guarantee on behalf of the issuer, to protect them from any future legal proceedings. Banks and other recipients of such letters will also be aware of the limited legal value of these documents and will accept them as an alternative to guarantees only in cases where the supported party has a standing of its own but needs additional security, and where the issuer is a company of such a rating that its reputation and moral standing would be severely affected by a default.

Duty-exempt guarantee

This form of guarantee is often used at exhibitions, fairs or in connection with installations or projects when machinery or equipment must be temporarily brought into the country. By issuing this guarantee in favour of the local customs authorities, customs duties are guaranteed should the equipment not be taken out of the country within the specified period.

Letter of indemnity

This guarantee is issued upon request of the buyer and in favour of eg a shipping company when the goods have arrived at port but without the buyer having access to the necessary bill of lading. The guarantee thus safeguards the shipping company from the risks and costs involved by delivering the goods without presentation of this title document.

Demand guarantees

The most usual interpretation of a guarantee is that it becomes payable when the issuing bank has verified that the principal has defaulted or is in breach of the contractual obligations, and that the beneficiary has suffered a loss or damages as specified in a claim document, submitted together with the demand for payment. This is the principle of a conditional guarantee, related to the underlying commercial contract.

Example of an advance payment guarantee issued by a bank, not related to the underlying contract (demand guarantee)

Messrs Polaris Communications Ltd
713 Road Salai
CHENNAY 63420, India

Guarantee No. 318/XY

Between you as 'buyer' and Amrode Services Ltd, Box 3468, Melbourne 8073 as 'supplier', an agreement has been signed according to contract HT4836 dated 25.01.13, regarding the supply of 575 Modulators model X/3, for a total contract amount of AUD 104,360.00

The 'supplier' is entitled to receive an advance payment of AUD 20,872.00 according to the contract. We the undersigned bank, therefore, hereby guarantee the repayment of the above advance payment on your first written demand, supported by your written statement, stating that the 'supplier' is in breach of their obligations under the above contract and specifying the details of such breach.

It is, however, a condition for claims and payments under this guarantee that the above advance payment has been received in full on an account with us in favour of the 'supplier'.

However, we shall not by reason of this undertaking be liable to disburse more than in total AUD 20,872 (twenty thousand, eight hundred and seventy-two Australian dollars only). This guarantee, issued under Australian law and jurisdiction, is to be governed by ICC Uniform Rules for Demand Guarantees, URDG, ICC 758[*] and remains in force until 25 November 2013, by which date (at the latest) your claims, if any, must have reached us in writing in order to be valid against us. After expiry, this guarantee will become null and void whether returned to us or not.

Melbourne, 15 March 2013

Australia Commercial Bank

Signature   Signature

[*] This reference to the ICC rules is to be included if acceptable to the buyer; see below, 'Reducing the risks with demand guarantees'.

In most cases it is usually clear if the principal has fulfilled the obligations or not, and if payment should therefore be made under the guarantee. However, sometimes this is not that easily established – the parties may have different versions of the events and the principal may simply instruct the issuing bank not to effect payment under the guarantee.

Such a claim could finally be settled in arbitration or end up in court if not agreed earlier by the parties. This procedure can take time, which further acts to the disadvantage of the beneficiary since it may delay the final completion of the transaction and thereby the entire value of the contract, despite payments or other commitments having already been made. This lack of perceived equality between the commercial parties has contributed to the introduction of a form of guarantee with a much stronger position for the beneficiary. In many countries, even within the OECD area, the beneficiary often requests the guarantee to be issued 'on demand' or on 'first demand'. This guarantee is then payable on the first demand from the beneficiary and without prior approval by the principal, or without having to prove to the issuing bank that a default has occurred. It is in that respect similar to a bank cheque, which the beneficiary can cash in at any time during the validity of the guarantee. This form of guarantee (also called simple demand guarantee or unconditional guarantee) puts the beneficiary (usually the buyer in the case of exports) in a much stronger position. The risk of improper use, or unfair or unwarranted calling as it is often known, will of course be much higher, even if such events are probably relatively rare.

A major disadvantage of a demand guarantee (from the principal/ seller's perspective) is not just the risk of unfair calling, but also that such a guarantee will automatically put the buyer in a stronger contractual bargaining position than might originally have been intended. During the life of the contract, and if and when disputes or other discussions arise between the parties, the buyer always has the option to call on the guarantee; even without ever doing so, the seller will be aware of the potential threat and the advantage that gives to the buyer.

Finally, it should be noted that once payment has been made under a demand guarantee it can be difficult for the seller to get such payment repaid, if not agreed with the buyer and then on their terms. The buyer will perhaps not be willing to take part in any arbitration or court proceedings, even if stipulated in the contract – and even if the seller is proven right in the end, that does not in itself guarantee repayment.

Reducing the risks with demand guarantees

In situations where the principal is unable to avoid issuing a demand guarantee, there are some measures that can be taken to help reduce the real risk of unfair callings. Since contract bonds/guarantees are an integral part of the terms of payment in the contract, such risks can often be covered by separate insurance, a 'bond insurance policy', which may be issued either as market insurance for shorter periods, often called bond/guarantee indemnity insurance, or for longer periods and more risky countries also by the export credit agency in the seller's country. This is explained in more detail in Chapter 5.

The 'unfair calling' cover under the insurance protects the seller should the buyer's demand in itself be unfair, but the calling could also be 'fair' from the buyer's perspective, but where the non-fulfilment is or may be due to political events in that country, effectively hindering the seller performing, for example through revoked or changed official approvals or permissions, or by many other reasons of a political nature.

The principal could also try to find a compromise between the two basic forms of guarantee, for example, by agreeing in principle to a demand guarantee, but only together with some form of descriptive documentation to support any claim, according to ICC rules, as shown in the above example. Even if the beneficiary will not accept an explicit reference to these rules, an alternative clause could be worded as follows:

> The demand for payment must be accompanied by your written statement that the principal is in breach of its contractual obligations and specify when and in which respect/s such breaches have occurred.

Even though such wording does not change the general nature of the demand guarantee and the right for the beneficiary to claim under it, it could act as a certain deterrent against potential unfair claims. It could also somewhat strengthen the position of the principal not only during the period of the contract, but also later on when trying to recover any amount unduly paid under the guarantee. The ICC has issued a booklet, *The User's Handbook to the URDG*, containing explanation to the rules and the way they are to be interpreted and applied.

Standby letters of credit

The standby L/C originated in the United States and has been widely used instead of guarantees by US banks for many years, mainly due to legal reasons, but is now recognized and used worldwide.

An example of a performance bond issued on the back of a counter guarantee, made on-demand by the local issuing bank

PERFORMANCE BOND NO BA 38769/C

Whereas our bank stands as joint and several surety for the debtor and as joint and several co-debtor for the definite guarantee fund of USD 150,000 (one hundred and fifty thousand US dollars), which the below-mentioned contractor is obliged to arrange, in order to ensure full performance of the contract 347 of 20 February 2013 between Shirat Shipyard Co, PO Box 29031, 02451 Istanbul (the 'buyer') and the 'contractor' Majestic Lift Machinery, PO Box 3465, Mumbai 60312, concerning delivery and installation of three heavy lift transportation systems.

We hereby undertake and state, on behalf of the bank, and as responsible representatives with full power to affix our signature that, in the event our bank is notified in writing by the 'buyer' that the contractor has violated the provisions of the contract and/or has failed to perform his undertakings completely or partially, the amount under surety will be paid in cash and in full, immediately and without delay to the 'buyer' or their order, upon their first written request, without the need to resort to any legal procedure or to issue a protest or to obtain a court order or the 'contractor's' consent.

This bond has been issued upon the counter-guarantee of India Trade Bank Ltd, Mumbai (NO 18346), dated 19 March 2013.

Ankara, March 28th, 2013

ARAB ORIENTAL BANK S.A.E.

Abdul Mohar   Akram R. Salidi

Comments

1   The wording is normally set by the standards of the local issuing bank, which has used the word 'bond' for what, in reality, is a guarantee.

2   The on-demand character of the bond is only too obvious, even underlining the rights of the buyer and the lack of rights for the seller.

3   The text contains no reference to validity or other limitation in time, and the bond may, therefore, continue to be in force under local law until it has been returned to the issuing bank. There is also no reference to applicable law, jurisdiction or any of the ICC rules.

Standby L/Cs can be used to support payments, both when due and after default, in cases of repayments of money loaned and advanced, or upon the occurrence or non-occurrence of an event in relation to financial or commercial transactions. The standby L/C is commonly described according to its purpose, often in the same terms as, for example, a contract guarantee, with the wording 'performance standby', 'advance payment standby' or 'bid bond/tender bond standby'. It could also be referred to as a 'commercial standby' and be an alternative to a payment guarantee, covering the obligations of the buyer to pay for goods or services.

The standby L/C could in most cases also be used by the principal as a strong alternative to demand guarantees, since the standby L/Cs are normally governed by their established and well-known ICC rules, thereby reducing some of the uncertainties that otherwise would be attached to the demand guarantees. (The standby L/C can of course also be used instead of a conditional guarantee; it is only a matter of its wording.)

The structure of the standby L/C is relatively similar to that of ordinary commercial L/Cs, which is one reason why the corresponding ICC rules are still more widely known and accepted than those for demand guarantees. This might also make it easier for the principal, often the seller, to be able to agree with the buyer to have a standby L/C issued instead of a demand guarantee.

The general advantages for the principal, but often also for the beneficiary, of having the undertaking governed by the ICC rules of the standby L/C are as follows:

- it has a defined terminology, but also gives examples of undesirable expressions that should be disregarded;

- it contains strict obligations for the issuing bank as to how to issue the standby and amendments, if any;

- it contains rules for presentation and examination of documents, partial drawing and multiple presentations;

- it contains rules on termination and cancellation, among others the issuer's discretion regarding a decision to cancel;

- it has a defined duration and must either have a fixed expiry date or permit the issuing bank to terminate the standby upon reasonable prior notice or payment.

The standby L/C also requires some form of statement or certificate as evidence of a default, and such documentation should at least contain:

1 a representation to the effect that payment is due because an event described in the standby L/C has occurred;
2 a date indicating when the statement was issued; and
3 the beneficiary's signature.

The standby L/C should be subject to the ICC rules ISP98, which are specially designed for standby L/Cs, or alternatively but less common, to the extent where they may be applicable, also to the rules of an ordinary commercial L/C (UCP 600). It is often made payable at sight at the advising bank in the buyer's (beneficiary's) country, against document(s) that the parties have agreed upon. Even if they cannot agree on any other documents, payment will only be made against at least the presentation of the above documentation.

The structure and design of guarantees

The practical structure and design of the guarantee or the standby L/C should be governed by the underlying commercial contract, its character, size and the structure of its terms of payment in general, but also with necessary regard to local practices. All these factors combined will determine the final structure and wording, but all guarantees, demand, conditional or standby L/Cs, issued directly or through an advising or instructing bank, should contain at least the following information:

● contract parties and the underlying commercial contract;
● the purpose of the guarantee and what it should cover;
● currency and maximum amount;
● time of validity and expiry date, if possible;
● last date when claims, if any, are to be presented;
● if and when supporting documentation should be presented;
● reference to the relevant ICC rules, whenever possible;
● the applicable law governing the guarantee.

Some of these points are of special importance and are commented on below.

Jurisdiction and applicable law

Commercial parties have the freedom to choose the applicable law, which does not necessarily have to be the same for both the commercial contract and the guarantee, even if it is to the advantage of both parties to use the same legal framework, which is almost always the case. Thus all guarantees should have a clear reference to applicable law and jurisdiction.

The question of governing law is a critical and particularly complex issue in international trade, with local laws based on different systems (for example common law in Anglo-Saxon countries, Continental law and Islamic law), but this matter is outside the scope of this handbook. However, if nothing is agreed, the law of the provider (the issuing bank) should generally apply according to the rules of the Rome Convention, but local law or practice could undermine even that principle in many countries.

When referring to contract guarantees in particular, the general advice is that the parties should agree to use the law and jurisdiction of the provider of the guarantee, as long as that country has a legal system that is internationally recognized and thereby should be acceptable to both parties. But even then, and particularly in the case of guarantees issued by local banks when the provider of the guarantee is that bank, the guarantee will normally be governed by the law of that country, irrespective of the instructions from the instructing bank.

Commencement and expiry dates

An important factor to consider is when the obligation comes into effect. A performance guarantee, for example, should not be operative until the buyer has fulfilled their corresponding obligations (ie not only to have an L/C issued but also its details approved by the seller) or that the advance payment is paid and all legal requirements and approvals are met.

Other stipulations could be that it should come into effect simultaneously with some other contractual event, for example a warranty guarantee that only becomes valid upon the return of a performance guarantee. The expiry date is equally important. Whenever possible a guarantee should expire on a specific calendar date, but it is worth noting that the rules governing expiry dates differ depending on laws and practices in different countries.

However, sometimes the parties cannot agree on a specific expiry date, perhaps owing to uncertainty about the date of delivery or completion. In such cases, the guarantee could be limited in time in relation to some other document, for example the shipping document, an approved test certificate or simply the issuing of another guarantee that is time limited (eg a performance guarantee to be replaced by a separate warranty guarantee with a fixed maturity).

In some countries the law prohibits time restrictions for guarantees but other rules may apply, for example that they will continue to be valid until the actual guarantee document is actually returned to the issuing bank, regardless of any specified time of validity. Many local issuing banks do not accept time limitations on a counter-guarantee, and to make it even more complicated, in some countries it is possible under local law to present a valid claim even after expiry if it could be argued that the event causing the claim took place or had its origin within the period of its validity. In such cases, the only way to release the instructing bank and the principal is through a confirmation to that effect from the issuing bank.

Regarding both conditional and, in particular, demand guarantees, where the beneficiary has a stronger position, it is quite common for a demand for an extension of the guarantee (extend or pay) to be forwarded to the issuing bank. If the guarantee is of a conditional type, that has to be part of a negotiation with the principal, but with a demand guarantee such a request is basically at the sole discretion of the beneficiary.

The risk for the principal (usually the seller) could also be lessened through some form of reduction of the outstanding amount during the period of its validity. For instance, the guarantee could contain reduction clauses that automatically reduce the maximum amount of the guarantee in line with specified events of due fulfilment of the contract, or against presentation of copies of the shipping documents. A reduction clause could read as follows:

> Our liability under this undertaking shall not exceed in aggregate USD ...
> and shall be automatically reduced by x per cent of the contract price of
> each delivery performed under the contract and the production to us by the
> company of a copy of a signed certificate of acceptance (or copy of the shipping
> documents) shall be conclusive evidence for this purpose.

The above uncertainties that can affect a bank guarantee, particularly if issued by a local bank in a country with a higher political risk structure, could be yet another reason for the principal (normally the seller) to use a standby L/C instead of a guarantee, if such an agreement can be reached with the buyer.

Summary and final comments on trade-related guarantees

- Banks normally request collateral for issuing guarantees and standby L/Cs, either under existing limits or under separate credit approvals, and the principal should know at an early stage what demands the issuing bank may have. Additional collateral and higher bank charges may also be requested for a demand guarantee, which usually carries a higher risk since the beneficiary may extend the expiry date (extend or pay).

- Bonds/guarantees issued by insurance companies covering the undertaking of the seller are sometimes used as an alternative to guarantees issued by banks. Such undertakings have the additional advantage of normally being issued only on the strength of the balance sheet of the seller; therefore not affecting existing bank lines, improving cash flow and thereby contribute to a more effective use of working capital.

- The guarantees should, as far as possible, be related to the underlying contract or have a reference to the contract (even if the guarantee is on demand). If it is to be issued by a local bank in the buyer's country, the exact wording should whenever possible be agreed in advance and be included in the contract.

- Whenever the buyer requests a demand guarantee, the seller should try to make such approval conditional on using ICC rules for demand guarantees or, alternatively, try to get the buyer to agree to a standby L/C with reference to its ICC rules.

- Finally, the beneficiary under a guarantee should always have inserted in the contract the name of the guarantee-issuing bank in order to be able to make a proper evaluation of the commercial and political risk on that bank, or any other issuing party, and their country. This also includes the wording, which may then be interpreted according to the law and practice in the buyer's country if nothing else is specified.

Currency risk management

Currency risk

Since the early 1970s, when the system of fixed currency rates finally collapsed, exchange rates between most countries have more or less floated. The possibility of coordinating alternative exchange systems along with the political ambition to do so has decreased over time, based on the realization that currency cooperation, in any meaningful sense, depends on close economic and financial cooperation.

Against this background most countries have chosen to deal with the relation between their own and other currencies and the corresponding currency exchange mechanism in their own way. The most common ways include:

- Allowing the currency to float freely on the currency market, even though this is sometimes limited through central bank market interventions or changes of interest rates, with or without the intention of moving the exchange rate in a certain direction. This is the case with most currencies used in international trade today.

- Allowing various exchange rates for different types of transactions, often a fixed or controlled rate for commercial transactions and a floating rate for financial transactions. This system was occasionally used in the past to create stable trading conditions, but it has been difficult to control and is not used today for any of the major currencies.

- Close cooperation with some specific currency but allowing free floating against others. One example is the Danish krona (DKK), which presently moves within a certain interval against the euro, but freely against other currencies.

- Pegging the currency to internally constructed trade-weighted currency baskets, either openly or secretly; both alternatives are relatively common among developing or emerging market currencies; see below.

- Pegging the currency, officially or unofficially, to a base currency, often USD, which is the case for many currencies in the Middle East, Asia and South America.

Pegging directly to other currencies may be a risky business in the long run if the underlying economic development is different between the countries involved, and could trigger sudden currency disturbances when the pegging collapses or is mistrusted by the markets. Such events could be dramatic, not only as a potential currency risk, but also because they can disturb the entire trade system and the whole economy of the country.

The euro (EUR)

The euro (EUR) has been a currency since the beginning of 1999 and is supposed to be introduced in additional EU countries over time. It floats freely against other currencies, which from a company perspective makes the risk similar to that of any other currency.

Please state your offered price in euro [EUR].

Dublin, february 2013

Despite increasing problems related to the diverging economic situation and the sovereign-debt crises in individual member states, the importance of the euro zone as a trade area makes the euro an important invoicing currency for many importing and exporting companies around the world. It makes price comparisons easier and increases competition, which will affect the choice of currency in offers and tenders and will, in the long term, also have repercussions on investment and production decisions, not only within the euro zone itself.

Even transactions between companies outside the euro zone may take place in EUR as part of larger trade contracts or as a method of balancing outstanding currency risks and minimizing transaction costs.

The Hong Kong dollar, which is the official currency of the Hong Kong Special Administrative Region of the People's Republic of China, has been pegged to the US dollar since 1983 without any problem. This has been done through a special currency board system, where the authorized local issuing banks are allowed to issue Hong Kong dollars only if they have the equivalent exchange in US dollars on deposit. This ensures the strongest possible pegging system with the whole monetary base backed with US dollars at the linked exchange rate/band.

Since 2005, the Yuan, which is the official currency unit used in the mainland of the People's Republic of China, has been pegged to a trade-weighted basket of foreign currencies, rather than being tied to the US dollar alone. It trades within a narrow band against this basket of currencies, where the exact composition and weighting is unknown by the market but strongly controlled by the authorities in order to manage the currency in relation to other currencies and avoid speculation.

The pegging of the DKK to the EUR seems to be an example of how a fixed currency cooperation can work smoothly and without friction in a pure market system even over longer periods, if based on similar economic development and strong commercial integration between the countries involved.

The currencies mentioned so far are mainly 'convertible currencies'. This means that they can easily be exchanged for other 'hard currencies' (eg USD, GBP, JPY and EUR) in an existing unrestricted and effective currency market. All currencies in the industrialized countries, but also many from the emerging market countries, are convertible in this sense.

Other currencies (not least from the developing countries) are generally perceived as politically or economically unstable, or under constant convertibility risk owing to currency restrictions and/or exchange controls within the country. Such currencies are, in practice, non-convertible and not traded on the major currency markets. If they are traded (often unofficially or in local currency trade only), or exchanged in single transactions, such trades are mostly subject to discounts, high volatility or other drawbacks. Many of these currencies are frequently used in regional trade, but they have a very small share of the world market, in particular in trade with the industrialized countries.

The currency markets

The currency market does not operate at any single exchange. Trading in foreign exchange occurs 24 hours a day – and as the day progresses, different banks are constantly on- and off-line. For example, as the European trading day comes to a close, trading in the United States is already under way. Likewise at the end of the US trading day, banks in Asia-Pacific are already open and trading. Hence, large corporations and multinational banks simply pass their foreign exchange (FX) orders around the globe to be executed as and when required.

Furthermore, extensive interbank trading among the larger international banks provides liquidity for everyone involved in foreign exchange, where the bank's clients include the corporate sector, central banks, brokers, hedge funds, insurance companies and private individuals. All these transactions represent a large trading activity; it is estimated that the daily average turnover of the FX market amounts to more than USD 2 trillion.

The spot market

The spot rate is the rate at which a foreig exchange trade can be immediately transacted. Most currency pairs exchanged will then be settled two business days later (T+2). If required, trades can also be settled on a different and later date; however, then a forward rate is agreed, described in detail below.

The reasons for transactions in the spot market could be:

- to settle a commercial transaction through buying or selling local currency;
- to settle a financial operation (eg transferring a loan in foreign currency to local currency or buying foreign currency for interest payments and amortizations);
- to balance or hedge an unwanted position in foreign currency; or
- to increase/decrease a currency position as a speculative move owing to expected future currency movements.

The spot trade

Currencies are normally quoted against the USD in the interbank market, even if nowadays most non-EUR European currencies are traded directly against the EUR rather than the USD. While major currencies are mostly traded directly (ie a direct quote for USD/JPY can be readily obtained as the currency pair is directly traded), smaller currencies are traded indirectly, mostly via the USD. Hence, there are two portions to the trade.

A currency table in January 2013 could look as follows for some larger currencies:

EUR/USD	1.3290 – 1.3293
USD/JPY	89.930 – 89.970
USD/SGD	1.2274 – 1.2280

The quotation is the banks' buy and sell (respectively) spot exchange rate for one currency unit, expressed in the number of units in the other currency. The difference is the spread, which varies between currency pairs.

Some currencies, including the EUR, GBP and some Commonwealth currencies, are sometimes seen expressed both ways, for example either EUR/USD or USD/EUR. In this chapter we have tried to use the alternative that is mostly traded in the interbank markets, but when evaluating or comparing currency data, the reader should generally be aware that both alternatives are sometimes used for a few currencies.

For currencies that are not directly traded against each other, the exchange rate is mostly calculated via some other major currency, so-called cross-rates. This can be seen from the following example, where the cross-rate for a smaller currency like the Swedish krona is obtained in the following way:

$$\text{Spot market exchange rates:} \quad \text{USD/SEK} = 6.5388 - 6.5425$$
$$\text{USD/SEK} = 1.2274 - 1.2280$$

$$\text{Cross rate: SEK/SGD} = \frac{1.2274}{6.5425} - \frac{1.2280}{6.5388} = 0.1876 - 0.1879$$

The spread in the interbank market, expressed as points or 'pips', is the 1/10,000-share of a unit of the currency. For major currency pairs it is usually within a few points. For less traded currency pairs it can be much larger, and the spread also tends to increase in an environment of falling liquidity and market disruptions. The spread towards customers will be considerably larger than in the interbank trade to account for a bank's trading profit, in particular when calculating cross-rates, even though larger companies with frequent trading in volume will often trade at a rate that is close to, if not at, the interbank rate.

The exchange rates towards the customers are normally quoted in one or in one hundred units of the currency, plus the applicable margin in each case, depending on currency, amount, competition and customer relationship.

Currency information to customers

The banks publish currency rates on a daily basis for the most commonly used currencies (as do most financial newspapers). However, these are by definition historical and are, in most cases, so-called 'fixing rates', established at about 11.00 or 12.00 local time during the day. For more current information, the customer must turn to their bank. Most banks have special customer desks within their trading teams, which give current currency information and advice as well as processing customer transactions. The rates they quote give a more accurate picture of the market at that particular time during the day. For larger amounts, it might also be beneficial to check with more than one bank but it must be done at almost exactly the same time to get a fair comparison.

Many larger banks have their own internet-based payment and currency information systems, where their customers can make payments and also get account and currency information to their own terminal. This information is constantly updated during the day, although not in real time.

More up-to-date currency information can also be obtained through some suppliers, delivering true real-time currency information. These systems, such as Reuters' treasury information services, are based on a constant currency updating by banks and brokers, which use these systems as a tool to promote their own quotations and trading teams in this market. These systems give the customer information almost as fast as within the banks themselves, as a base for a more profitable currency trading of their own and/or for more effective management of their currency positions. These currency information systems are now widespread, not only among financial institutions, but also among traders and larger corporations.

The forward market

Currencies traded for settlement on a day later than T+2 are traded at the forward rate. The forward contract creates an obligation between a bank and its customer to exchange a fixed amount of one currency for a second currency at an agreed rate and date. The settlement date can be any business day and it is not unknown for forward agreements to stretch a number of years.

The reasons for using a forward transaction could be the same as for a spot transaction: to settle a commercial or a financial transaction, to balance a currency position or as speculation, but with the difference that the settlement is at a future date.

Determination of forward rates

Forward rates are usually available in most currencies that can be traded in the interbank spot market. However, the trading in interbank forward rates is somewhat different since these rates are, between the banks, not quoted as real currency rates but as differences from the spot rates, so-called 'forward points', reflecting the currencies involved and their respective interest rates and the length of the period. The forward point differential in each deal forms a contract in the form of a currency swap, where the banks agree to exchange a fixed amount of one currency for another currency at spot rates, and after a specified time reverse the transaction at forward rates determined by the same spot rate adjusted by the point differential originally agreed in the currency swap.

The advantage with this trading system is obvious: forward points are easier to compare over different periods, they are more stable over time and are not changed automatically with the spot rates, which are constantly changing. These forward points can then easily be converted to ordinary currency rates when quoted to a customer outside the interbank market. The forward points are simply added to or subtracted from the spot rate, according to whether the values are positive (higher offer than bid points) or negative (higher bid than offer points). This will give the forward exchange rates, also often called 'outright forward rates'. For example, if the USD/SGD interbank spot rate is 1.2274 – 1.2280 and the three-month currency swap rate is 24 – 9, which indicate a very small difference in interest rates for that period, then the three-month outright forward rate is 1.2250 – 1.2271.

The forward points as well as forward currency rates in general are basically determined by the interest rate differential between the two currencies involved. This can also be explained as follows, since a future exchange rate can always be established in a more complicated way. Presume that a Singapore exporter is expecting an incoming payment in USD in three months' time but wants to cover the exchange risk in this alternative way. Instead of doing a forward contract, they borrow USD on the market and exchange it into SGD at the same time at the prevailing USD/SGD spot rate. The borrowed USD amount will carry a cost determined by the USD interest rate for the period until it is repaid at the due date through the incoming export payment. However, the SGD amount received by the spot exchange will have a corresponding interest revenue for the same period, determined by the SGD interest rate, and this interest rate differential is the real cost (or revenue) for this way of hedging the export transaction.

This interest differential between the two currencies, which can be both positive and negative, could then easily be recalculated into a set of forward points or into outright forward rates as described above. The interest rates involved are thus the basis for any forward currency rate, but the system with currency swap rates used by the banks is the only system simple enough to create constant interbank trading. But the background is nevertheless the same in relation to the spot rate: the forward rate is obtained by adding/subtracting the difference between the borrowing and the lending interest rates for the two currencies up until the due date.

Forward currency rates are thus not based on what banks 'expect' them to be, but based on the interest rates of the involved currencies, as established on the free and unregulated international money markets. However, interest rates themselves are influenced by a number of external factors, such as expectations about future interest movements or by new or changing economic or political facts or expectations. In such cases the market participants tend to act accordingly and in a more one-sided direction, with an upward or downward pressure on interest rates and consequently on the forward currency exchange rates as well.

Currency exposure

As can be seen from most charts and surveys, currency movements have been relatively volatile in recent years, making currency exposure an even more important aspect in international trade, as well as foreign investments, particularly if the currency risk is outstanding for longer periods. Even for those currencies that are stable over a longer time-span this is no protection when it comes to new transactions, primarily for two reasons.

First, a historical perspective can never be taken as proof for future currency development, particularly when past development has been strong and a correction might be more likely. Second, it is quite usual that these long-term trends are quite opposite to the short-term development, and it is this short-term trend that is more important when evaluating the risk aspects of most trade transactions. It is the actual exchange rate that is relevant, whether this is established through a spot or forward transaction.

To evaluate currency risks, every company must know what types of risk may occur and to decide what risks should be covered in that particular case. The currency exposure for a company, or the 'translation exposure' as it is also called, is often divided into two separate parts: balance exposure and payment exposure.

Balance exposure is, in principle, an accounting risk, which may appear in the company's books when consolidating foreign assets. When assets and liabilities are converted into the consolidated accounts of the group for accounting purposes, these figures will be calculated at different exchange rates, and might then give a distorted picture of the real value of the assets. For example, assets which are financed through a foreign currency loan are normally included in the consolidated statements at the acquisition rate, whereas the corresponding loan is valued at the higher of the acquisition rate and the rate when closing the accounts. Therefore, moving exchange rates will always have an effect on the accounts of the business, either positively or negatively. However, these exchange adjustments may be inaccurate if they do not reflect the true value of the assets and are not in themselves accompanied by any cash flow consequences.

Payment exposure, on the other hand, involves the flow of payments in foreign currencies, within the parent company and its subsidiaries, in connection with sales and purchases of goods and services, interest payments and dividends, etc. This currency exposure is real and realized when the transactions occur, and the effective exchange rates instantly affect the cash flow of the company and the operating result of the group. In the following text, we will deal with payment exposure only, since this is related to trade transactions.

Most companies have different attitudes to currency exposure, depending on factors such as currency volumes, its composition over time and what currencies are involved. Even the attitude towards risk within the company is important, as laid down in its general financial strategy. Often you will find one of the following three main alternatives when dealing with currency risks:

1 To try to keep the currency exposure as low as possible at all times and to cover the risks systematically as they occur, in order to minimize the overall currency risk.

2 To aim at a selective coverage to keep the currency exposure within specified limits set by the company. The most common ways of

achieving this are covering only certain currencies, only amounts above certain limits, only exposure over certain periods of time or to use some form of proportionate coverage. A combination of these alternatives is most often chosen.

3 Not to cover the exposure at all, an alternative which may be chosen when the volumes and the outstanding exposure are small in comparison with the total business of the company, perhaps in combination with past experience about the strength of their own currency.

Most companies use one of the first two alternatives, as is described at the end of this chapter, actively trying to limit or minimize the currency risks involved in their business.

Currency position schedule

Before any hedging of currency risks can take place, the company must first get a broader overall picture of the company's present and future currency risks (ie proportions, currency, volume, timing and if they are 'firm' or 'anticipated'). This must be done within the framework of a comprehensive set of rules and guidelines on currency risk management specific to each company.

If such management covers several units, for example foreign subsidiaries, the schedule must be such that each unit's position could be monitored while at the same time they are aggregated to a grand total. However, in many companies it is common practice to strip the subsidiaries from exchange risks as far as possible or to have them covered internally within the group in order to concentrate all currency risks to the finance department of the parent company.

By using a rolling position schedule for each currency (eg on a daily, weekly or monthly basis, as shown below), the company will get a fair picture of future currency flows and a good background as to how to hedge the net positions. (Please note that the schedule is for illustration purposes only; in practice they are usually computerized with much higher sophistication.) To make these positions as reliable as possible for management, they should include not only known inflows and outflows but also outstanding offers or tenders together with other less certain transactions (often within brackets) in order to update the positions over time. How this can be achieved in practice is shown at the end of this chapter.

TABLE 4.1 Practical example of a currency position schedule

	Currency position in USD (000s)					
INCOMING Week No.	**20**	**21**	**22**	**23**	**24**	**25**
Currency invoices, due[1]	185	20		1.200	70	200
Currency account assets	50			30		
Currency overdrafts						
Other liquid currency assets						
Firm contracts, not delivered[2]	150				120	
Firm offers outstanding[3]					(100)	
% additional sales (recalc.)[4]					(200)	
Others		30		50		
TOTAL INCOMING	**385**	**50**		**1.280**	**190** **(490)**	**200**
OUTGOING						
Unpaid invoices[5]		170	30			300
Currency loans[6]				1.200		
Accepted offers						
Other outgoings						
TOTAL OUTGOING		**170**	**30**	**1.200**		**300**
NET	+385	−120	−30	+80	+190 (+490)	−100
HEDGED	−200	−50	+10		−150	+50
RISK EXPOSURE[7]	+185	−170	−20	+80	+40 (340)	−50

1 Incoming payments should be based on earlier experience, and rather too late than too early for slow payers or uncertain countries. Should the payment arrive earlier than expected, it could always be converted into the base currency or placed as an interest-bearing deposit until used.

2 Same as above to a higher degree, based on the uncertainty of shipment date.

3 Firm offers or tenders must be within brackets until acceptance.

4 Many companies with a stable flow of export earnings over time often use a rolling system where a certain percentage of expected but not yet contracted earnings are included in the schedule. This is described in more detail below in 'Practical currency management'.

5 Unsettled outgoing payments are easier to calculate and can often be paid somewhat later than scheduled, but also earlier if a rebate can be achieved.

6 Loans in foreign currencies are sometimes used to hedge future export earnings as an alternative to a forward contract.

7 The risk exposure should be reasonably balanced over time, but not necessarily at all times if the balance fluctuates around an acceptable average exposure level.

Hedging currency risks

The most common methods of hedging currency exposure are as follows; in practice, a combination of these alternatives is often used:

- choice of invoicing currency;
- currency steering;
- payments brought forward;
- forward currency contracts;
- currency options;
- short-term currency loans;
- currency clauses;
- tender exchange rate insurance.

The alternatives are described below, mostly from the perspective of the exporter in order to simplify the text, but the conclusions are just as valid for the importer.

Choice of invoicing currency

Three different types of currency can be involved in any cross-border trade transaction:

1 the seller's currency;
2 the buyer's currency, if it is a common convertible currency;
3 a third country currency, often USD.

If not easily agreed at an early stage, the relative market position of the various currencies, along with the competitive situation, will often decide the final choice of currency. If the buyer has a strong and well-known currency, this will facilitate the seller's decision to agree to that currency as a base for the contract – even if the preferred choice was their own currency. However, the seller should, for obvious reasons, be careful about using currencies other than those commonly used in international trade.

Invoicing in their own currency is the easiest way for the seller to eliminate the currency risk, provided that they have their basic cost structure in that currency. On the other hand, it transfers the currency risk to the buyer, which could make it more difficult for them to evaluate the profitability of the transaction and may increase the risk for the seller of not getting the business, particularly if the buyer receives other, more competitive offers in their own currency.

In many overseas markets it is therefore very common to use a third-party currency, often the USD. This is particularly the case if the local currency is officially or unofficially pegged to that currency, or if it is so widely used in the country that invoicing in USD becomes normal practice. This is also the case within many business areas, such as energy, raw material, agricultural products, defence materials, shipping and aircraft, as well as within many service areas such as trading, insurance and transport. It may, therefore, often make commercial sense to accept invoicing in foreign currency if the seller can evaluate the currency risk and hedge it. The questions to consider are:

- Is the invoicing currency freely convertible and actively traded?
- Does it have the trading volumes needed to give it market stability?
- Is it stable in the interbank markets for loans and deposits?
- Is the forward market working properly for the volumes and time periods that may be applicable to the transaction?

Currency steering

In some cases the company can influence or manage their own currency position, particularly if having both incoming and outgoing payments in the same currency. It may then be possible to match parts of the payment flows through the choice of currency. If this is possible, the company may use one or more currency accounts for that purpose. Such accounts can be opened with most banks and used like any other account, including the use of overdrafts (see Figure 4.1).

How such currency accounts are used in practice is part of the overall currency management within the company, together with the structure of the currency flows and the interest rates that can be obtained for both loans and deposits. These aspects will also decide whether to keep balances on currency accounts for shorter or longer periods or to transfer them back into the base currency account.

Payments brought forward

It is always advantageous for the seller to persuade the buyer to agree to an earlier payment from a liquidity point of view but also to reduce the currency risk if invoicing in a foreign currency. However, the buyer will almost certainly see such premature payments as a corresponding disadvantage unless they can gain some other concession from the seller. For ordinary transactions with a short time-span such premature payments, compared to what is considered normal practice, will therefore seldom be agreed.

When it comes to larger transactions and periods longer than ordinary open account terms, and in foreign currency, the question could be more important. The seller could then try to agree with the buyer to divide the payment into part-payments (as is shown in Chapter 8). Such an agreement will often contain at least some prepayment together with the main part-payment at delivery, even if the seller also has to arrange for a payment guarantee in favour of the buyer, covering any pre-delivery payments.

FIGURE 4.1 Summary of the use of currency accounts

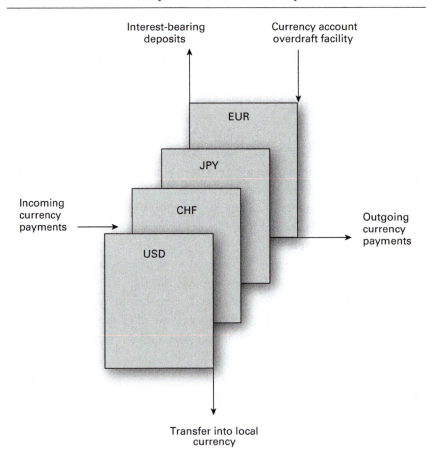

The seller could also act internally within the company to ensure an early receipt of payments, for example by more prompt deliveries, sending the invoice and having all the documentation ready for presentation at the bank immediately upon shipment, and then having an effective system in place for tight credit control.

These aspects, together with the right choice of terms of payment at the outset, are some of the most important steps the seller can take on their own, both as a method to make the currency schedule more precise and minimize the currency risks involved, but also as part of effective cash management.

Forward currency contracts

The most commonly used method of hedging currency risks is through a forward contract with a bank, whereby the company can fix the value in local currency at an early stage but with delivery of the foreign currency at a later date.

Through the forward contract, the company agrees with the bank to sell or to buy the invoiced currency at a certain rate with a fixed delivery date. This forward rate may be higher or lower than the spot rate at that time, but it is not what the bank expects it to be at the due date, but mainly a function of the interest levels of the two currencies for the period in question, plus the bank's margin (as described earlier in 'Determination of forward rates').

A forward contract can be issued in one or more parts with separate maturities and due dates, in order to match the payment flows or to hedge the total risk balance. But it is a fixed agreement with the bank and should normally be done only when the underlying contract is signed and/or when payment can be anticipated with some accuracy. If that is not the case – if the payment may be delayed or in the worst case not take place at all – the company may end up with a new currency risk when having to honour the forward contract with the bank. If in such cases the company cannot use the contract for any other purpose, the bank must be contacted for a cancellation, at a price that depends on currency, volumes and not least the fixed maturity, since both the interest differentials and the bank's margin tend to increase over longer periods.

Forward contracts can be issued over very long periods, for some currencies up to 5–10 years, even though for commercial transactions periods from three/six months up to a year are most common. These shorter periods are also the most liquid, whereas for longer periods the spreads, and thereby the cost, may increase owing to a more illiquid market, but with great variety between different currencies.

If the exact date for the incoming payment cannot be determined in advance, the forward contract can, in most cases, be prolonged or shortened in time after agreement with the bank, even if it could involve an additional cost. Another alternative is to arrange the contract at the outset as a period instead of a fixed date during which the currency may be delivered to or from the bank. Such contracts, called 'forward option contracts' (not to be confused with currency options, described below), will give higher flexibility to the company, but at a less favourable rate, depending on the length of this open period.

However, the larger the company or its currency volumes, the more it will tend to arrange contracts not for individual business transactions, but for outstanding balances over time, calculated according to the currency schedule. Such hedging of balances or part balances will always create greater flexibility and is normally more cost-effective than covering individual transactions. How this is done in practice is shown at the end of this chapter.

Currency options

The currency option is totally different from a forward contract. The holder of the option has the right, but not the obligation, to buy or to sell a particular currency at an agreed rate and date. It may therefore be used as an alternative or as a supplement to a forward contract.

The currency option could be used when an offer or a tender is outstanding and when the seller does not know if the deal will be won or not. Should this be the case, the company could later make use of the option to cover the currency risk. If the deal is lost, the seller may simply abstain from doing so, or if the value of the currency has changed in their favour, the option might have a value of its own and the seller might sell the option contract back to the bank at a profit.

There are two types of currency options: put options and call options. Purchasing one of these options gives the holder the right (but not the obligation) to buy (call) and to sell (put) one currency against another. Consequently, every currency option involved both a call option and a put option. The agreed price at which the exchange of currencies takes place under the contract at the agreed expiry date is called the 'exercise price' or the 'strike price'. For example, a US exporter may take a currency option to buy US dollars against the South African Rand (US Call) and sell SA rand against the US dollar (Rand Put). At maturity, when receiving the Rand, they choose the best alternative price – either from the prevailing spot market price at the time, or the price specified in the option.

The holder of the option also pays a premium for the contract itself, but normally no additional commission or other charges. This up-front cost can be seen as an insurance premium which is determined by factors such as interest level, the length of the contract, market conditions, expected currency volatility and at what strike price the option shall be exercised, compared to the spot market rate at that time. The bank may thus offer the company a number of different strike prices, both above and below the spot rate at that time, which leaves them with a combination of several strike prices and premiums to choose from.

As a direct comparison between the rate of a forward currency contract and the break-even price for a currency option (when adding its strike price and the premium paid), the option contract will usually be more expensive than the forward contract. But that is to be expected. In a currency option the company has a choice that is not available in a forward contract. On the other hand, if the exchange spot rate moves further than the strike price (the intrinsic value), the owner of the option can earn a substantial profit.

Currency options as a means of hedging a commercial exchange risk have not yet reached the same level as forward contracts for many reasons. This market does not have the same depth and liquidity as the forward currency market and it is therefore more difficult for the banks to hedge options compared to forward contracts – making the options more expensive. However, if the bank can use a currency option towards a customer as an additional hedge for an existing imbalance in its own portfolio, or as a counter-trade against another transaction, the bank may price the option accordingly.

The option market is understandably also more traded and liquid for the larger currencies used in international trade and for shorter periods, although together with an increased use for commercial purposes, currency options might become more and more competitive. It is estimated that 5–10 per cent of all commercial currency hedges are completed today in the form of options. However, the company should always check the alternatives and see the currency option as only one of several methods, which combined should hedge the overall currency position. The option may be more expensive but, in conjunction with other hedges, it can be worth the cost.

Currency derivates

A currency derivate is a generic term for specific types of products that banks and other currency traders derive from the basic exchange rates.

The main types of derivates that have been described in this chapter are:

- currency swaps;

- currency forwards; and

- currency options.

However, currency derivates, and in particular currency options, are often constructed by banks and currency traders in a number of different ways, depending on the purpose, and can for larger amounts often be tailor-made for a specific transaction.

The earlier description in 'Currency options' refers to what is called the simple option, or 'the vanilla option', which is an often-used expression for the standardized option traded in a foreign exchange market. But there are many other forms of options, for example in the form of a combined currency forward and option contract or as a basket option where the holder has the right to exchange a basket of currencies against a single currency at expiry date, or vice versa. There is also the collar option, which consists of a simultaneous purchase of put and call options for the same principal amount and maturity but with different strike prices. The user maintains full protection against adverse movements, but gains due to favourable exchange rate moves are limited to the strike price of the sold option.

Another form of currency derivate nowadays quite often used in international trade is the so-called 'cap and floor' contract where the seller (and/or the buyer) can take advantage of favourable price movements to the upper end of the contract range while remaining protected against moves below the lower end of the contract range. Within that range, the contract settles at the spot rate and the customer pays a net premium based on the structure of the set limits.

Short-term currency loans

A loan in a foreign currency is primarily a form of finance, but can also be used by the seller to hedge the value of a future incoming foreign currency payment, as described above. By immediately exchanging the loan amount into local currency at the spot rate, the seller avoids future currency risks on that amount, and on the due date of the loan it will be repaid by the incoming currency payment. The hedging cost will then be the interest on the loan less the reduced interest on the current account. The seller may thus end up with a total cost for this type of hedging which will be similar to the cost of a forward currency contract for the same period.

The use of a currency loan as a hedging tool is also part of the total cash management of the company together with other methods used to cap or minimize the total currency balance and overall liquidity.

Bill discounting

Banks may discount bills of exchange that the seller receives from the buyer (or sometimes promissory notes, which are often used for longer credit periods). Such discounting, as with short-term currency loans, is primarily a method of refinancing, with the currency exchanged at spot rate and the debt being repaid to the bank at maturity out of the proceeds from the bill. The practice of discounting is described in Chapter 6.

Currency clauses

When both commercial parties want to avoid the exchange risk, it can be tempting to use some form of currency clause with the intent of sharing or dividing the risk between them. With a 'cap and floor' agreement with the buyer (or individually arranged with a bank), an Australian exporter may, for example, accept EUR as the invoicing currency, but with a fixed exchange rate floor against AUD. If the EUR weakens below the floor rate during the contract period, the seller would then automatically be compensated through receiving a correspondingly higher EUR amount. The parties could also agree on a similar cap to the buyer's advantage, thereby paying a lower amount if the EUR strengthens above a certain exchange rate.

When it comes to larger amounts and longer time periods in particular, when the exchange rate developments may be a major issue for the parties, such clauses could be an alternative for sharing the currency risk. But should the clauses be made more complicated, what might have been a straightforward agreement at the negotiating table can soon turn into disputes or disagreements later on, when one of the parties wants to make use of it. A good piece of advice is therefore to stick to the simple 'cap and/or floor clauses' for shorter periods and for the major currencies only, and to contact the banks for advice should more complicated currency clauses be discussed.

Tender exchange rate insurance

The exchange risk during the period when the bid or tender is open is one of the factors that can make the transaction particularly risky. The seller risks losing money when tendering at a fixed price in a foreign currency –

while obviously wanting the tender to be successful, the seller could lose out in the contract if the currency weakens during the period between submitting the offer or tender and winning the contract.

Insurance against tender exchange risks are provided for shorter periods by some insurers in the private market, often called 'tender exchange rate indemnity', and in some cases also by the country's export credit agency (see Chapter 5). The private market insurance could be an alternative to currency options if that is not a realistic alternative owing to the costs involved or other practical reasons. Insurance might also be a better alternative than inserting currency or escape clauses in the contract, clauses which often seriously weaken the value of the offer.

These insurance policies are generally construed to mitigate the drawback of having to quote a firm offer in foreign currency with a currency risk that could be outstanding for a period of time. The insurance conditions are basically quite straightforward, sometimes also with a requirement to pay to the insurer any 'surplus', should the invoiced currency have increased in value during the period. The seller pays an up-front fee, often only a smaller part of the total premium, combined with agreed terms for the remaining part, depending on the bid becoming successful or not.

A tender exchange rate indemnity can be given in the most commonly traded international currencies normally up to a year, but the availability and the cost involved also depend on the time period and market conditions at the time of the cover. As in any other currency hedge, many other situations could also arise during the contract period, such as if the contract should fail, be prolonged, amended or abandoned. The indemnity should have to cover these eventualities, and will therefore, as with any insurance, be based on individual terms and conditions for each single transaction.

Practical currency management

The most common methods for hedging currency risks have already been described, but an equally important question is how they are managed and hedged in practical terms within the company, and how the currency aspects are dealt with during the whole process from negotiation until the sales contract is concluded and payment is received.

Most companies have internal systems for establishing their currency position, and rules and limits for dealing with currency risks. These systems may often be quite simple for the smaller company with a limited risk exposure, but often they are much more sophisticated and computerized. It all depends on the volumes and currencies involved, and the more stable the currency flows are over time, the easier they are to forecast, even over long periods ahead.

Many exporting companies with large currency invoicing also have a rolling currency position schedule, comprising both fixed and estimated currency flows, for example, inserted to 100 per cent for contracted deals and with a lower and variable percentage for future non-contracted deals, depending on probability and the time period covered. Many companies even cover their main positions years in advance on such a rolling basis to achieve the best possible currency rate stability over a longer period.

Such a long-term portfolio is constantly updated with new or changed contracts, from a low to a higher percentage if the contract is already in the books, inserted in full for a completely new contract, or reduced with anticipated contracts that were not accepted or did not materialize as planned. When the payment is finally received, it will be booked at the rate of the forward contracts or against other hedges falling due at that time and to the percentage that the hedge covers the individual transaction. Any excess amount not taken against a hedge is booked at the prevailing spot rate.

When determining the internal and calculated rate of exchange to be used within the company in price discussions, offers and tenders, the rate applied is often based on an average currency rate, including the hedges, calculated from the currency schedule over the relevant period. It is then up to the appointed staff to communicate these internal rates within the company as they change. The periods covered in such currency schedules depend on the stability of the forecasts, on risk acceptance and how quickly the cost structure to the final customers can be changed. They are also constantly changing in both size and maturity, depending on external currency fluctuations and verified or anticipated changes in company sales.

When it comes to less used foreign currencies, and for smaller or medium-sized companies generally, the currency transactions are normally smaller and less stable, and thereby harder to predict for longer periods. The seller must then often establish internal currency rates for individual transactions, instead of a calculated average currency rate, and thereafter cover the transactions on a case-by-case basis.

As shown earlier, low-inflation countries with stable economies often have low interest rates and thereby often a premium in their forward currency rates (ie higher forward than spot value). The opposite is true for countries that for any reason have higher interest rates (ie a lower forward than spot value). But irrespective of the method used, the forward currency rates are generally the basis for how smaller companies establish the internal currency rate for individual transactions when preparing an offer or tender, and before actual hedging is arranged.

FIGURE 4.2 Establishing internal currency rates

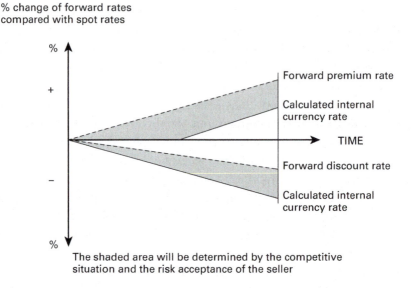

% change of forward rates
compared with spot rates

Forward premium rate

Calculated internal
currency rate

TIME

Forward discount rate

Calculated internal
currency rate

The shaded area will be determined by the competitive
situation and the risk acceptance of the seller

Nowadays, the difference between forward and spot rates for shorter periods is relatively small for the more commonly used international currencies, owing to a similar economic policy in these countries and consequently less spread in interest rate levels. But, for other currencies, this difference may be higher. Nevertheless, if the seller follows the principle of using the forward currency rate as the basis for offers and tenders, then the following method could be used for covering the individual transaction, with a cautious approach, as shown in the graph above.

For currencies with a forward premium, the seller can use the spot rate as a base for the internal rate during the sales negotiations, with a percentage increase for longer periods, depending on the angle of the forward premium curve and the competitive situation. For currencies with a discount, the actual forward rate can be used as a base, adjusted with a further discount, depending on the volatility of the currency, the period and the competitive situation.

Other techniques used in setting internal currency rates or covering the currency risk during the quotation stage could be, as an alternative or as a complement, to work with currency options and include the premium in the quotation price. Alternatively, the seller could reduce the validity of the outstanding offer or tender, or insert a price clause covering adverse currency fluctuations. But, as pointed out earlier, all such clauses have a competitive disadvantage.

Export credit insurance

A mutual undertaking

Previous chapters have dealt with the different forms of risk that can occur in an international trade transaction, risks that have to be covered through the terms of payment. But, in many cases, that may be difficult to achieve, because the buyer does not accept the proposed terms, the bank is unwilling to take the risks involved, or the remaining risks may be considered by the seller as being too high.

The terms of payment must be negotiated in the same way as other parts of the contract, in which both commercial parties often have to make a compromise. In many countries there are established practices in the way payments are made and it may be difficult to agree with the buyer should the terms differ too greatly from these practices – particularly if they expect other suppliers to offer more competitive terms. In other situations, the seller may have difficulty in finding financial institutions that are willing to accept the inherent risks in the discussed terms of payment, in particular related to the political and/or commercial risks in many countries in conjunction with short-term financing, not to mention medium- or long-term periods.

In these cases it is crucial to try to structure the deal in a way that enables the seller to maximize the combined cover that can be obtained from banks, financial institutions and separate export credit insurance companies or institutions. The seller must then explore, in advance, what is achievable before commencing negotiations with the buyer. Having the knowledge and capability to structure such transactions, together with banks and/or insurers, is of vital importance for the seller when dealing with political and commercial risks that might otherwise make the transaction difficult or even impossible to deal with.

Export credit insurance

Export credit refers to the credit that the seller offers the buyer in the contract for sale of goods and services (ie a supplier credit) or credits given to finance such a sale (ie a buyer credit), described in Chapter 6.

Export credit insurance is normally divisible into commercial and political risks. The commercial risk is that which rests with the buyer, ie their ability to pay for what has been purchased. The political risk is that associated with the buyer's country and includes losses arising from such events as the cancellation of an import licence, war and the prevention by the authorities in the buyer's country of the transfer of the foreign exchange required to pay the seller.

This chapter focuses on how the export credit insurance market works in general terms for exporting companies, for short and long periods, together with a description of the two main areas within this sector: the private sector insurance market mainly covering the shorter periods, and the market for government-supported insurance, covering the longer periods and/or more complex export markets.

It should be stressed that government-supported insurance schemes through national export credit agencies (ECAs or just 'agencies') are established in only about 40 industrialized or emerging market countries (see separate box later in this chapter), even though this covers a large part of total world trade. However, the role of the agencies and the cover they may give to promote exports from these countries are also of great importance to buyers in most countries, since they fulfil an important role in supporting the transfer of goods and services and, indirectly, provide knowledge and expertise to many countries, particularly developing countries; in many cases this would not have happened without this support.

Insurance is based on a mutual relationship between the parties involved, where both the insurer and the insured (in this case the seller) enter into obligations towards one another. This is a major difference compared with a guarantee or bond, which is a one-sided obligation based on specified conditions.

Many forms of export credit insurance have been created to cover different parts of the transaction, for example coverage from shipment only or also including the production period. Each insurance cover is based on special terms and conditions, which the seller has to check with the preconditions applicable to the individual transaction. The most common of these conditions are related to the seller's own risk in the transaction, qualifying or waiting periods or conditions precedent, for example that an L/C has been issued, certain permissions in the buyer's country have been obtained or that certain guarantees have been received by the seller.

However, the seller also has obligations towards the insurer; for example, that the uninsured percentage should be retained during the whole insured period or, alternatively, that it might only be transferred under certain conditions. Other conditions could be that specified time limits must be adhered to or adverse changes regarding the buyer or the transaction should be reported, and/or that important changes to the transaction have to be approved by the insurer.

Risks not covered by export credit insurance

Export credit insurance cover is, in principle, limited by two main factors:

1 the percentage of coverage, or inverted, the uninsured percentage that the seller is not allowed to lay off to any third party; and

2 the qualifying period – the period before settlement of the claim takes place.

However, you should always go through all aspects of non-coverage with the insurer, especially in situations where tailor-made coverage is needed.

When calculating the size and potential cost of these uncovered risks, the seller must assume that the maximum risk occurs not only when delivery obligations have been fulfilled but before receipt of the first payment from the buyer. This risk also depends on whether delivery is in one or more shipments, the buyer is to pay in one or more part-payments, and/or separate credit terms are connected to the deal. However, the maximum risk not covered by the insurance can always be determined in advance.

To calculate this risk and its inherent costs, three factors have to be considered:

1 capital risk – the amount of capital not covered by the insurance, which the seller has to retain at their own risk;

2 interest risk – the corresponding uninsured parts of any credit given to the buyer, calculated on estimated interest payments during the credit period, multiplied by the average interest rate;

3 settlement risk – the interest due for the period before payment is made under the insurance.

The seller should also consider other important issues that may vary between insurers, for example risk cover and settlement rules when invoicing in a foreign currency.

Incorrect, misleading, changed or unreported circumstances may, in the worst case, lead to the insurance being reduced or revoked. The seller must also take reasonable action during the insurance period to prevent or mitigate potential damage or losses under the insurance. It is, therefore, important for the seller to ensure that staff, who might not be aware of the conditions of the insurance, do not make changes or give concessions to the buyer that may jeopardize the insurance cover. This applies in particular to the longer government-supported insurance. In the private sector insurance market, the normal situation is that all the commercial buyers (the debtors of the insured seller) are pre-evaluated and individual credit limits established for each buyer. The seller then only has to ensure that the individual credit limits are available and are part of the credit insurance contract. Even though many standard and special terms may apply, these terms are part of the same credit insurance contract and should therefore be well known to the seller's staff.

If used correctly, export credit insurance can be a crucial part of the whole structure of the deal, whether it is to cover ordinary day-to-day short-term export transactions or the additional risk of an offered medium-term credit.

The private sector insurance market

Goods and services exported to the most developed OECD countries on credit periods less than two years (consumer goods, raw materials and certain lighter capital goods) can only be covered by the private sector according to established OECD rules, while government-supported insurance is usually only allowed for longer periods or for covering other countries where the private insurance market generally is less competitive.

For periods of one to two years, the commercial risk is the main risk element for exports to most OECD countries. But where both the commercial and political risks are increased, the terms of payment are generally shifted from open account terms to terms based on documentary payments, with stronger control over the goods until payment is received. For non-OECD countries, where the commercial/political risk is even greater, bank guaranteed terms of payment, usually in the form of an L/C, are often the norm.

The usual condition for obtaining insurance is that it covers the delivery of goods or services. However, the risks during the production period up to delivery can also be included, based on a signed contract between the parties.

This basic payment structure is consistent with the structure of the market sector credit insurance, covering mainly commercial risk on shorter periods, or the combined commercial/political risk on government or semi-official institutions. Political risk cover can sometimes be added to the policy for commercial buyers. The market sector insurance core business therefore comes from industrial countries, or countries in industrial development, in which relevant financial company information can be obtained and where the legal framework and financial systems are reasonably efficient.

The advantages of an international network are also used in the marketing of other services provided by insurers in the market sector; for example, issuing various types of export-related guarantees or bonds (mainly contract guarantees/bonds) in competition with the banks, or services related to the credit risk policies, such as credit risk assessment and collection of overdue payments.

The main advantages of private export credit insurance, taken from different leading insurance companies, are:

- capped and calculable costs;
- economic security;
- rapid and professional settlement of claims;
- access to experience from various business sectors in many countries;
- professional coverage of clients and outstanding claims;
- access to an international network with local representation;
- large databases of customer information;
- release of administration and resources from clients;
- increase in borrowing capacity from banks;
- expanding sales to existing customers;
- developing sales into new international markets;
- professional credit management overview of receivables.

One of the advantages of market sector credit risk insurance, emphasized by the insurers themselves, is that their combined services and not just the insurance tend to reduce the outstanding risk in the markets in which they operate, for example through local representation in the buyer's country and more professional supervision.

The development of more sophisticated models for risk analysis, together with new techniques for database handling and the establishment of an international network, has led to a rapid restructuring of this segment of the insurance market, which (apart from a large number of local and specialized insurers) now consists of only a few companies with a global presence.

The cost structure for market export insurance is based on a number of factors such as risk assessment, customer relations, the volume of business generated and the competition. This means that the premium for individual transactions or for a package of transactions can vary considerably between insurers, even when considering the differences in risk cover and in other terms and conditions that may apply.

Many credit insurance companies or brokers have standardized systems on their websites, so-called credit insurance cost-benefit analysis, where the seller can do a simple analysis evaluating their total export portfolio. By inputting the insurable yearly export sales, the average gross margin and an estimated average or worst-case loss ratio, this analysis shows not only the direct cost involved but also what incremental sales are necessary to pay for the corresponding average credit insurance premium.

Not surprisingly, the seller will probably find that in most of these general and standardized calculations, the premium is a relatively small investment for covering the potential loss, and that the additional sales needed to cover this loss are of such magnitude that they justify almost any credit insurance programme. This is before taking other indirect advantages into account.

However, even if standardized calculations do not give the whole picture, the seller should study the cost-benefit of using a general credit insurance cover in their particular case, based on the seller's own preconditions and assumptions. A general cover often gives the best outcome in such an analysis owing to the business volumes involved and the automatic spread of risk for the insurer, and any new individual deal could be added to the cover at beneficial rates. When this analysis is done, it is easier for the seller to compare other alternatives and to make an informed decision as to whether to use such credit risk cover programmes. Another important evaluation for the seller is to look at the consequences of non-payment of larger invoices.

The insurance policies offered in the market sector are generally individually structured and can be combined with many other services, and the seller should try to find the optimal combination for them, either directly or through an insurance broker. By doing so, the seller can also check the various preconditions that might be needed for entering into a potential transaction or to cover a risk portfolio, for example the terms of payment required. This may also give a better picture of the costs involved in relation to different levels of risk coverage, together with a better analysis of how the risk is assessed by an individual insurer. This is why it is so important to establish early contact with banks and credit insurers when it comes to new transactions or unfamiliar markets or buyers.

Most of the larger private sector providers of export credit insurance (as well as public export credit agencies) are members of The Berne Union, the leading international organization within this area; see the list of members at **www.berneunion.org.uk**.

Market sector insurance cover

The dominant insurers tend to structure credit insurance policies in the international market in a similar way, but often with different product names and including additional, optional services.

One general feature of this market is the tendency to strive to cover not only individual deals or single buyers, but primarily all of the seller's export transactions. This enables the insurer to obtain larger volumes of business with a more diversified risk structure, and to take advantage of the international network and additional services included in the offer. The description of the market sector insurance below is, therefore, of a general nature in order to highlight the basic structure of these insurance products. However, it also shows the different levels of services, the diversity of services and how these policies can be adapted to the needs of the individual seller based on business structure, risk aversion and affordability.

It goes without saying that every request for insurance is evaluated according to the risk involved, which means that certain buyers and/or countries may not be insurable. Or, if they are, it could be at a low percentage indemnity and/or a prohibitive premium.

Standard export credit insurance

Most market sector insurers have designed a range of export credit policies suitable for small- and medium-sized businesses, with cover against non-payment of debts owing to commercial and/or political risks. These policies are highly standardized in order to be cost-effective, often combining both domestic and export sales, with a risk assessment on the individual buyer and an indemnity level of up to 90 per cent. They are generally structured and priced in order to induce the company to include most of its receivables, often combined with additional services for more effective credit control, and with collection and litigation support as additional and mostly optional services.

To facilitate the practical day-to-day handling of the credit limit process, the larger insurers may also offer their customers internet access to their internal underwriting systems, thereby enabling the seller to manage their credit limits online in the most efficient way, including:

- applying for credit limits on new or existing customers;
- monitoring current portfolios under existing limits;
- making amendments to, or cancelling, existing buyer limits.

An additional advantage of standardized insurance – particularly important to small, growing businesses – is access to increased levels of export finance and the added security this cover will give the lender.

Tailor-made credit risk insurance

Many insurers offer more sophisticated integrated insurance packages, tailor-made for larger companies with greater volumes of receivables (both domestic and global). They can also include global risk cover for the group's requirements and risk limitations on the turnover covered by the policy. Even insurance packages for smaller businesses are often more or less tailor-made, though mostly not as complicated and of a more standardized character.

However, products and services offered as tailor-made solutions tend to differ significantly between both countries and individual insurers based on established domestic practice, customer demand and the particulars in each case, and it is not within the scope of this handbook to elaborate on this insurance cover in more detail. Exporters with this particular need should always contact a professional insurer for optimal cover based on their individual requirements.

Political risk insurance

Apart from the political risk that is directly associated with the commercial risk in an individual transaction, many market credit risk insurers (or other insurance companies) also cover pure political risks associated with trading or investments in countries where such cover may be needed. The most common market insurance policies in this area are described below.

Contract repudiation indemnity or contract frustration policy

There are different names for this kind of cover. It is an insurance that can be combined with the commercial risk on a company in many developing countries, but covering related risks of a more political nature such as changed or revoked approvals, licences, guarantees or other circumstances directly or indirectly caused by the government or any other public body. The cover can also include protection for similar events when interference from such institutions makes it impossible for the seller to fulfil their contractual obligations towards the buyer.

Bond/guarantee indemnity insurance

This insurance provides cover against so-called 'unfair calling' of bonds or guarantees issued on behalf of the seller, related to the export sale. This includes both genuinely unfair callings, but also (what might be called) 'fair callings', but caused by a public body or other political interference, which makes it impossible for the seller to perform their obligations under the commercial contract and which might therefore trigger the calling under the guarantee. (See also 'Reducing the risks with demand guarantees' in Chapter 3.)

Investment insurance

This insurance covers events such as confiscation, expropriation, nationalization or deprivation of the investor's fixed or mobile assets overseas. The cover can also be extended to include war, civil war, strikes, riots, terrorism, regulatory changes, currency inconvertibility, business interruption and the inability to recover leased equipment, but since they are mostly long term by nature, they are mainly covered by the export credit agencies (ECAs) as described in 'Investment insurance' later in this chapter.

Export credit agencies (official export credit institutions)

Most industrialized and emerging market countries have established ECAs with roughly the same objective: to support exports from their own countries. There is, however, no such thing as a typical ECA.

Most ECAs are part of the 'Berne Union' (International Union of Credit Insurers), the leading international organization in the field of export credit and investment insurance, with members from both the public and the private sectors. The majority are however official export credit institutions that deliver guarantees and insurance on behalf of the national governments in a variety of ways. Some are government departments or agencies, while

TABLE 5.1 Export credit agencies

ECAs (often also named EXIM-banks) have an important role in securing the export transaction or its finance in many countries, but the structure, the programmes and the terms of cover may differ. The exporter must therefore turn directly to their local ECA, as shown below, to find out what is applicable in the specific potential or actual transaction. But the buyer may have the same interest, for example when negotiating the finance options with the seller.

Australia EFIC – Export Finance & Insurance Corporation	**www.efic.gov.au**
Austria OeKB – Oesterreichische Kontrollbank Aktiengesellschaft	**www.oekb.at**
Belgium ONDD – Office National du Ducroire	**www.ondd.be**
Brazil SBCE – Seguradora Brasileira de Crédito à Exportação S/A	**www.sbce.com.br**
Canada EDC – Export Development Canada	**www.edc.ca**
China SINOSURE – China Export & Credit Insurance Corporation	**www.sinosure.com.cn**
Chinese Taipei TEBC – Taipei Export–Import Bank of China	**www.eximbank.com.tw/ en-us**
Czech Republic EGAP – Export Guarantee and Insurance Corporation	**www.egap.cz**
Denmark EKF – Eksport Kredit Fonden	**www.ekf.dk**
Finland FINNVERA – Finnvera plc	**www.finnvera.fi**
France COFACE – Compagnie Française d'Assurance	**www.coface.com**
Germany EH Germany – Euler Hermes Kreditversicherungs–AG	**www.agaportal.de**
Hong Kong HKEC – Hong Kong Export Credit Insurance Corporation	**www.hkecic.com**
Hungary MEHIB – Hungarian Export Credit Insurance Ltd	**www.exim.hu**
India ECGC – Export Credit Guarantee Corporation of India Ltd	**www.ecgc.in**
Indonesia ASEI – Asuransi Ekspor Indonesia	**www.asei.co.id**
Israel ASHRA –The Israel Export Insurance Corp. Ltd	**www.ashra.gov.il**
Italy SACE – Istituto per i Servizi Assicurativi del Credito all'Esportazione	**www.sace.it**
Jamaica EXIMBANK JAMAICA – National Export–Import Bank of Jamaica Ltd	**www.eximbankja.com**
Japan NEXI – Nippon Export and Investment Insurance	**www.nexi.go.jp**

TABLE 5.1 *continued*

Korea KSURE – Korea Trade Insurance Corporation	**www.ksure.or.kr**
Malaysia – EXIM Bank Malaysia Export Credit Insurance Berhad	**www.exim.com.my**
Mexico BANCOMEXT – Banco Nacional de Comercio Exterior SNC	**www.bancomext.gob.mx**
Netherlands ATRADIUS	**www.atradius.com**
Norway GIEK – Garanti-Instituttet for Eksportkreditt	**www.giek.no**
Poland KUKE – Export Credit Insurance Corporation	**www.kuke.com.pl**
Portugal COSEC – Companhia de Seguro de Créditos, SA	**www.cosec.pt**
Singapore ECICS – ECICS Ltd	**www.ecics.com.sg**
Slovak Republic SLOVAK EXIM – Export–Import Bank of the Slovak Republic (Observer)	**www.eximbanka.sk**
Slovenia SID – Slovene Export Corporation Inc.	**www.sid.si**
South Africa ECIC – Export Credit Insurance of South Africa Ltd	**www.ecic.co.za**
Spain CESCE – Compania Espanola de Seguros de Credito a la Exportacion	**www.cesce.es**
Sri Lanka SLECIC – Export Credit Insurance Corporation	**www.slecic.ik**
Sweden EKN – Exportkreditnämnden	**www.ekn.se**
Switzerland SERV – Swiss Export Risk Insurance	**www.serv-ch.com**
Thailand THAI EXIMBANK – Export–Import Bank of Thailand	**www.exim.go.th**
Turkey TURK EXIMBANK – Export Credit Bank of Turkey	**www.eximbank.gov.tr**
United Kingdom ECGD – Export Credits Guarantee Department	**www.ecgd.gov.uk**
United States US EXIMBANK – Export–Import Bank of the United States	**www.exim.gov**
Multilateral institution, ICIEC – Islamic Corp for the Insurance of Investment & Export Credit	**www.iciec.com**

SOURCE: The Berne Union

others are private insurance companies (as in Germany and France, for example) which, apart from doing insurance business on their own account, also act as an agency on behalf of the respective government, typically for credits over two years. This section deals with these official institutions only.

Even if the obligations are guaranteed by the respective state, official ECAs should operate with reasonable confidence of breaking even in the long term, charging customers premiums at levels that are sufficient to cover the perceived market and buyer risks and administration costs. In addition to these costs, some also include a 'reserve margin' in the premium rate to accommodate potential individual large losses or general country/regional payment moratoriums. They also make every effort to recover amounts paid in claims, either directly from individual buyers or borrowers or through the Paris Club of Official Creditors.

The OECD has regulated the ways in which the official ECAs operate, in order to restrict the potential for governments to use their ECAs to win export contracts by offering to their own exporters terms and conditions that are too favourable. To stop this 'race to the bottom', the major exporting nations have negotiated the OECD Arrangement on Officially Supported Export Credits, also known as the 'Consensus' or the 'Arrangement' (described in Chapter 6). The Consensus covers export credit support on periods of two years or more and includes the length of credit for different types of goods; repayment structures, minimum advance payments and maximum credit limits; minimum government-supported interest rate levels; and premium rates for sovereign/country risk.

It is worth noting that the EU and many other developed countries do not allow member states to issue state-supported insurance/guarantees for commercial risks to most OECD countries on periods of less than two years, an area that should normally be covered by the private insurance market. However, for other countries there is no such restriction, and in these cases many agencies issue insurance/guarantees for shorter periods.

The agencies also work together in purely commercial matters, primarily in transactions involving suppliers from several different countries. In order to facilitate such transactions, one of them will normally take overall responsibility and cover the entire package (according to its rules), with reinsurance from the other agencies covering their suppliers. These 'one-stop shop' programmes have several advantages for the project and for the lead supplier, which needs to have contact with only one agency.

Competition and matching

The primary objective of the official ECAs is to supplement the private insurance market by assuming credit risks that this sector is unable or unwilling to accept at competitive terms. There are, however, two areas of business where the OECD has tried to eliminate excessive competition between the countries in order to safeguard an equal playing field for government export support: commercial matching and tied aid matching.

Commercial matching is related to decisions taken by individual agencies giving special advantages to their domestic exporters. Since the establishment of the Consensus between the major OECD countries in the 1970s, a system of transparency has been introduced together with strict notification and consultation rules. Any deviation from agreed practices automatically leads to a matching procedure, where other agencies are free to give the same terms to their exporters competing for the same business.

Tied aid is government-to-government concessional financing of public sector projects, primarily to the poorest developing countries. The financing is often provided as a jointly arranged financial package by the government aid agency, together with support from the official export credit agency, covering the risk on the commercial part of such a loan. The terms for this type of finance can be far better than any other terms available, often with maturity up to 20 years and with extremely low interest rates.

In order to limit the use of tied aid for projects that should be commercially viable, and to separate them from real revenue-generating commercial projects, the major OECD countries have agreed certain standards for this type of financing. One is that such financing should contain at least a mathematically computed 'grant element' of at least 25 per cent to be considered concessional.

Government aid can also be formally 'untied' but combined with conditions that directly or indirectly favour exporters from a particular country. Real untied aid projects provided for developing and emerging market countries is a big potential market for suppliers from most countries; see Chapter 7, 'Multilateral development banks'.

Some general principles

The agencies always apply some general rules or restrictions to their guarantees and insurances, but often with different terms and interpretations depending on the countries involved, covering:

- foreign content or components;
- used or refurbished equipment;
- local costs;
- environmental and human rights aspects;
- illegal practices and anti-corruption guidelines.

A few agencies, such as the US Exim Bank, may also sometimes apply additional restrictions, for example shipping requirements with vessels from their own country for larger transactions, or economic or national impact assessments for strategic equipment, but such aspects are not dealt with in this book.

Individual agencies have somewhat different rules regarding cover for foreign content or components of the delivery. Some support relatively low levels of foreign content (normally 15–30 per cent), while others may support higher levels on a case-by-case basis, depending on size, structure, buyer country and other supplier countries involved.

Used or refurbished equipment may also be eligible for support, but in most cases this depends on factors such as contract value, the origin of manufacture, foreign content, domestic costs for refurbishment, whether the equipment has been previously exported, and the remaining useful life of the equipment.

Local costs for goods and services that are related to the transaction, but are incurred in the buyer's country, may also be eligible for support up to a certain percentage of the contract value. Such costs are primarily associated with projects or larger transactions, including installation or construction, and should relate to the exporter's obligations as verified in the sales contract or in a separate exporter's certificate, but originating in the buyer's country.

In most cases up to 15 per cent of the value of the exports can be covered for locally originated and/or manufactured goods and services. However, restrictions may apply as to the size and nature of the transaction or the project.

The OECD has also issued strict guidelines for a much broader perspective of government-supported international trade, for example its effects on the environment, sustainable development and human rights in the buying country. The larger the transaction and the more it is related to the infrastructure of these countries, the more important these considerations become.

Illegal practices are also receiving more attention (ie facilitation payments, money laundering, bribes and other corrupt practices). The area of corrupt practices was discussed in Chapter 1, but most agencies currently demand separate anti-corruption statements from applicants for insurance cover.

Insurance or guarantee

The terminology varies between institutions; some prefer to call all their cover 'guarantees', irrespective of whether they are issued as insurance or as a guarantee.

Others use the term 'insurance' when issued in favour of the exporter, normally with an excess as part of the cover and with other conditions attached as in ordinary insurance, and the expression 'guarantee' when issued to the lending institution normally covering 100 per cent of both capital and interest and payable on demand at default of the loan.

In this book we mainly use the term 'insurance', unless referring to a specific type of guarantee.

Different forms of insurance/guarantees

The insurance issued by the official ECAs has to comply with the rules laid down by the OECD and other directives. However, within that framework they are free to structure their programmes to meet the specific demand from their domestic business community. There are some basic programmes that are very much the same but differ with regard to name, terms and conditions, premiums and simplified procedures; or are specifically aimed at smaller companies, which is a special target group for most agencies.

The description below illustrates the diversity of cover available in different countries, but most agencies issue only some of these policies, even if under different names. More details can be found on the website of the respective agency, where full descriptions of available insurance can be found.

TABLE 5.2A Export credit insurance/guarantees

Exporter policies	
Single-buyer export insurance policy	Credit protection for general short-term credit sales, made by an exporter to a single foreign buyer (see below)
Multi-buyer export insurance policy	Same as above, this policy allows the exporter to insure all sales to eligible foreign buyers
Lender policies	
Working capital loan guarantee	This policy offers pre-export working capital loan guarantees to commercial banks, providing liquidity to the exporter to support new export transactions or related contract guarantees (see Chapter 6, 'Working capital insurance/guarantees')
Buyer credit insurance policy	Protects lenders financing the export of goods and services directly to foreign buyers, both on a short- but more often on a medium-term basis (see Chapter 6, 'Normal terms and conditions in buyer credits')
Supplier credit insurance policy	Protects lenders that finance or purchase export-related receivables from the exporter on a non-recourse basis (see Chapter 6, 'Refinancing of supplier credits')
Bank letter of credit policy	This policy protects banks against losses on L/Cs, when they are not prepared to confirm the L/C without such cover, owing to the uncertainty of the creditworthiness of the issuing bank (see Chapter 2, 'Level of security')

TABLE 5.2B Other forms of insurance/guarantee

Bond insurance policy	Protects the exporter against the risk of 'unfair calling' under a contract guarantee issued in favour of the buyer (see below and Chapter 3, 'Reducing the risks with demand guarantees')
Project and structured finance guarantee	A wide range of guarantee solutions may be offered for project suppliers and their international customers, covering limited recourse lending and structured financing (see Chapter 7, 'Project finance')
Leasing insurance policy	Cover may also be given to the leasing industry in the form of either an operating and/or a financing lease policy (see Chapter 7, 'Export leasing insurance')
Foreign currency insurance policy	Cover may also be available for transactions in foreign currency under most of the policies described; however, this is usually restricted to a fixed percentage or a maximum exchange rate. Cover may also be available during the bid/tender period (see Chapter 4, 'Tender exchange rate insurance')
Overseas investment insurance	Covers the exporter or the financial institution against the political risks on long-term foreign investments (see below, 'Investment insurance')

The standard export credit insurance policy

The most common export credit insurance policy (the name may vary between agencies) covers the risk for the seller for non-receipt of payment under an export contract, owing to commercial and/or political risks. The coverage is normally up to 90–95 per cent, with a three- to six-month waiting period, and the seller must retain the risk on the uninsured part, which cannot be laid off to a third party.

Commercial risk involves the insolvency of the buyer or failure either to pay or not fulfil obligations in any other way according to the contract within a certain period, often three to six months from the due date and, as a consequence of this failure, the seller suffers a loss on the insured contract. Political risk involves political, social, economic, legal or administrative events outside the exporting country that prevent the buyer fulfilling the contractual obligations, or create difficulties or restrictions of such a nature that the seller and/or buyer cannot fulfil their obligations.

These policies are generally issued in two different forms, either as a pre-shipment policy covering the buyer's obligations from the time the contract is signed and other related conditions are fulfilled, or as an after-shipment-only policy. The pre-shipment policy is by far the more common, since it not only covers payments (if any) to be made by the buyer before delivery, but also any other contractual obligation, the failure of which makes the seller suffer a loss. Such insurance also strengthens the seller's option to arrange additional pre-shipment finance through banks or other institutions.

As with all insurance policies, a maximum amount of loss is stipulated in each case (denominated in local currency), but within that limit, claims could also be settled in another currency if that is the valid currency of the claim (even if the currency risk is sometimes covered under separate policies). Insurance premiums are individually set, based on the assessment of the risk, the insured value and the length of the risk period.

Application procedures

Every agency has established standard procedures for dealing with requests or proposals for cover, following the normal business cycle of its customers (most market insurance companies apply a similar structure). The first stage is often in the form of a preliminary response, in oral or written form, when the seller is in the early internal process of discussing or preparing the offer. This response is without commitment, outlining only basic details for cover (if any) together with indicative terms and conditions.

The second stage is usually a conditional offer, issued upon request by the seller when preparing an offer or a tender for contract. This offer, often fixed for a period of 90–180 days, is more detailed, specifying the cover and the premium, but is subject to certain terms and conditions, and to the business details supplied by the seller.

The third and final stage comes when the contract is secured (subject mainly to external approvals and documentation), when the conditional offer is confirmed and the insurance policy is issued, which specifies the final details and terms and conditions, with a validity for a period of 90–180 days to allow time for documentation and fulfilment of all outstanding conditions in the contract. With this in mind, it is important for the seller to ensure that any signed contract is conditional upon the final issue of the insurance or guarantee, but also that any material changes thereafter in the commercial contract should have prior approval from the agency.

Investment insurance

This form of insurance covers events such as confiscation, expropriation, nationalization or deprivation of the investor's fixed or mobile overseas assets. The cover can be extended to include war, civil war, strikes, riots, terrorism, regulatory changes, currency inconvertibility, business interruption, and the inability to recover leased equipment. This cover can be obtained from both the private insurance market sector, but mainly from the export credit agencies for longer periods.

The insurance programmes may differ in detail between the countries but are generally based on the same principle to cover the investor against the political risks in connection with their overseas investments (whereas the commercial risk is up to the investor/supplier to assess and to cover separately, if needed). However, the cover can extend to breach of contract, where the host government or a local authority causes the underlying reasons, also often including the indirect consequences in case such events damage or prevent normal business operations related to the investment.

The schemes mainly provide cover for: 1) overseas direct investments as shareholder equity, loans or guarantees; 2) bank loans to an overseas company, when used for investment or purchase of goods from that country. These insurance programmes have, over time, become very important for many investors, which are often export companies creating production, storage or sales facilities abroad to strengthen their business opportunities in the region.

The programmes generally cover long-term investments, some as low as USD 10–20,000 and with cover up to 90 per cent for up to 10 or 15 years. During this period the investor can apply for annual renewals, sometimes at unchanged terms and conditions, including premiums, even if the situation in the country deteriorates. At the same time, the investor must normally take the long-term view on the investment in order to benefit from the cover, with an intended investment period of at least three to five years, or in the case of loans, with the same duration.

Export credit insurance – a summary

The commercial risk, often in conjunction with the political risk, is mostly the main risk for sellers in their overseas trade. As has been shown in this chapter, there are many different options for covering these risks through credit insurance.

The private insurance market covers primarily short-term commercial risk, sometimes in combination with political risk, but mainly for shorter periods up to two years, and is most competitive for a package of export risks and not just individual transactions.

The ECAs cover both the shorter periods, with a minimum of six months up to two years, depending on the status of the importing country, but mainly periods longer than that, where the private insurance market is less competitive. However, for most, but not all, OECD countries they are only allowed to cover the commercial risk on periods of two years and more.

It is generally recommended that the exporter should establish a basic risk strategy and a policy on how to make use of insurance cover when the commercial/political risks involved cannot be fully covered through the proposed or agreed terms of payment.

Trade finance

06

Financial alternatives

Being able to give or to arrange finance as part of an export transaction is increasingly important, both as a sales argument and to meet competition from other suppliers. This applies particularly in the case of heavier capital goods or whole projects, where finance is often an integrated part of the package, but it may also apply to raw materials, consumer goods and lighter capital goods for shorter periods.

The length of credit is often divided into short, medium and long term, even though such classifications are arbitrary and depend on the purpose. Short-term credits are normally for periods up to one year, even though the typical manufacturing exporter would normally trade on short-term credits of 60 or 90 days, perhaps up to a maximum of 180 days. Periods between one and two years may be described as both short- and medium-term depending on the purpose, whereas periods from two to five years are medium-term and periods above that are long-term credits.

In general, the buyer often prefers to split the payment for capital goods (machinery and installations with a considerable lifespan) into separate instalments over longer periods, perhaps with the intention of matching the payments against the income generated from the purchased goods. In such cases, the seller may have to offer these longer credit terms to be competitive.

The credit period is usually calculated from the time of shipment of the goods, or some average date in the case of several deliveries. However, in practice, payment is seldom made at that early stage and some form of credit is therefore included in most transactions. The seller may prefer to refinance such credits through ordinary bank credit facilities, especially for shorter periods and smaller amounts. However, in other cases the financing has to be arranged in some other way, which can also affect the structure of the transaction.

Trade finance

The expression 'trade finance' generally refers to the financing of fluctuating working capital needs for either single or bulk trade transactions. This financing should, in principle, be self-liquidated through the cash flow of the underlying transactions.

Trade finance is a major issue for both seller and buyer. In this book the focus is mainly on the exporter's situation, although the text will be as easily understood by readers who want to view it from the buyer's perspective.

Typical trade finance lending is, whenever possible, secured by the export goods and/or future receivables or other trade debt instruments such as bills of exchange, thereby assuring any external lender that the incoming cash flow will first be used for repayment of any outstanding debt before being released to the seller. This self-liquidating aspect of trade finance is generally more secure for the lender compared to other forms of working capital facilities and could therefore facilitate a higher lending ratio and often better terms than would otherwise be applicable.

Another aspect of trade finance involves different ways of obtaining security that will enable the seller to extend such credits, often directly through the terms of payment, or in combination with separate credit insurance. Such risk coverage and the terms under which it can be obtained have a strong influence on how export credits can be structured, but they also affect the terms of payment and other conditions related to the transaction, particularly for longer periods. Figure 6.1 provides a summary of the most frequently used techniques for financing or refinancing international trade and the following text is structured accordingly.

Of the alternatives, only one or two may be of interest in each case, depending on the particular area of business or trade cycle of the transaction, that is, the period from the time when the first costs are incurred for ordering raw material or other goods, until shipment and final payment from the buyer. However, the trade cycle also covers the time from when the first risks have to be incurred, for example agreements with other suppliers or simply the need to change internal procedures or preparations for the new production.

This trade cycle can be relatively similar for most products within one and the same company, depending on the area of business, or it can be unique for every transaction. The character of the trade cycle will also differ between most suppliers and will determine the structure of the terms of payment, as well as the method of dealing with different trade finance alternatives.

FIGURE 6.1 Summary of trade finance alternatives

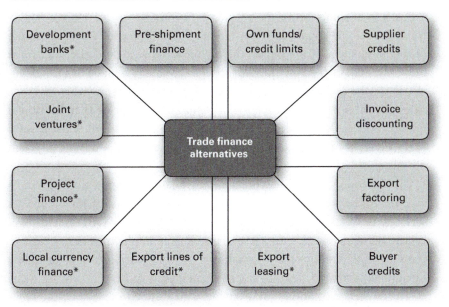

*See Chapter 7, Structured trade finance

Pre-shipment finance

The expressions 'pre-export finance' and 'pre-shipment finance' (sometimes also called 'packing finance') are defined as the temporary working capital requirement needed for the fulfilment of one or several specific export transactions. This covers the cash flow (and guarantees, if any) related to costs of raw material and other goods, labour, equipment and overheads, until final payment – or until the earlier stage where receivables or debt instruments are received from the buyer, which can be refinanced, either with or without recourse to the seller.

The period before delivery is often the most difficult part of the export transaction, particularly when trading on an open account basis. In that stage of the transaction the seller has only a sales contract, not a bill of exchange or other debt instruments related to the trade, nor any of the shipping documents that come with the actual delivery; for example, copies of the bill of lading and the invoice, showing that delivery has taken place and that a trade debt has been created.

For ordinary day-to-day transactions, the most frequent method of arranging pre-delivery finance requirements is through existing or additional bank credit limits, without involving the specific sales contract and/or the additional security, if any, created by the method of payment. However, when a business expands or, in the case of individual larger or more complex transactions, when existing limits are fully used or needed elsewhere in the ordinary business, it is important to know how to find the additional means to finance the new transaction until payment is made or until documents can be produced, which are necessary for the refinancing. In some cases the sales contract in itself can be used for creating that additional finance during the pre-delivery period, for example if and when a third party (ie a parent company) is in any way related to the buyer's payment obligations.

The difficulty of arranging pre-shipping finance in connection with open account trading is a major reason for the development of the SWIFTnet services and products, described in Chapter 2. 'The SWIFT system' is a central data information database that will increase the transparency of the transaction and reduce the uncertainty for the participating bank, enabling them to expand also their pre-shipment finance.

The existence of an L/C or a payment guarantee in favour of the seller could strongly facilitate the pre-shipment finance requirements in many ways. The advantages of having the L/C made transferable are also obvious: they will automatically transfer not only the financial cash flow but also security from the seller to their suppliers, who might use the transferred L/C for their own pre-shipment arrangements.

Many banks also extend special 'export loans' on the basis of the L/C up to a certain percentage of its value, with or without the L/C and its future proceeds pledged to the bank. Both the percentage and the collateral will most certainly vary depending on the many aspects to be considered by the bank, for example the issuing bank, the size and maturity of the L/C, its terms and conditions, the nature of the goods and, perhaps equally important, the knowledge and experience of the seller.

The advantages of an L/C as a pre-shipment finance instrument also apply to a payment guarantee issued by the buyer's bank in favour of the seller, but perhaps not to the same degree. The payment guarantee (supposed to be a normal trade-related and conditional guarantee as described in Chapter 3) is more like a credit risk umbrella covering the general payment obligations of the buyer according to the contract. But it does not contain a mechanism, such as an L/C, where the issuing bank automatically has to pay, irrespective of the buyer's consent, when certain specified terms and conditions are met. Even though it is thereby less precise than an L/C, most banks will nevertheless regard such a guarantee as an important instrument for increasing the seller's credit limits.

In a mutually advantageous business negotiation and when the commercial parties know each other well, the buyer may even be willing to make further concessions in the payment structure to accommodate the seller and their need for additional pre-delivery finance. In fact, the buyer has already done so indirectly by agreeing to an L/C as a method of payment in the first place, or by having it made transferable. If agreeing to support the seller's pre-delivery cash flow, this could be done through inserting a 'red clause' in its terms, even if such clauses are now relatively rare in international commercial trade. A red clause allows the seller to make use of an agreed part of the value of the L/C before delivering the documents, sometimes earmarked for payment only for some specific purpose. By inserting such clauses in the L/C, this pre-delivery part-payment will, in fact, become an advance payment. However, advance payments in general are otherwise mainly used only as part of an overall part-payment structure, with the larger part being payable at shipment and with one part up-front and one part as a deferred payment; this type of split is often used in contracts containing more than just delivery obligations, such as installation or maintenance and over a longer period.

Even if any form of advance payment received by the seller has to be secured by a conditional bank guarantee in favour of the buyer, and thus issued under the seller's existing credit limits, it is still to their advantage both from a cash-flow and a collateral perspective. Such a guarantee cannot be drawn upon by the buyer as long as the seller fulfils the contractual obligations and therefore involves no additional risk; for that reason such a bank guarantee may be issued with other, less stringent security requirements from the issuing bank, compared with ordinary lending.

Working capital insurance/guarantees

When dealing with pre-shipment finance, one also has to look at the sales contract between the commercial parties and how that could be used as a financial tool. Both private market insurers and ECAs may offer pre-delivery cover (see Chapter 5, 'Different forms of insurance/guarantees'), even if structured differently and with different requirements on the status of the buyer or on the terms of payment.

Such cover can be issued in the form of an insurance policy to the exporter or directly as a guarantee to an authorized lending institution, thereby enabling the seller to obtain a loan to finance their export of goods and services, to be used for the following purposes:

- purchase of finished products for export;
- cost of raw materials, equipment, supplies, labour and overheads to produce goods and/or provide services for export;
- work in progress and finished export goods;
- support standby L/Cs or other arrangements serving as contract or payment guarantees;
- finance of open account or term receivables.

With such a working capital or pre-shipment guarantee, the seller should be able to increase their borrowing capacity considerably in comparison with normal lending criteria. Such insurance/guarantee may cover up to 90 per cent of the loan amount and with a maturity to match the underlying cash-flow requirements, typically from six months up to a year.

The existence of separate credit insurance will increase the security of the transaction and will have a strong influence on the bank's decision on additional finance. This interaction between the seller, the insurer and the bank (ongoing during the entire negotiation process with the buyer) may be the key for securing additional pre-finance needed for the transaction.

This procedure also gives the seller feedback on the terms on which the insurer and/or the bank may be willing to participate and what might be required from the seller and from the terms of payment in the sales contract. Having achieved that, the seller will have secured the support needed from these institutions, covering both the risks involved and the cash needed as pre-shipment finance.

Supplier credits

Supplier credits are the most commonly used method of trade finance, mainly for shorter periods but to a lesser degree also for medium-term periods. The credit's structure is determined by its time-span and size, the buyer's country and the method of payment agreed in the sales contract – details that determine not only the seller's risk exposure but also the structure required by the financial institution, should the credit have to be refinanced at a later stage.

The possibility of the seller agreeing to a supplier credit is determined by how it can be refinanced, either through existing bank limits for smaller amounts and shorter periods, or by separate discounting or refinancing of the finance instrument that becomes available at shipment or shortly thereafter. The credit terms that can be offered by the seller are also important as a sales argument and as a competitive advantage – or at least as a means of being on an equal footing with competitors.

Sometimes the terms of such short credits can be made particularly advantageous for the buyer as part of the offer, even if the seller compensates themselves in another part of the contract. The problem for the buyer is that it is not easy to see if the price has been increased because of the favourable credit terms, and if so, by how much. There is also a risk that the seller may overcompensate for the risks in their credit offer if the buyer is unfamiliar or if the seller cannot evaluate the commercial risk correctly. The buyer, on the other hand, may ask for a quotation to include both cash against delivery and a supplier credit alternative in order to be able to make a fair comparison.

The buyer may even start the negotiations based on cash against delivery or short-term open account terms to allow for new and longer credit negotiations, when the price discussions are more or less concluded. It will then be more difficult for the seller to add the credit costs to the price and these will have to be part of a separate negotiation in which the buyer again tries to get the best solution – or arranges the finance elsewhere or, in the worst case, chooses another supplier altogether.

Irrespective of how the negotiations proceed, there are some general questions that the seller must evaluate before offering a supplier credit, such as:

- To what degree is the requested credit changing the commercial and/or the political risk involved in the transaction?

- Can the buyer be expected to take any open credit costs?

- Should the financial costs be included in the original price offer or should the seller be proactive by keeping the credit terms open as a separate question to be discussed with the buyer?

- How can such credit be refinanced?

- In the case of foreign currency invoicing, how should the currency risk be evaluated and covered?

In cases of shorter periods and smaller amounts, these questions are easily dealt with, but in other cases they may be one of the major aspects of the transaction.

Short-term supplier credits

The most common form of short-term supplier credits is in combination with open account payment terms; that is, the contract is based on a future payment transfer, and the invoice specifies the date when payment must be received at the seller's account. However, the seller has no other security for the buyer's payment obligations. Sometimes, particularly for periods over three to six months, even short-term credits are arranged through a bill of exchange to be accepted by the buyer at delivery, thereby replacing the open credit with a documented debt instrument, payable at a specified later date.

The seller may nevertheless also enclose a bill of exchange with the invoice even when trading on open account and on shorter payment terms (30–90 days), showing the delivery date together with the corresponding payment date. This could have its value even if the bill is not to be accepted by the buyer because it connects the sales contract with the delivery and the buyer's corresponding payment obligations. This is the same procedure as used in connection with documentary collections, payable at presentation.

The seller should also evaluate whether it would be beneficial to offer both cash against delivery terms and short-term credit on favourable terms as alternatives; however, if choosing the latter, only conditional upon the buyer's acceptance of a bill of exchange when presented together with the invoice. A short, well-documented supplier credit could have advantages for both parties, compared to open account payment terms, for the following reasons:

- it could be an additional advantage for the seller from a sales perspective;
- the buyer can use the credit for improved cash-flow management, perhaps at more favourable terms, but with the strict obligation to pay at maturity – with the risk for noting and protest of the accepted bill if not paid;
- the seller has the advantage of an accepted finance document that is easier to refinance at an earlier stage, if needed;
- the seller can plan liquidity more exactly at the outset, knowing that payment on maturity is highly likely; and
- the seller may wholly or partly include interest in the bill of exchange, compared with a later overdue interest (which in practice is very difficult to receive).

The difference between open account payment terms and the accepted bill of exchange is also greater than one might first expect (even with the same maturity date). With open account terms, the buyer has a stronger case for negotiating with the seller prior to payment, should it be considered that the delivery was not in accordance with the agreement. It could be anything from time of delivery to shortcomings in the quality or quantity of the goods – the main point is that the buyer may refuse to pay until the matter is resolved.

However, by accepting the bill of exchange at or about the time of shipment, the buyer has an unconditional obligation to pay, irrespective of any real or alleged shortcomings discovered later in the delivery. If the claim is correct, the buyer will probably get compensation; however, the bill must be paid at maturity, irrespective of the ongoing discussions with the seller.

When documentary collection is used as the method of payment together with supplier credits, the documents will be released against acceptance of a bill of exchange with a fixed maturity. The documents are exchanged against the bill, normally without any further security for the seller. But, if the supplier credit is given as part of an L/C (with documents against acceptance), the banks involved will determine the procedure and will also check the accuracy of the documents. Upon approval, the bill of exchange will be accepted (by one of the banks as a banker's acceptance and not by the buyer) and can then easily be discounted by the seller on favourable terms, mostly without recourse.

Medium- and long-term supplier credits

Supplier credits of two years or more are usually arranged in connection with the sale of machinery, vehicles, equipment or other capital goods, and with credit documentation that tends to be more complex than for shorter periods. In these cases separate financial documentation is often used, with or without supplementary bills of exchange – or promissory notes with the same but more summarized wording compared to a complete loan agreement.

When bills of exchange or promissory notes are refinanced externally, the seller often has a prearranged agreement with a bank or financial institution, specifying the details, including the security required for such refinancing to take place. In any case, the seller is likely to have such refinancing agreed as part of the transaction, with all preconditions in place before delivery.

With longer supplier credits, two questions are important for both commercial parties to agree upon: 1) the choice of currency; and 2) the choice of fixed or floating interest rate. The choice of currency need not be the same as the invoicing currency, even if that is normally the case. However, if the parties agree to a separate financing currency, they also have to agree at what future date, and at what exchange rate, the change from invoicing to financing currency will take place.

The buyer's possible currency deliberations are described in Chapter 4. The outcome may be a 'neutral' third-party currency, often USD, which also has good liquidity over longer periods and, therefore, is possible to hedge at reasonable terms. However, if the currency of the credit is not the buyer's home currency, then the buyer takes the currency risk, or the hedging cost, until final maturity (often with a substantial risk or cost if it is either not hedged at all or hedged against a weaker currency).

Example of a promissory note (issued under a medium-term supplier credit agreement)

Promissory note No. 10

For value received, Bayala Machinery Group Bhd, 2 Jalan Tong Shin, 50201 Kuala Lumpur, Malaysia (the buyer), hereby irrevocably and unconditionally promises to pay, on 21 June 2018, to Pierson & Henders Ltd, 4 West Regent Street, London EC2 4LP (the seller), or order, the principal sum of one hundred and thirty-five thousand US dollars (USD 135,000) and to pay interest on said amount from and including the date hereof at the rate of five per cent (5 per cent) per annum. Interest shall be payable semi-annually in arrears on 21 June and 21 December each year, commencing on 21 December 2013, calculated on the exact number of days and a year of 360 days, and any overdue payment should be calculated on a day-to-day basis at an interest rate of 7 per cent, until payment is made. Both principal and interest is payable in USD at First Commercial Bank, 3 Tower Hill Street, London EC2 3JK, in favour of the lawful holder of this note, without set-off or counterclaims and without any deduction for present or future withholdings or taxes.

This note is one of a series of ten (10) promissory notes in the aggregate amount of USD 1,350,000, of the like form and tenor except their number and date of maturity, issued pursuant to the Contract Number DN/8318/26, entered into between the buyer and the seller on 3 February 2013. The contract cover sixteen (16) 280 KW diesel generating machines, the delivery of which is fulfilled according to contract and unconditionally approved by the buyer by signing this note.

Each one in this series of notes is covered by the enclosed separate bank guarantee issued by Bank of Berhad, 304 Sultan Road, 50230 Kuala Lumpur, Malaysia, a currency transfer guarantee by the Central Bank of Malaysia and by a legal opinion issued by the law firm Derr & Whitney, Kuala Lumpur.

The laws of the United Kingdom shall govern this note, and the courts of England should settle any legal dispute.

Date and verified signatures

The box on the previous page shows an example of a promissory note, the last note in a medium-term supplier credit over five years with 10 equal and semi-annual instalments and fixed interest rate. As can be seen in the example, a bank guarantee as well as a currency transfer guarantee from the central bank may sometimes be required to make the notes acceptable for refinancing (in this example by a UK forfaiting institution under UK law).

NB: The above example is an illustration only; any debt instrument should always be subject to legal scrutiny in each particular case.

The choice of fixed or floating interest in a medium- or long-term supplier credit is primarily the buyer's, if a fixed rate alternative can be obtained through the refinancing bank. That is most likely in the larger trade currencies, either as direct refinancing or through interest swaps, which are separate contracts with the bank, exchanging floating for fixed interest rate under a fixed period of time. Such contracts in the larger trade currencies can be obtained at reasonable rates for very long periods.

Refinancing of supplier credits

In one way or the other, the exporter has to finance or refinance the supplier credit extended to the buyer; some of these methods have been mentioned. As a summary, some of the most used forms of refinancing supplier credits on short- or medium-term periods are:

- bank loans and trade finance limits;
- invoice finance facilities;
- export factoring;
- forfaiting;
- other medium-term refinancing.

The last point, other medium-term refinancing, is mainly relevant only to larger or more complex supplier credits, when both the collateral and the structuring of the documentation itself will become more complicated. Such deals are often covered by export credit insurance and state-supported export credits, sometimes involving not only the exporter's own bank but also special export banks. Such supplier credits are therefore – when it comes to their refinancing – very similar to the structure of buyer credits, which are separately described later on this chapter.

Bank loans and trade finance limits

The most common method of refinancing short-term supplier credits is simply by using the seller's existing bank credit limits, often the current account and its overdraft facility, based on general collateral pledged to the bank in the form of fixed or floating charges on the company's assets. This refinancing is then done at a floating interest rate determined by the lender as for any other domestic loan, normally based on the prime or base rate of the country, set by the central bank.

This form of domestic bank finance is mainly used to finance ordinary trade transactions based on open account payment terms, and since they represent the major part of international trade, the banks are also the main refinancing source of this shorter end of trade finance.

If the transaction is made in foreign currency, the seller may alternatively take a separate loan in the same currency to refinance the supplier credit, thereby also covering the currency risk involved. Such a loan could also have beneficial interest advantages if the currency in question has a lower interest rate than the domestic currency. The currency loan will then immediately be changed into local currency at the spot rate and repaid by the incoming payment from the buyer. The cost for such a currency loan as compared to a domestic base or prime rate loan will be based on the following factors:

- the bank's refinancing costs, which are generally based on the interbank money market rates in that currency and for that period, as explained in more detail at the end of this chapter ('The international money market');
- the bank's interest margin as determined by the amount, customer relationship and market competition;
- the cost for any currency hedge (which in this example is not needed since the loan is automatically hedged by the incoming currency from the buyer).

Apart from these basic forms of general bank finance, banks also offer different forms of trade-related loans based on the individual transaction, normally connected to documentary collection and L/Cs, where if necessary the documents and the corresponding flow of money can also be pledged to the bank as additional security.

In connection with documentary collection, the banks may give advance payment against documents under collection to a certain percentage of their value (up to 70–80 per cent), often under a separate and more favourable trade-finance limit, to be used for self-liquidating trade transactions. The accepted short-term trade bill of exchange, normally three to six months, may also be discounted under such a limit.

In case of an L/C payable by acceptance, some banks may offer separate 'export loans' up to a percentage of its value, available from the time of its issuing. At the time of presentation of documents, the advising bank (if that is the place where the L/C is payable) or the issuing bank will accept the bill of exchange, which can then almost automatically be discounted and the net proceeds paid to the seller.

After delivery, there are additional finance alternatives offered by both banks and finance companies in connection with open account trading, covering the short-term credit of normally 30–90 days included in most trade transactions. At that time, the seller has fulfilled their delivery obligations and a payment obligation on behalf of the buyer has been created, evidenced at least by the seller's invoice, indicating actual shipment. It is true that the buyer may have objections to how the delivery has been executed, but unless that is the case it should be possible to refinance that invoice in one way or the other to generate immediate cash for the seller, less interest and fees involved in the refinancing.

The main alternatives available after delivery, based on the invoice alone are described below. They are relatively similar and consequently often treated as synonymous with each other, but in this book we make the main distinction between the following two basic areas:

- *Confidential financing*, where the finance is a transaction between the seller and the bank/finance company, of which the buyer is not aware. This facility is referred to as 'invoice discounting' below.

- *Notified financing*, where the buyer is fully informed about the finance transaction, normally through an assignment on each invoice to a third party. This facility is referred to as 'export factoring' below.

The parties offering these services are either banks or bank-owned finance companies, which receive most of their business through referrals within the group, larger and independent finance or factoring companies, or smaller niche players concentrating on certain segments only. Since pure invoice discounting or other invoice finance facilities are a quite straightforward service offered by banks and their finance companies and also by a number of other institutions, the general term 'provider' is generally used in this connection, whereas 'factoring company', or 'factor' as it is commonly known, is used in the area of export factoring.

However, there are probably few areas within international trade finance where both terminology and procedures differ so much as to how such refinance is carried out in practice in all its different forms. The segmentation into *invoice discounting* and *export factoring*, and the detailed description below, may therefore not always be valid in all countries, but it nevertheless has a pedagogical advantage that will enable the reader to understand the concepts and make use of them to their advantage according to their individual circumstances.

Invoice discounting

Invoice discounting (also called invoice finance or invoice lending depending on the nature of the facility) can briefly be described as the provision of finance against the security of a bulk of receivables, mostly but not always secured by an earmarked floating charge or a specific debenture.

Invoice discounting is a confidential facility; it is also mostly a pure lending facility where the title to the invoice and the right to the proceeds remain with the seller. It gives cash payment of a certain percentage of a bulk of receivables, and invoice discounting is therefore mostly used when the seller already has an internal system in place for effective credit control.

Invoice discounting can accommodate most of the seller's invoices based on open account payment terms on a rolling basis; however, as it is confidential, the buyers are unaware of the facility and the seller is responsible for sales ledger administration and later collecting procedures, should that be necessary.

Some providers integrate invoice discounting with other services, such as credit information, credit insurance and debt collection, to make this combination more competitive at a reasonable cost. Even if these 'packages' are constructed somewhat differently, this combined service has even more similarities with factoring, seen from the seller's point of view.

It is important to remember that there is no typical invoice discounting or invoice finance facility since they differ not only between countries but also between providers in one and the same country. However, the main features of an ordinary invoice discounting facility used for trade finance purposes may include the following aspects:

- The buyer is unaware of the arrangements between the seller and the provider.
- The provider may arrange the opening of a separate bank account in the name of the seller, where all trade payments must be paid. This

account, along with the invoices, could be, but is not necessarily, pledged to the provider as security.

- The seller may be required to send copies of invoices to the provider to be included under the facility, in order for them to keep the pool of eligible invoices constantly updated. New invoices are included, and paid invoices, together with unpaid and long overdue invoices, are deleted.

- The provider will make the facility available to the seller at an agreed percentage of the underlying invoices in the 'pool'.

- The provider may send the seller regular statements in order for the seller to check against the export invoice ledger, and the seller may be obliged to send to the provider copies of that sales ledger at intervals for control purposes.

Invoice discounting is suitable for most companies and is particularly useful for smaller and rapidly growing companies whose balance sheets would not be sufficiently strong to allow for the volume of ordinary credit limits they may need for their expanding business. Such facilities mostly cover both domestic and export transactions in order to reach administrative advantages and critical mass, with foreign buyers mainly from developed and neighbouring countries where open account payment terms are normally practised.

Invoice discounting is a 'with recourse' form of lending up to a certain level of the face value of the invoices, often 70–80 per cent, based on a risk assessment and mostly secured by either a general pledge on all the company's assets or a specific and unsecured debenture covering invoices not already pledged. The finance percentage offered is not only based on the invoices themselves, but also on their average distribution regarding amounts, buyers and countries. As it is a confidential facility based on invoices only, the general credit standing of the seller is most important, as is their experience and track record, and the aggregate of all these criteria will determine the percentage lending value and the cost structure.

In most cases, invoice discounting could be used as an ordinary overdraft facility at the seller's discretion, set by the volume of the underlying eligible invoices, forming a pool of available borrowing under the facility at any time. As the value of the pool of invoices fluctuates, more or less money will be available. In case of maximum utilization in conjunction with re-duced total invoice value, or in case of non-payment when the invoice will be deleted from the pool, the seller may even have to repay money in order to keep the agreed percentage.

Invoice discounting can release liquidity instantly at a high percentage of the underlying receivables and because of the nature of the facility it can also be made relatively cost-effective, especially when covering both domestic and export sales, hence its popularity in many countries. Some providers also offer these facilities via the internet, which facilitates the practical day-to-day handling for both parties and gives the seller an instant picture of usage and availability at any time. The cost depends on the services involved, but the facility is often charged for by means of a flat fee related to the agreed total limit and an interest rate for actual usage that is usually higher than a normal overdraft facility, together with additional handling charges, based on volume and the work involved.

Export factoring

Factoring is a special form of short-term finance where a finance company (the factor) purchases the seller's receivables and assumes the credit risk, either with or without recourse to the seller. Factoring is still mainly used in the industrialized countries and within trading areas with a relatively similar structure of harmonized laws, rules and procedures. It is generally more complex, involving not only finance but also additional services, and in many countries it is therefore used more selectively and often for larger individual amounts compared to invoice discounting finance. *The principles of export factoring are basically the same as for domestic factoring and therefore only a few paragraphs in this chapter refer specifically to export factoring.*

In its original form, the seller entering into a factoring agreement sells the receivables to the factor, mostly also relieving themselves of the credit control and debt collection functions, which are assumed by the factor against a fee. In such a case, the factor also gains the title to the invoice and the right to the proceeds, and takes future decisions, if any, regarding collection and other measures, including the legal work in the event of non-payment. The seller will display a notification on the factored invoices, informing the buyer that the invoice has been transferred to the named factor, together with instructions on how payment is to be made directly to them in order to discharge their payment obligation. The seller also sends copies of the invoices and the shipping documents to the factor, but often the factor issues the invoices themselves upon instruction from the seller.

The factor starts with a credit assessment of the seller and the general structure of their trade and previous experience, followed by an assessment of the different buyers, including any insurance cover, to establish individual lending limits on the buyers and a total credit limit for the seller. Factoring could have the following advantages for the seller:

- a better risk performance than for other finance alternatives through the credit information services included;
- more punctual payments from the buyers, aware of the sale of the invoices to the factor;
- the borrowing value of the invoices could be higher than through ordinary bank lending, thereby increasing the seller's total liquidity;
- the seller can often make use of additional administrative systems to reduce workload.

Factoring is mostly in the form of 'with recourse factoring' with up to 90 per cent of invoice value, with the provision that if the buyer fails to pay the invoice after a set period of time, the factor will be repaid by the seller. In some cases factoring can be provided as 'non-recourse factoring', where the factor stands the risk in the event of bankruptcy or liquidation of the buyer. In these cases the seller will never be requested to repay the discounted invoice to the factor and can then remove the invoice from the receivables in the balance sheet. However, they may have to pay interest for the agreed waiting period after the due date, normally 60–90 days, as specified in the factoring agreement. Most such non-recourse factoring relates to larger individual transactions, either based on good corporate names with little risk or secured by separate credit insurance or similar security.

It is often said that factoring is more expensive than similar bank services, in particular export factoring, but such a comparison could be somewhat misleading as the services are difficult to compare. In most cases factoring does lead to considerably more punctual payments, better control of outstanding receivables and less administrative workload for the company. The factoring services are generally more efficient with regard to slow payers and in these cases the use of a factor can have an effect – and the seller avoids straining the business relationship.

Apart from the interest charged, a flat service fee is also charged on every invoice factored, the size of which depends on workload and services included, numbers of factors involved and the total factoring turnover. The seller should therefore complete a cost/revenue valuation in relation to the services offered – and needed – compared with other alternatives, for example invoice discounting finance.

When it comes to export factoring in particular, there are in principle two basic forms, either 'two-factor export factoring', where the seller's domestic factoring company uses local correspondents (either an independent company or a branch) in the buyer's country within a chain of cooperating factors, or 'direct export factoring', without such a local factor being involved. From the seller's perspective, there is a big difference between these two alternatives, when it comes to the risk involved and to cost.

The use of domestic factors or branches of an international organization will mostly increase the overall cost structure, but has the big advantage of a local presence and knowledge of the buyers. The local factor will also have full knowledge of the legal aspects of factoring in that country and how it operates in practice, and of debt recovery and similar procedures, should that be necessary at a later stage. This overall knowledge and experience of both the seller's factor and their correspondents abroad will finally decide in what countries export factoring should be used as a viable alternative to other forms of finance.

Figure 6.2 shows the two-factor alternative, in which the seller's factoring company cooperates with a domestic factor in the buyer's country. Nowadays this form is the most-used system for export factoring.

FIGURE 6.2 Export factoring*

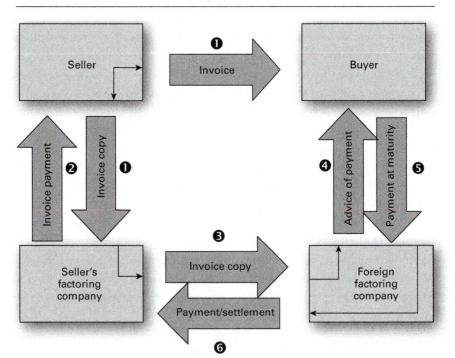

* Explanations relating to the numbering are included in the text.

Some major global providers of credit information (see Chapter 1) have also expanded their services into the credit risk management area, thereby offering in-house combinations of purchase of invoices, credit information, credit insurance and debt collection. These services combined are relative similar to export factoring, and are sold within their own organization through a network of branches around the world, in competition with the established factoring companies.

Forfaiting

Refinancing of medium- or long-term supplier credits is mostly handled by the commercial banks, often together with, or in competition with separate export banks specializing in the longer periods of export finance.

The medium- and long-term finance market also includes the special forfaiting institutions, which have a long tradition in financing international trade. They are mainly located in the larger financial centres such as London and New York, but do not have the same importance today owing to increased competition from commercial and international banks. Forfaiting basically means the surrender of an unconditional future right to a trade-related claim through accepted and freely negotiable bills or notes, in return for the receipt of prompt payment.

Forfaiting, whether through specialized departments within the banks or through traditional and independent forfaiting houses, is a special type of discounting of trade-related and mostly fixed-term-interest bills of exchange with different maturity dates, which can range from 180 days to seven or even 10 years, without recourse to the seller. When it comes to risk evaluation of both individual buyers and countries, the forfaiters are well placed in trading these negotiable financial instruments, by spreading the risks through risk participation and distribution through other domestic and international credit risk insurers, using established reinsurance and syndication techniques.

Forfaiting risks are generally based on security in the form of first-class corporate risks with an acceptable political risk, or otherwise with different combinations of bank guarantees, standby L/Cs, undertakings from ministries of finance in the case of sovereign buyers, with or without currency transfer guarantees from a central bank. The diversity of the operations, often with the forfaiters specializing in different countries or commodities, may therefore create different risk evaluations and credit decisions among these institutions, influenced also by their existing exposure and limits.

If a deal is acceptable, the forfaiting house will issue a firm or a conditional facility letter to the seller, specifying the terms and conditions for discounting and the interest level and fees to be applied. The example of a promissory note shown earlier in this chapter illustrates the terms and conditions that would be acceptable by a forfaiting house to discount such notes without recourse, in that case secured by a separate bank guarantee covering the payment obligations of the buyer in combination with a currency transfer guarantee from the central bank.

Forfaiting normally requires larger transactions to be cost-effective, with a minimum of at least USD100,000 per item, and the procedure is mostly quite simple; at receipt of the bills or notes according to the terms in the facility letter, the discounted net amount is paid to the seller without recourse.

More information about forfaiting can be obtained through the International Forfaiting Association, IFA, which has about 150 members and is the worldwide trade association for commercial companies, financial institutions and intermediaries engaged in forfaiting; **www.forfaiters.org**.

Buyer credits

Buyer credits are given directly to the buyer or the buyer's bank in connection with the export transaction. This enables the seller to receive cash payment at delivery and/or at different stages of construction or installation, while at the same time a longer-term credit is extended to the buyer. Buyer credits are normally used for larger individual transactions, particularly when the transaction involves more than just delivery of goods or covers a longer contract period, and often also when the delivery is tailor-made to the specifications of the buyer.

Buyer credits may be given in two different forms, either directly to the buyer's bank, 'bank-to-bank credits' for further on-lending to the buyer, or directly to the buyer, 'bank-to-buyer credits', then mostly covered by a guarantee from the buyer's bank. However, since this difference is relatively small from the perspective of the seller, we shall deal with both these forms as bank-to-buyer credits below.

When exporting to industrialized countries, but also to many emerging market countries, buyer credits are usually arranged on pure market terms. However, outside these countries it is seldom possible to finance transactions of this nature on longer terms on the open market; they need to be backed by additional security, mostly in the form of export credit insurance. The seller should then coordinate the commercial negotiations with the buyer and with both the chosen bank lender and the insurer so that the

FIGURE 6.3 Supplier and buyer credits – a comparison

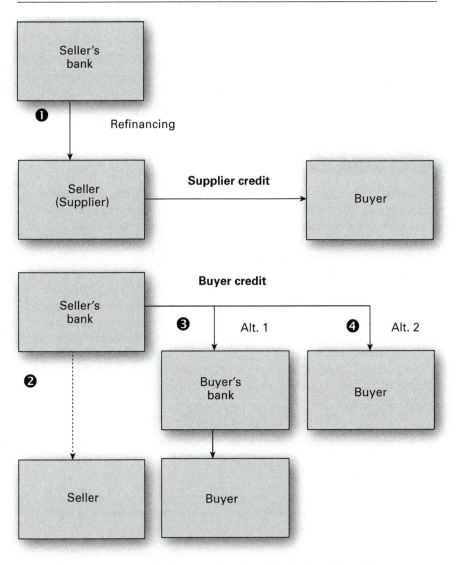

1 Refinancing is done through a bank or some other financial institution, with or without recourse to the seller.

2 Credit amount is normally 80–85 per cent of contract value and the buyer instructs the seller's bank to pay directly to the seller under the credit agreement.

3 With bank-to-bank credits, the seller's bank has the buyer's bank as counterpart, which forwards the credit to the buyer, often with the same/similar documentation.

4 With bank-to-buyer credits, the seller's bank has the buyer as a direct counterpart in the same way as the seller in the commercial transaction and will, in these cases, request a third-party guarantee, normally from the buyer's bank, covering the obligations under the credit agreement.

contract and the corresponding loan agreement can be developed in parallel during the negotiating process.

One of the important aspects of buyer credits is how they relate to the underlying contract. Financial credits are principally unrelated to the obligations between the commercial parties, and that also applies to buyer credits when the buyer normally has to approve the delivery in connection

Export credit banks/financial institutions

In most countries the actual lending of export credits is made through commercial banks, either on their own without additional support, or with such support, mostly in the form of guarantees from export credit agencies, when the credit risk (commercial and/or political) is otherwise deemed too high. These agencies, on the other hand, are basically insurance or guarantee institutions, but they very seldom give direct loans themselves.

In many of the larger exporting countries, however, the financing is also done through special export credit banks or similar financial institutions, owned or partly government owned as official export institutions, even if the practical aspects of loan documentation and loan administration may remain in the hands of the cooperating commercial banks during the lifetime of the loan. But the official lender is then the export credit bank, which also funds that lending on the international markets, being capitalized in such a way that they achieve the very best terms for their funding.

As official institutions, their structure and activities may include:

- administration of state-supported export credit schemes as well as extending loans on commercial terms based on market funding, both floating and fixed rates of interest;

- lines of credit (see Chapter 7) established with major banks in their main importing countries, providing export finance facilities also for smaller export transactions based on pre-arranged loan documentation;

- administration of grants in tied or untied mixed or concessionary credits to developing countries on behalf of the government aid agency (see Chapter 7, 'Multilateral development banks');

- financing of long-term investments and acquisitions made by domestic businesses in their internationalization process.

Most export credit banks also have the additional advantage that, as official export institutions, they may avoid having to pay withholding tax on interest that would otherwise be applicable in some buyer countries, resulting in even lower interest rates being offered to their customers.

with entering into the loan. The outstanding contractual risk at that time, if any, for the due fulfilment of the seller's obligations is then normally covered outside the loan agreement by a separate performance guarantee in favour of the buyer, in order to keep the commercial contract and the financial credit separate while protecting the buyer at the same time. Should that procedure not be suitable, the loan may contain recourse clauses towards the seller until the obligations of the seller are approved by the buyer, involving a corresponding credit risk for the bank lender on the seller during that period.

The loan agreement and its final wording have to be approved by all parties – the buyer, the seller, the banks and the credit insurer, if applicable. It is normally based on the same principles as an ordinary international loan agreement, but also includes the relevant parties to the commercial contract so that the two agreements harmonize during the disbursement period. Thereafter, they should be seen as two totally separate agreements.

Normal terms and conditions in buyer credits

Buyer credits can be arranged in almost any way and on terms decided between the parties, as long as it is done on market terms without government support. However, when such support is needed, the credit terms must also comply with the Consensus rules, as described below.

The exported goods should qualify for credit periods of at least two years, with 15 per cent of the contract value as advance payment and a maximum of 85 per cent credit, with disbursement, repayment and interest structured according to the Consensus rules. However, for buyer credits, the minimum contract value is normally considerably higher compared to ordinary supplier credits, since this type of financing is mainly applied to larger and often tailor-made transactions, which are more difficult and costly to arrange.

Buyer credits may be given in most trade currencies, at both floating and fixed-term rates. Officially supported rates may also be given, particularly on a fixed-interest basis, even if the market rates often can be as competitive, particularly in a low-interest environment. Other finance techniques such as 'interest-swaps' are also available to offer competitive fixed market rates for long-term credits and larger amounts through the international money or capital markets. If possible, offers can also be made to provide the loan, or part of it, in the buyer's local currency. (See Chapter 7, 'Local currency finance'.)

The Consensus – a summary

The OECD has stipulated a number or guidelines for restricting state-supported export credit competition between countries, often referred to as the 'Arrangement' or the 'Consensus'; it contains guidelines for minimum and maximum credit periods, amortization structure, minimum advance payment and, above all, minimum interest rates.

The minimum credit period for which these rules apply is two years, with repayment in equal half-yearly instalments (plus interest); the first is due three to six months after the starting point of the credit, which is normally acceptance or the 'mean acceptance date' in the case of several deliveries. It could also be commissioning or physical possession relating to whole projects. A minimum payment of 15 per cent has to be paid before the starting point of the credit.

Buyer countries are divided into two groups. Group I consists of the industrialized countries and some of the countries that are members of OPEC (Organization of Petroleum Exporting Countries). Group II includes most developing countries. This classification is made automatically, based on World Bank statistics of per capita gross national income (GNI).

The maximum credit period for countries in Group I is up to five years; however, in exceptional circumstances this may be extended to 8.5 years after international pre-notification, which means that other competitors should get the same advantage, so-called 'matching'. For countries in Group II the maximum credit period is 10 years, but shorter periods may apply for certain commodities and lower contract values.

The minimum level for state-supported fixed interest is based on OECD guidelines – the CIRR-rates (Commercial Interest Reference Rates), which are revised monthly, based on the assumption of what they might have been if finance had been available. The two types of CIRR are contract CIRR and pre-contract CIRR, which is 20 basis points higher. The advantage of the pre-contract CIRR for the seller is that they can submit a cost-free offer to the buyer based on a fixed interest rate at the date of the application, which can then be held during the negotiations for up to 120 days. The contract CIRR must be applied for before signing the contract and will be the rate applicable at contract date, so in this case the parties will not know the exact rate in advance. After contract, the rates so determined will be held for another 180 days to allow time for credit documentation.

More detailed information can be obtained from commercial or export banks, or directly from the ECAs listed in Chapter 5.

The loan agreement in a buyer credit contains the same standard clauses as in every other international loan, such as conditions precedent, default clauses and applicable law, along with legal opinions regarding both the loan and the sales contract, showing that they are compatible, legally enforceable and duly executed. It must contain confirmation of receipt of the stipulated advance payments, and other relevant details of the commercial contract must be included. The disbursement clauses also have to be properly documented. Most buyer credits are disbursed directly to the seller in one payment or related to the seller's successive performance, and the loan amounts will be payable against certificates of completion countersigned by the buyer, according to a preliminary draw-down plan and timetable as an appendix to the agreement.

The international money market

Apart from purely domestic finance, based on prime or base interest rates fixed by the domestic central bank, the market commonly used for the refinancing of trade finance is the international and unregulated money market or markets, operating within financial centres in different time zones. These markets trade in short-term currency loans and deposits, whereas the expression 'capital markets' refers to long-term periods, usually only for larger amounts and with fixed interest, for example through bonds and other long-term instruments.

Often the term 'euro currency' is used for deposits traded on these markets, referring to funds that are held by a bank or other party outside the home country of the specific currency, but it now has nothing to do with Europe or the Euro, even if that was where originally a major part of these funds were held. The prefix 'euro' is thus nowadays a reference to deposits outside the jurisdiction of the local central bank, first of all in the currencies of the four major economies, USD, EUR, JPY and GBP, but this reference may be applicable to any other currency as well. For example, 'Eurodollar' for USD held outside the United States, and 'Euroyen' for JPY held anywhere outside Japan.

The money markets are no physical marketplaces but a general description of the trade itself, carried out in different currencies between numerous lenders and borrowers. The major banks, both domestically and internationally, play a central role through their internal interbank deposit trading, which is crucial for both liquidity and stable market conditions – in the same way as banks operate in the currency market. For short-term loans and deposits in different currencies, this interbank money market is often referred to as the name of the financial centres where the main banks are operating; for example, the London Interbank Market, where the corresponding interest rates are referred to as London Interbank Offered Rates (LIBOR).

London is by far the largest money marketplace, not only in the European time zone, and is also the financial centre to which many commercial contracts or agreements worldwide are referred regarding interest rates for most trade currencies, even though other financial centres in different time zones are also often used to specify the interest rate for the main international currencies.

There are a number of other financial centres where interbank money market rates are quoted; for example TIBOR, the Tokyo Interbank Offered Rates, where for example the free and unregulated money market rates for the Euroyen are quoted, which are published daily by the Japanese Bankers Association. These constantly fluctuating money market rates are often different from the domestic base or prime rates in the same currency, which are regulated by the domestic central bank and mostly changed only at intervals to regulate economic activity within the country. This difference between domestic and free money market interest rates in the same currency could be quite significant in times of credit crunches or turmoil on the money markets and these unregulated rates are therefore the best indicator of the real cost of short-term money in that currency.

When it comes to the euro currency itself, European banks have established an interbank reference rate called EURIBOR (Euro Interbank Offered Rate), which is the benchmark rate of the interbank euro money market that has emerged since 1999, sponsored by among others the European Banking Federation. EURIBOR is the rate at which euro interbank term deposits are offered between prime European and international banks, computed and published on the Reuter screen.

During the day, an interbank reference rate is fixed in most currencies, to be used as the reference rate in, for example, contracts and loan agreements. Most such rates are published daily by central banks or bank associations through different online information systems or separate web pages, usually at 11.00 am local time, for periods up to a year. They are also quoted in the newspapers as the established short-term international interest rates for the most common currencies. However, as the market interest rates change continuously during the day, more accurate information is available either through the banks' own internet-based information systems or through direct contact with their trading departments. For participants actively trading directly in the market, there are also specialized online systems available, with almost identical and instantly updated currency and money market information.

Floating interest rates related to trade finance are often based on these interest rate fixings, even if more details have to be specified in each individual case; for example, 'USD LIBOR three months interest rate, at 11.00 am on (date) as shown on (screen website)'. To be even more precise, many loan agreements also often refer to the average interest quotations from some specifically named major banks in that market (reference banks), to get the interest rate absolutely identified and fixed without referring to a general marketplace. The total interest rate for the customer also includes the margin as applied by the lending bank(s) in each individual case, or as specified in the loan agreement.

Trade finance transactions are generally based on bills or notes when it comes to supplier credits, but more frequently on separate loan agreements for buyer credits and structured trade finance transactions, as described earlier in this chapter. Short-term bills of exchange are often combined with a fixed interest for the entire period until the due date, with the capital amount and interest rate compounded into a fixed amount to be paid at maturity. Promissory notes are often made in the same way, but for longer periods they have to be more detailed and are usually designed as short loan agreements, based on either a floating or fixed interest rate.

For buyer credits (bank-to-bank or bank-to-buyer credits) and other forms of structured finance, a separate and detailed loan agreement is always used for these longer periods. If based on a floating interest rate they also contain a clear definition of how the interest should be calculated and fixed for each short interest period, with a successive number of roll-over periods of, for example, three or six months until final maturity. The borrower can often choose the length of these roll-over periods and at the end of each such period interest is due, together with amortization, if any.

Many loan agreements also give the borrower the option to change currency at the end of each interest period, but combined with a maximum amount expressed in one base currency in order to cap the total outstanding loan in case of adverse currency exchange movements. This structure, with different optional currencies, floating or fixed interest rates and variable loan periods, can be adapted to suit the changing circumstances of the borrower during the lifetime of the loan and makes the international money market a very flexible source for short-, medium- or even long-term trade finance, based on a variety of financing techniques.

One of the advantages of longer-term loans based on short-term roll-over periods is that they are simple to use and so flexible that, in principle, they can be adapted to any trade or financial transaction for almost any period. The disadvantage for the borrower on longer periods can be the floating rate, which makes the credit costs difficult to evaluate in advance, but this problem is easily resolved in most cases.

In Chapter 4, the forward points system was described as the basis for establishing currency forward rates. The technique is similar for changing floating interest rates into fixed rates through interest swap agreements. A five-year loan based on, for example, three-month LIBOR may thus be changed into a fixed interest rate loan at any time during the loan period. This is done through a separate interest rate swap agreement with a bank, whereby the borrower agrees to receive the floating rate needed to service the loan and deliver fixed interest rates to the bank under the swap agreement.

However, such a swap agreement contains an additional risk for the bank should the borrower default during the period of the loan, thereby not being able to deliver the fixed interest. It is, therefore, subject to a separate credit decision within that bank, but the technique and the market liquidity make it possible to hedge the interest rate for very long periods. In the most-traded currencies this can be done up to five or 10 years, thereby eliminating the potential disadvantage of using the money market's short-term interest rates.

Structured trade finance

07

The expression 'structured trade finance' is used in many different situations and is not generally defined. In this book it has the meaning of prearranged or tailor-made trade financial techniques or structures, designed for individual transactions or projects, arranged by, or in cooperation with, specialized financial institutions.

International leasing

Leasing in its simplest form is a means of delivering finance, broadly defined as 'a contract between two parties where one party (the lessor) provides an asset, mostly equipment, for usage to another party (the lessee) for a specified period of time, in return for specified payments'.

Leasing is a medium-term form of finance for machinery, vehicles and equipment, with the legal right to use the goods for a defined period of time but without owning or having title to them. The lease is normally divided into two separate categories:

1 *The operating lease* – where the lessee is using the equipment but where the risk of ownership with all its corresponding rights and responsibilities is borne by the lessor, who also buys insurance and undertakes responsibility for maintenance. Furthermore, the duration of an operating lease is usually much shorter than the useful life of the equipment and the present value of all lease payments is therefore significantly less than the full equipment value. In most respects, the operating lease is equivalent to rental and, under most jurisdictions, the equipment consequently remains on the books of the lessor.

2 *The financial lease* – where all practical risks of ownership are borne by the lessee, who uses the equipment for most of its economic life with or without the ultimate goal of acquiring it at the expiry of the lease at an agreed and often nominal cost. From the outset, the lessor

therefore expects to recover from the lessee the capital cost of the investment along with interest and profit during the period of the lease (often called a 'full payout lease'), and where in most cases under the tax laws of most countries, the equipment has to stay on the books of the lessee.

The distinction between these types of lease is not always that clear in reality and many leases are frequently structured in one way while being defined in another, usually owing to potential cost or tax advantages. However, in most countries where leasing is frequently used, such as the United States, tax authorities or the domestic Accounting Standards Board has laid down specified conditions for a lease to be classified as an operational lease.

When the sales contract between the supplier and the lessor, and the leasing contract between the lessor and the lessee have been signed, the equipment is usually delivered directly from the supplier to the lessee, who is the end-user of the equipment. Following approval of the delivery by the lessee, the lessor remits the payment to the supplier. The equipment, together with the leasing contract, constitutes security for the lessor, sometimes together with a limited or full supplementary repurchase agreement with the manufacturer/supplier. But most of the risks, rights and obligations in connection with the use of the equipment rest with the lessee.

The lessee leases the equipment for a period that corresponds to either the economic lifetime of the equipment or a shorter period thereof, with monthly or quarterly lease payments, based on annuities, which could be adapted to the lessee's own fluctuating liquidity situation during the year. At the end of the lease period, the equipment is either returned to the lessor or the lease is extended for a new agreed period; however, the lease contract could also include an option for the lessee to buy the equipment at the prevailing market value at that time or at a fixed percentage of the original lease value.

This is a general description of a lease, also shown in graphic form in Figure 7.1. The principles are basically the same irrespective of whether it is a domestic transaction or an export or international lease, the obvious main difference being that in the latter case the parties are located in different countries. However, that difference could have a major impact on the trans-action and how it is executed.

The most common form of lease in connection with day-to-day export is when a leasing company in the 'buyer's' country is buying the equipment from a foreign supplier and leasing it to a lessee (the buyer) in their country. Such a lease should be regarded more as a domestic lease, mostly arranged in local currency and with other parts of the contract also adapted to local conditions. It may be arranged or initiated by the seller as part of the offer

FIGURE 7.1 Summary of a lease transaction

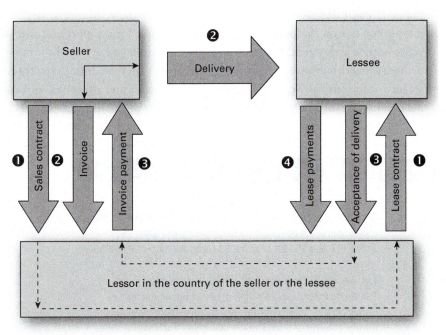

Explanations to the numbering are included in the text.

and normally leads to cash payment for them upon acceptance of the delivery by the buyer (the lessee), but with continued responsibility for any contractual repurchase, partial guarantee or other undertaking the seller may have to enter into with the foreign lease company.

Cross-border leasing

When the lessor and the lessee are located in separate countries, the expression 'cross-border leasing' or 'structured leasing' is often used. This type of lease is sometimes structured to take maximum advantage of differences in tax and depreciation rules between countries. This may produce a most competitive solution, often generating an effective total cost for the lessee lower than the best commercial interest rates. To produce such results, the lease agreements are sometimes structured to involve more parties than the original ones; for example, an investor in a third country who might legally, and from a tax perspective, also be the formal owner of the equipment, thereby creating depreciation in several countries on the same equipment. Such leases are frequently used in connection with big ticket deals such as aircraft, large computers, ships, railway carriages and other rolling transport vehicles.

Local authorities have understandably tried to prevent the excessive use of such tax-driven arrangements and there is a constant battle between financial engineers on the one hand, trying to find new solutions, and the tax authorities on the other, trying to cap their use for tax purposes. Most cross-border leases are considerably less complicated and are used for more ordinary-sized equipment as an alternative to other medium-term trade finance solutions, in which ownership, depreciation and other tax aspects may be important but not crucial to the execution of the transaction.

Short-form summary of an international lease contract

§ 1
- Definitions, parties involved and the description of the equipment.
- Conditions precedent for executing the agreement.
- Terms of lease and for prolongation, cancellation or termination.

§ 2
- The lessee's receipt and final approval of the equipment.
- The terms for the lessee's right of use of the equipment.
- Requirements for a separate service agreement between the supplier and any local agent of choice in the country of the lessee.

§ 3
- Choice of currency, the lease calculation and terms of payment.
- Rules for default interest.

§ 4
- Geographical area for the equipment to be used and rules for movement.

§ 5
- Rules for VAT payments for leases and residual values.
- Rules for payments of import duties or any other taxes.

§ 6
- Conditions, if any, for transfer of the lease agreement.

§ 7
- Discharge for the lessor against claims from the lessee for fault or deficiencies in the equipment and the lessee's responsibility for any third-party claims or damages in the country of operation.

§ 8
- Rules for insurance and arrangements in case of damage or total loss.
- Rules for current inspection of equipment by selected third party.

§ 9
- Lessor's right to repossess the equipment.
- Rules in case of use of lease option or return of equipment.

§ 10
- Rules for legal actions, applicable law and definition of force majeure.

§ 11
- Guarantees, or other security, if any, to cover the obligations of the lessee.

Even for ordinary cross-border leases, detailed knowledge of the legal consequences is crucial, as are the tax implications. For example, VAT – should it be paid, and in what country and by whom? The aspect of legal ownership also has to be addressed, which may depend on factors such as the length of the lease in relation to the life of the asset, transfer of ownership, the discounted lease payments in relation to market value, any options for 'bargain price' sales, etc. These aspects are also the actual basis for determining whether the transaction is to be deemed an operational or a financial lease in many countries, which could have economic consequences for both the lessor and the lessee.

Legal ownership is thus an important factor to consider in each case, not only in relation to pure economic advantages and commercial and political risks, but also with regard to legal and economic consequences in the event of damages and claims from any third party (which may be governed in accordance with the laws of the country where the equipment is used).

Within industrialized countries, however, where most lease transactions are made, the applicable law for governing the lease contract, as well as definitions for tax and accounting purposes, is becoming increasingly similar. In other markets, where that might not be the case, the lease is usually arranged through a local leasing company to avoid these and any other third-party risks. If the lease is part of, or connected to, larger projects it will probably come under the general framework governing the project as a whole.

A cross-border lease can be arranged in most international trade currencies, based on floating or fixed interest rates in accordance with the structure of the annuities in the contract. Other advantages for the 'buyer' could be 100 per cent finance, flexible annuities and the use of a source of finance that will not affect the existing credit limits with their banks. The buyer (the lessee) may have an option to replace the equipment with newer versions and may also benefit financially from tax benefits in their country. It is up to them to compare the advantages and cost of leasing with other financial options, and for the seller to explore these options with a leasing company in their own country, in order to be able to offer the most competitive financial solution.

Export leasing insurance

Many ECAs offer cover for export leasing transactions to facilitate this form of export finance, adapted to the structure, product and size of the deal, sometimes in the following two forms, reflecting the basic lease structure:

1 *Operating lease policy*, predominantly based on a less than full payout and no transfer of title at the end of the lease period, together with a value depreciation cover to be borne by the lessor. The insurance may cover both periodic and fluctuating lease payments as well as most political risks after a repossession period due to government actions, including expropriation, confiscation and licence cancellations, with coverage of up to 95 per cent depending on the nature of the transaction and risks covered.

2 *Financing lease policy*, mainly based on a non-existing residual value at the end of the lease period. It is therefore quite similar to a policy covering an ordinary medium-term credit, requiring a 15 per cent advance payment from the lessee with equal (plus interest) or annuity-based repayments and with coverage of up to 95 per cent of each lease payment as they fall due.

Most lessors are eligible as policyholders, provided the equipment is leased to a lessee outside the exporting country, in combination with similar rules on domestic manufacture, material input and foreign content restrictions, as in other ECA insurances. The premiums adhere to OECD guidelines, reflecting the risk elements and the period of the transaction. More information can be obtained directly from the relevant ECA; see the list in Chapter 5.

Lines of credit and local currency finance

Lines of credit

As mentioned earlier, buyer credits are usually arranged in connection with tailor-made transactions, requiring a relatively high contract value to be cost-effective. This is one reason why many commercial banks in exporting countries have established separate lines of credit directly with foreign banks in countries where there is a substantial and established trade pattern, to be used for smaller and more ordinary transactions.

Lines of credit, which may be arranged by both commercial and special export banks, are often backed by an ECA insurance or guarantee, given to the bank arranging the line of credit, covering each individual commercial contract to be financed. The advantages for the seller in such an arrangement are that these lines of credit and their corresponding export credit insurance, if needed, are already in place at the time of negotiation with the buyer, especially identified for low-value contracts.

Each established line of credit specifies the framework for the finance, such as goods, currency, minimum and maximum value of contracts, conditions precedent, applicable law and most other standard clauses in an ordinary international loan agreement. However, the credit terms must be consistent with the OECD Consensus rules, if backed by an ECA guarantee. This established framework makes it easy to add only the specific details of each commercial contract as they materialize. Such lines of credit are intended as general-purpose lines to be used to finance a number of contracts from different exporters, but could equally be used as a framework for the financing of a specific project with deliveries from a number of suppliers from the same country.

More details on banks and countries where such lines of credit are in existence can be found at the website of the national ECA (see Chapter 5) or directly through the major banks; the seller can thus find out in advance if such limits are available in their particular case.

Local currency finance

Most of the export credit alternatives available directly to the buyer have so far been described as based on finance in the larger international trade currencies, which implies a currency risk for the buyer unless that risk can be hedged or balanced by a matching inflow in the same currency. For buyers in industrialized countries this is usually not a big problem. However, to hedge a strong currency against a currency with a potential devaluation risk – or convertibility risk owing to a change in law or regulations – can be very expensive. The buyer is also seldom in the fortunate position of having a constant inflow of foreign currency or being able to generate such earnings from the purchased goods. Consequently, many buyers have taken huge currency losses from entering into overseas export credits in recent years.

For that reason, many buyers outside the industrialized countries may prefer finance in their own local currency, either for the whole credit amount or part of it, despite the higher interest rate usually incurred. The financial consequences of a local currency credit could at least be more calculable, even with a floating interest rate. Such local finance, however, would probably not be available to the buyer without a credit guarantee covering the risk involved on behalf of the lender. Many ECAs have therefore introduced schemes based on the buyer credit structure, with up to 100 per cent unconditional guarantee to the financing bank, even if only for selected domestic currencies. Such loans are raised in the buyer's country and financed by a local bank, based on the Consensus credit terms.

Such loans would normally be at floating rates owing to the difficulty of swapping these into fixed-term rates at a reasonable cost and for the periods required. Other criteria also have to be fulfilled owing to the implications for the country concerned. The local currency has to be convertible in some sense and the local market needs the capacity to support the finance without major impacts. It also has to be approved by or at least acceptable to the local financial authorities.

If the commercial contract is in USD or some other commonly traded currency, which is usually the case, at some point in time there has to be a conversion into the local currency of the loan agreement. The parties have to agree when the exchange should take place and, consequently, who should stand the currency risk during the period between signing the contract and the time of conversion into local currency. More information about the availability of local currency finance can be obtained from the relevant ECA; see Chapter 5.

Project finance and joint venture

Project finance

Project finance in its original meaning is normally related to larger individual private or public sector projects, for example factories, power plants, larger construction or infrastructure projects, sometimes of national interest in the buyer's country. They are generally to a high degree based on the revenues of the project itself, mostly secured on its assets and less on the creditworthiness of the buyer, as this party is frequently only a single-purpose company or a partnership with limited equity.

Such projects can take years until a signed contract and an effective loan agreement stage are reached, sometimes because of internal political or local controversy as to its real or alleged social, economic or environmental consequences. Such projects also incur more pre-contract costs than ordinary export contracts, not only because of their length but also through feasibility studies and appraisals, legal and technical costs and necessary approvals by a number of local authorities.

In many of these projects, finance is the key question, or rather how to arrange and structure the necessary collateral for such finance. The World Bank, through its International Finance Corporation (IFC), and some of the regional development banks are often involved in larger projects of national interest, together with international banks and the national ECAs from the supplier nations. But the final solution for the project finance will inevitably be as complex and tailor-made as the project itself.

Owing to the cost and work involved, such projects usually have a high minimum support value, and the credit periods may be up to 15–20 years with flexible loan structures and amortization periods reflecting the structure of the project. Other requirements are mostly that support, at least from the commercial banks, should be given as senior debt and risk sharing on an equal basis with other lenders.

It is not within the scope of this handbook to elaborate more on this often highly complex area, but more information about project finance and the criteria and preconditions for participation can be obtained directly from the domestic agency or export council or through the larger commercial banks.

Joint ventures

In many developing countries and/or emerging market countries, the seller could be asked to participate as co-owner of the project, or even be required to do so in order to secure the contract. The buyer may have many reasons for such a request and local authorities may even have it as a requirement of the successful bidder before giving import licences or currency approvals. In other cases, it could be advantageous for the seller and their future business prospects with a particular buyer, or for the long-term goal of establishing a permanent base and a competitive advantage in the country or region.

The local partner may hope that a joint venture will not only offer capital or equity advantages, but also the benefits of technical knowledge and management along with the international marketing expertise that an international partner can provide. The authorities can also look for potential advantages in the form of a widened infrastructure, additional exports and the creation of new jobs.

The establishment of a joint venture often requires significant management resources from the seller and it may take years before the advantages can be seen; before then, many legal, cultural and management differences may have to be solved. On the other hand, many host nations clearly see the advantages of joint ventures and can back them in many ways through local support or market benefits. Today, most countries accept foreign majority ownership as well as foreign management, which may increase the potential value for the international company of such ventures but also mitigate any potential internal frictions.

Development finance institutions

To facilitate the creation of joint ventures in developing countries, the International Finance Corporation (the World Bank) is actively participate in assisting such joint ventures or partnerships. Many industrialized but also some emerging market countries have established similar corporations on a smaller scale, so-called development finance institutions (DFIs), to promote and/or support companies, mostly from their own country, in forming such joint ventures in primarily the developing or emerging market countries.

DFIs are private sector development finance vehicles, generally directly or indirectly owned and funded by governments. Although their charters and their project focus may differ, depending on the trade marketing or investment profile of the home country, they also have many similarities.

Business opportunities

One of the practical services offered within most exporting countries when it comes to projects, joint ventures or similar real or potential transactions is the information given by government institutions, trade or export councils or similar organizations. The purpose of this service is to spread such information among the country's own business community, which is gathered by or through their embassies, consulates or trade representatives around the world, often in combination with information provided by multinational development banks or United Nations institutions.

When this service is available in a country it is mostly restricted to the local business community to give a competitive advantage and, therefore, the companies normally have to register in some form, sometimes with a profile of their own business, to receive information from specific markets around the world relevant to their product/services. This information may be given as a free internet-based service or as a service to be charged for.

The information may be divided into different categories, such as:

- specific private sector opportunities: including enquiries from overseas agents and distributors looking for business contacts or other potential opportunities found locally by the trade representatives stationed overseas;

- tender or public sector opportunities: including invitations to pre-qualify for larger projects;

- joint venture or investment opportunities: with information about requests or possibilities for manufacture, investment or distribution in overseas markets;

- multilateral aid agency business opportunities, with details of overseas plans, proposed or approved by multilateral funding agencies.

For more information about this export service, which is available in some form in most countries, the exporter should contact the trade organization in their country.

DFIs normally operate in developing or emerging market countries with a low or middle per capita income eligible for such investments according to international agreements (the OECD's DAC list). Their objectives are to support economic development in the country of investment while at the same time supporting co-investors from their home country to the benefit of their own country.

The projects are mostly based on cooperation between reputable local partners and the foreign co-investor in order to strengthen the viability of the joint venture, particularly in smaller or medium-sized production, trade or marketing set-ups, when this combination of local and foreign know-how may be a precondition for its success. Participation by the DFIs can take different forms.

The DFIs operate with a large spectrum of investment or financial tools to suit the individual project, such as equity, loans or guarantees, but also quasi-equity or mezzanine instruments such as preference shares, convertible or subordinated loans and management buy-ins or buy-outs. The equity investments are generally only minority stakes ranging from 10 per cent upwards, and with a clear strategy of how to exit the project when viable, normally within a period of three to seven years.

The projects often involve participation with other institutions, particularly in the case of larger joint ventures, and then mostly in the form of partnerships with other DFIs or with the multilateral development bank in the region. More information about DFIs in different countries can be found on the following websites:

- Association of European Development Finance Institutions (EDFI), **www.edfi.be**;
- Association of African Development Finance Institutions (AADFI), **www.aadfi.org/**;
- Association of Development Financing Institutions in Asia and the Pacific (ADFIAP), **www.adfiap.org/**;
- Association of National Development Finance Institutions in Member Countries of the Islamic Development Bank (ADFIMI), **www.adfimi.org/**.

To support overseas long-term investments, including this form of joint venture, the national ECAs and many market insurers can provide insurance cover to companies and investors or directly to the financing banks against the political risks on equity, loans or guarantees invested in the project. These overseas investment insurance programmes are described in Chapter 5, 'Investment insurance'.

Multilateral development banks

Over many years, a number of multilateral and regional development banks have been established, with the main purpose of supporting projects vital for economic development within the region.

The best known of these institutions is the World Bank, which is not a bank in the common sense, but consists of five unique organizations, of which the best known are the International Bank for Reconstruction and Development (IBRD) and the International Development Association (IDA). Each institution plays a different but important role in the main mission of the World Bank, namely to reduce global poverty and improve living standards. The IBRD is the main lending agency and raises most of its money in the world's financial markets by selling AAA-rated World Bank bonds, usually to financial institutions, pension funds and other institutional money managers, as well as to central banks. The IBRD focuses on middle-income and creditworthy poor countries, while the IDA focuses on the poorest countries in the world. Together they provide low-interest loans, interest-free credit and grants to developing countries for education, health, infrastructure, communications and many other purposes.

When pursuing business opportunities in projects financed by the World Bank, it is essential to understand that the governments, or their departments or agencies, in the developing countries are the borrowers of money for specific projects and are also responsible for procurement. All contracts are therefore between that borrower and the supplier, contractor or consultant. The World Bank's role is to ensure that the borrower's work is done properly, that the agreed procurement procedures are observed, and that the entire process is conducted with efficiency, fairness, transparency and impartiality.

The International Finance Corporation, which is also part of the World Bank Group, operates on a commercial basis, providing a mix of finance (loans, equity finance, risk management products and intermediary finance). It is active in promoting projects for the development of private industry by participating as shareholder or lender in joint ventures vital to the country and with reasonably good prospects. The World Bank Group also includes the Multinational Investment Guarantee Agency (MIGA), guaranteeing the political risks for investments and projects in many developing countries.

A number of regional development banks have also been set up, based on the same principles as the World Bank, but with a more regional purpose. These are the African, Asian, Inter-American and Islamic Development Banks and their development funds for lending on 'soft terms' to projects of special importance for regional development. These institutions also have finance agencies similar to the IFC model to promote private industry within their regions.

The regional development banks not only participate in projects as a lender or a guarantor but frequently also, and more directly, in feasibility studies and promotion of the project itself, even as co-arranger. Their involvement often takes place together with international banks and ECAs from supplier countries, but also in cooperation with local governments, which are often the borrowers or the guarantors of the loan. This gives these projects a high political and financial priority within the country and an added reassurance to co-partners, suppliers and creditors that they will be financially secured, not only during the construction phase but also during the entire repayment period.

The development banks have a high international rating due to their ownership, capitalization and proven financial record and can therefore often offer their borrowers better than market terms, for example through lower interest rates and longer repayment periods. However, they can cater for only a small part of the finance requirements. Therefore they also contribute to the development of different forms of leveraged finance, such as co-joint or parallel financing techniques together with other sources of finance, for example international major commercial banks, special export banks and aid agencies from industrialized countries.

The projects supported by the development banks are often very attractive for potential suppliers, not least because they receive cash payment through the finance arranged by the banks. The rules for tender for projects financed by or through the development banks may vary, but bidding is often restricted to companies from the bank's member countries. However, most industrialized countries are also non-regional members of these banks and their national businesses are thereby eligible to bid even for such restricted contracts.

It is not within the framework of this book to describe these development banks in detail (although the European Development Bank is described in summary below because it has a more direct link to international trade than the other institutions).

Some larger regional development banks

Regional development banks are important for promoting and supporting larger international trade transactions and projects in their respective regions. Further information about their activities can be found on their websites. It is recommended that the seller trading in the areas covered by these institutions study these websites, since they often provide valuable information and links to other local institutions that could be of interest:

African Development Bank (AfDB)	**www.afdb.org**
African Development Fund (AfDF)	**www.afdb.org**
Asian Development Bank (ADB)	**www.adb.org/**
Asian Development Fund (ADF)	**www.adb.org/ADF/**
European Bank for Reconstruction and Development (EBRD)	**www.ebrd.com**
European Investment Bank (EIB)	**www.eib.org**
European Investment Fund (EIF)	**www.eif.org**
Inter-American Development Bank (IDB/BID)	**www.iadb.org**
International Bank for Reconstruction and Development (IBRD) World Bank	**www.worldbank.org**
International Development Association (IDA), World Bank	**www.worldbank.org/ida**
International Finance Corporation (IFC), World Bank	**www.ifc.org**
Islamic Development Bank	**www.isdb.org**
Multinational Investment Guarantee Agency (MIGA), World Bank	**www.miga.org**
Nordic Investment Bank	**www.nib.int**

European Bank for Reconstruction and Development (EBRD)

The EBRD, established in London in 1991, is a development bank with a somewhat different profile from the other development banks and therefore probably more relevant for exporters and suppliers from most countries involved in ordinary trade as well as for investors in the 30 countries where it presently operates.

The bank is owned by the member countries of the OECD and by many emerging market countries, the European Union and the European Investment Bank, and has a capital base of not less than EUR 20 billion. Its main objective is to support countries from central Europe to central Asia, including many former Soviet republics, plus the southern and eastern Mediterranean areas. It describes its goal as follows:

> To provide financing for banks, industries and businesses, both in new ventures and investments in existing companies. It also works with publicly owned companies, to support privatization, restructuring state-owned firms and improvement of municipal services ... and promote policies in these countries that will bolster the business environment.

The EBRD is the largest single investor in most of the markets in which it operates. Although one of its core businesses is the finance of larger projects, it is involved in many other areas as well – the bank has so far invested over EUR 50 billion to almost 3,000 single projects. The bank invests only in projects that could not otherwise attract financing on similar terms.

Apart from larger projects, the bank has also been involved in several hundred thousands of additional smaller transactions, promoting small businesses in particular, crucial to nurturing a private sector economy in these countries. This is mainly done through co-financing and/or facilitating domestic funding for other financial institutions or banks, and by supporting local commercial banks, equity funds and leasing consortiums. Through these arrangements EBRD makes loan financing and/or guarantees available to such companies for domestic or international trade, covering a wide range of goods and services including consumer goods, commodities, equipment, machinery and construction as well as technical and other support.

Terms of payment

08

Terms of payment and cash management

Through the terms of payment, the objective of both parties is to optimize the outcome and profitability of the transaction within the framework of an established and acceptable risk level. However, from the seller's perspective, the terms of payment can also be used as an additional sales argument to strengthen their competitive edge, in the same way as other parts of the contract. This makes it important to understand the structure of terms of payment and how they could be used in conjunction with guarantees, different forms of finance solutions and separate export credit insurance. Such a framework also raises the question of how to use the capital resources in the most efficient way. Anyone who controls these matters will be a better negotiator and able to conduct more profitable business.

In most cases, effective cash management means minimizing the use of capital while at the same time using the resources available to support the core business of the company. Good cash management could, for example, involve the seller offering the buyer a medium-term supplier credit in order to be more competitive, providing the risk is curtailed and that such credit is deemed to be necessary to get the deal.

Effective cash management could also include the seller taking the decision to delay, restructure or cancel a transaction if the risk structure is outside an acceptable level, for example if the buyer is not fulfilling part of the contract through the late or incorrect issuing of an L/C. This is why the structure and wording of the terms of payment are so important – particularly when things do not develop according to plan and when both parties begin to scrutinize the wording. There must never be any doubt as to how the seller, for example, can or may act in different situations without risk of damages, callings under guarantees or other countermeasures from the buyer.

It is through the correct structuring of the terms of payment, in conjunction with any additional security arrangement, that both parties should be able to determine, in advance and with a high degree of accuracy, when, where and how payment will be made. That will also determine what capital resources are needed during the different phases of the transaction, which is the basis for all cash management, particularly in international trade where some risk elements are more difficult to evaluate.

The different structures of practical terms of payment shown below must of course be adjusted to the individual preconditions in each case. But when payment can be anticipated with accuracy within a narrow timescale, it can also be incorporated into the payment flow of the company in advance, with optimal effect on its liquidity planning, making the necessary capital requirement easier to calculate and finance, and any currency risk easier to cover.

Contents of the terms of payment

When negotiating with the buyer, the seller needs to determine the detailed terms of payment to be included in the sales contract. This can be a complicated process in which, initially, both parties could have different views. For more complex transactions, new buyers or countries with an increased political risk, the terms of payment are often among the last areas to be agreed.

When entering into negotiations it is essential to know what details the terms of payment must contain and what minimum requirements the seller must adhere to in order to maintain the expected level of security. These minimum requirements are:

- *when* payment should take place (time of payment);
- *where* payment should take place (place of payment);
- *how* payment should take place (method of payment).

In the case of several payments, each part has to be treated as a single terms of payment – this also applies to guarantees issued under the contract.

Time of payment

The seller and buyer may have different views on when payment should take place: the buyer may want to make the best use of a competitive situation by having the seller finance the purchase through a short- or longer-term supplier credit on attractive terms, whereas the seller would probably prefer payment on delivery or with a shorter deferred payment covering the shipping period only.

The negotiations will determine when the payment will take place, or in the case of larger contracts or longer contract periods, when the different part payments will take place – both before and after delivery – mostly along with the larger part payment at delivery.

However, the possibility of offering supplier credits has become increasingly important as a sales argument. Even with smaller transactions it is quite normal to offer short-term credit for 60–90 days, including the period of transportation. In other situations, involving larger transactions, both seller and buyer may have a common interest in having the deal financed through a third party, often separate bank-to-bank or bank-to-buyer credits. This will give the seller cash payment on delivery while the buyer gets bank financing (on even better terms than they could have achieved on their own), which could at best also wholly or partially balance the cash flow generated from the purchased goods.

The size of the transaction, the delivered goods and the length of the credit discussed and the security for it will finally decide what credit terms can be offered and may bridge the gap between the different views of time of payment.

Place of payment

The question of where payment should take place must be defined, since it determines the fulfilment of the obligations of the buyer. This also relates to what form of payment is used. L/Cs are normally payable at either the issuing or the advising bank. This means that either of these banks takes responsibility for transferring the payment to the seller – but only after the documents have been approved.

The situation is similar when a documentary collection is used as the method of payment – the difference being that the buyer has fulfilled their obligations when paying or accepting a bill of exchange against the documents at the collecting bank. It is then up to this bank to transfer the payment according to the instructions originating from the seller.

In the relatively few cases when payment by cheque is agreed upon, it must be made clear whether the seller will accept a commercial cheque or a bank cheque (also referred to as a banker's draft). It is up to the parties to decide if the buyer's obligations have been fulfilled when the cheque is sent, when it has been received by the seller or when it has been cleared in the banking system and the payment is available to the seller as cleared funds. This includes the question of who covers the postal risk, should the cheque be delayed or lost.

In the case of bank transfer, the place of payment must be decided by the parties involved. The seller wants the payment to be received by their bank before accepting that the buyer has fulfilled their payment obligations, whereas the buyer may consider their obligation to have been fulfilled when they pay the amount at their local bank. For payments within most OECD countries, this may be a matter of only two to three days' difference, with the reliable and fast international transfer systems most banks operate in these countries through the SWIFT system. However, there are other reasons why the place of payment should be clearly defined.

Irrespective of the transfer system used, a payment out of a country might depend on currency regulations or be delayed for other reasons. These could include incorrect handling or slow practices in general, bank strikes or other forms of force majeure, or simply insufficient or incorrect payment instructions from the buyer, which could cause a long delay.

The question of where the buyer fulfils their payment obligations in connection with open account payment terms is always a matter for the parties to agree. If no such agreement is made, disputes may arise later on, and may then have to be decided by the applicable law. In most countries, the law stipulates that the debt should be paid at the domicile of the creditor, namely the seller. It is therefore also in the buyer's interest that the place of payment is stated in the terms of contract, particularly with larger amounts, when every day's interest is important.

The place of payment should therefore be defined as being at the premises of the seller's chosen bank and account number, and the corresponding SWIFTBIC codes should always be included in the terms of payment to secure accurate and rapid transfer.

Summary of the structure of the terms of payment

Listed below is the basic structure of some of the most commonly used terms of payment, grouped in order of their advantage to the seller.

TABLE 8.1

Terms of payment	Comments
A: Payment before delivery	
1. Without advance payment guarantee.	1. Gives the highest security for the seller.
2. Against contractual advance payment guarantee.	2. As above, based on due fulfilment of the contract.
3. Against an 'on demand' advance payment guarantee.	3. Gives less security for the seller (seldom used alternative).
B: Payment at delivery	
1. Letter of credit, documents against payment.	1. High security – dependent on the strength of the issuing bank – and if confirmed or not.
2. Documentary collection, documents against payment.	2. Dependent on the buyer honouring the documents – and which documents are included.
C: Payment after delivery	
1. Letter of credit, documents against acceptance.	1. Same security as **B** but with later payment.
2. Payment secured by payment guarantee.	2. The security is dependent on the issuing bank and the wording of the guarantee.
3. Documentary collection, documents against acceptance.	3. As **B**, but after the release of documents the risk is solely on the buyer until payment.
4. Bank transfer.	4. Risk on the buyer until payment.

Methods of payment

How payment is made depends on the role of the banks involved and affects the security offered to both buyer and seller. As described in Chapter 2, 'Different methods of payment', payments can, in principle, be divided into two main categories: 'clean payments' and 'documentary payments'.

Clean payments (bank transfers and bank or corporate cheques) are primarily used when the parties have agreed on open account payment terms, meaning that the buyer must pay according to the contract after receiving the seller's invoice specifying the payment date. With the absence of any other security for payment offered by the buyer, clean payments (or rather bank transfers) are regularly used within industrialized or neighbouring countries or in conjunction with other security, for example credit insurance.

Documentary payments are used in situations other than those mentioned above, when the need for additional security is greater, whether the underlying reason is the buyer, their country or the nature or size of the individual transaction. The documentary payments are divided into documentary collections (bank collections), when the buyer has to pay or accept a bill of exchange to obtain access to the documents for collection, or L/Cs where the seller is also guaranteed payment if the documents presented are in accordance with the terms of the L/C.

Structure of the terms of payment

Based on when, where and how a payment is to be made, the parties can, in principle, design many different combinations. Examples of some frequently used terms of payment are given in this section, showing what they should contain, as a platform for adapting them further according to the specific situation.

No examples are given for the use of cheques as this form of payment is not frequently used in international trade and has no main advantage over a bank transfer. However, should payment through corporate cheques be allowed by the seller (as is sometimes practised by large buyers because of its cash management advantages), or payment through a bank cheque, this has to be agreed between the parties on a case-by-case basis, and then follow the basic structure and wording of the bank transfer, as shown in the box below.

Bank transfer (bank remittance)

To ensure that payment will be received by the seller's bank at maturity, it is up to the buyer to arrange the payment through their local bank some days prior to this date. The possibility of receiving overdue interest for shorter periods is often limited in practice, but the mere mention of it could have a positive effect on timely payment. (See also the example overleaf, where the open account transaction is secured by a separate bank guarantee.)

> Structure of terms of payment based on bank transfer in open-account trading
>
> 'Payment through bank transfer, which shall have reached (name and address of the seller's chosen bank (with full details of the SWIFTBIC code and customer account numbers), not later than 90 days from date of invoice, which shall be the same as the date of shipment. Interest on arrears at x % pa is charged from maturity date until payment is received.'

Bank guarantee

As additional security covering the open account sale, the terms of payment could stipulate that the buyer should arrange a bank guarantee covering the payment obligations according to the contract – particularly if the transaction includes a longer supplier credit.

A bank guarantee has to be issued under the existing credit limits with the buyer's bank but it should, in reality, come without any additional risks for the buyer (in the case of a conditional guarantee), provided they fulfil the payment obligations already agreed. Such a clause could have the wording shown in the box below.

> Structure of terms of payment combined with a bank guarantee
>
> 'The buyer has to arrange a payment guarantee issued by ... (the name of the buyer's bank) for USD [amount] – in favour of the seller, covering the buyer's payment obligations according to contract. The guarantee shall be advised through ... (the name of the seller's bank) and shall have reached that bank not later than 30 days from date of contract and be valid for 30 days from last delivery as stipulated in the contract.'

This wording, referring to the underlying sales contract, makes it a conditional guarantee, payable only after the applicant's approval (the buyer in this case) or after the issuing bank has been satisfied that the buyer has defaulted in their contractual payment obligations.

Documentary collection (bank collection)

By specifying the chosen collection bank at the buyer's location, as the example below indicates, the documents can often be sent directly to this bank by the seller's bank without delay.

Unless the buyer's bank is not a particularly small local bank, it is normally advantageous for the seller to agree to use the buyer's main bank, where the buyer may also have to give good reasons for unduly delaying payment or acceptance. However, it should also be advantageous for the buyer to have the documents sent directly to their own bank.

It is important to agree in advance which documents the buyer needs and it is also up to the buyer to decide if additional details should be included; for example, latest shipping date, port of loading and destination in the bill of lading, or endorsement instructions for the shipping and insurance documents. However, overly detailed specifications are not necessarily beneficial for the seller, who might want some flexibility in shipment and documentation details (while still adhering to the stipulations in the contract).

The expression 'clean on board' in the bill of lading in the example is a standard expression indicating that no damage or defective condition of the goods or their packing could be noticed at the time of loading. As a document of title, it should also be endorsed in blank or to any other party as agreed in advance.

Structure of terms of payments based on documentary collection

'Payment through documentary collection at first presentation of documents through (complete name and address of the chosen bank at the domicile of the buyer, where the documents should be presented).

'Payment should be effected against presentation of the following documents:

- at sight bill of exchange drawn on ... (the buyer);
- invoice in triplicate;
- certificate of origin issued by ...;
- insurance policy, issued by ...., covering ... (value and risks);
- full set of clean-on-board bill of lading, blank endorsed.

'All collection charges (alternatively, bank charges outside the seller's country) are to be paid by the buyer. Interest on arrears at x % pa will be charged on overdue payments and is to be paid together with the documents.'

Letters of credit

In most cases it is satisfactory to specify the terms of payment as shown in the L/C example in Chapter 2, as long as there is a clear reference to the underlying contract. The same comments apply as for a documentary collection.

Under the new ICC rules UCP 600, all L/Cs are by definition irrevocable and therefore there is no need to specify this fact in the terms of payment, but on the other hand there is no harm in doing so. Since this tradition of referring to an L/C as being irrevocable has been so fundamental, this practice will probably continue for some time to come, but we have decided to follow the ICC definitions in the examples in this chapter and not use this old expression.

The L/C is often issued in such a way that it may at first glance appear to be in accordance with the contract, but nevertheless contains minor details that could make it difficult for the seller to comply totally with its terms, or create uncertainty if that will later be the case. In this example, the seller therefore has reserved the right to have reasonable amendments made in order to be able to comply with the terms of the L/C, as long as they do not violate the contract.

Structure of terms of payment based on a letter of credit

'Payment through letter of credit, payable at sight with and confirmed by ... (the agreed advising bank). The letter of credit shall be issued by ... (the agreed issuing bank) and shall have reached the advising bank in form and substance acceptable to the seller in accordance with the contract, not later than 60 days from the date of the contract.

'The letter of credit, which must give reference to the contract number and date, shall be valid for three months and be payable against the following documents:

- at sight bill of exchange, drawn on the advising bank;

- invoice in triplicate;

- packing list;

- certificate of origin, issued by ..., covering ...;

- full set of clean-on-board marine bill of lading, blank endorsed and showing (shipping date, ports, etc).

'Partial shipments and transhipments are not allowed. Bank charges outside the seller's country are to be paid by the buyer.'

Both the detailed agreement concerning the L/C and the subsequent handling of documents require a high degree of care so that the seller obtains the advantages and security upon which the transaction is based.

Unfortunately, it is very common for buyers, particularly in developing countries, to vastly underestimate the time it takes to get all the necessary approvals and permissions in order for the issuing bank to issue the L/C. This delay will immediately affect the seller and their planning of production and delivery. At some point in time a decision may also need to be taken between having to take additional costs without having the security on which the transaction is based, or to postpone the production, delivery or some other obligations, and the seller must reserve the right to do so according to the contract.

With this in mind, it is crucial that all time limits and delivery obligations agreed by the seller are based not on the date of the contract alone, but also on the time when the seller has received and approved the L/C, and that the seller's own obligations will only come into effect when that has been achieved.

Composite terms of payment

With larger transactions over longer periods, it is quite normal for the payment to be divided into part-payments in order to satisfy both parties. The combination of the size of the transaction and the time period between delivery by the seller and final acceptance by the buyer could otherwise lead to unacceptable risk and liquidity consequences for either or both parties.

The risk for the seller might increase through the nature of the product and the size of the transaction, particularly if the goods are tailor-made with a long timescale between production and final delivery. However, the buyer will also take an increased commercial risk in the case of payment being made before the final acceptance of delivery. The terms of payment built around these transactions will, therefore, follow the sequence of the contract itself, from contract date, production and delivery periods, installation, test runs, acceptance by the buyer and final warranty periods. Such terms are often combined with different forms of guarantee covering both the seller's and the buyer's mutual obligations during this period.

With regard to machinery and equipment, it is relatively common that both the payment before delivery and on/after completion varies between 10 and 15 per cent in order to achieve a reasonable balance between the parties, with a main payment at delivery of about 75 per cent.

As can be seen from the example below, nothing is mentioned about confirmation of the L/C, which would indicate that the seller in this case is satisfied with the credit standing of the issuing bank and the political risk in that country. In this example, the parties have also agreed to let a separate inspection company have the final say when the last payment is to be released, which will also be the time when the seller has fulfilled their contractual obligations. Separate instructions have to be given to the inspection company to carry out such an inspection.

Structure of simple composite terms of payment

'Ten (10) per cent of the contract value through bank transfer to be received by ... (the advising bank below) not later than 30 days from contract. The amount is to be paid to the seller against an advance payment guarantee issued by the advising bank in favour of the buyer, according to the text on page xx in the contract.

'Seventy-five (75) per cent of the contract value on delivery through letter of credit, payable at sight with ... (the agreed advising bank). The letter of credit shall be issued by ... (the agreed issuing bank) and shall have reached the advising bank in form and substance acceptable to the seller in accordance with the contract, not later than 45 days from the date of the contract. The letter of credit, which must give reference to the contract number and date, shall be valid for three months and be payable against the following documents:

- at sight bill of exchange, drawn on the advising bank;

- invoice in triplicate;

- packing list;

- certificate of origin, issued by ..., covering ...;

- full set of clean-on-board marine bill of lading, blank endorsed and showing (shipping date, ports, etc).

'The letter of credit shall permit partial shipments and transhipments.

'Fifteen (15) per cent of the contract value upon signed installation certificate, issued by (the name of a control and inspection company agreed by the parties) to have reached (the advising bank) not later than 30 days from such signing.

'All bank charges outside the seller's country are to be paid by the buyer.'

The example below shows terms of payment combined with a long-term supplier credit. When released, the bills will not be covered under the L/C but by a separate guarantee by the issuing bank, issued directly on the bills. It can also be presumed that the seller has an additional firm offer from a bank or a forfaiting house to discount the bills without recourse to them at their release. However, the wording of the terms of payment must always be checked against such an offer so that the seller can be absolutely sure that all conditions can be met when presenting the bills for discounting.

Structure of composite terms of payment combined with a long-term supplier credit

'Five (5) per cent of the contract value before delivery, through a bank transfer which shall have reached ... (the advising bank below) not later than 30 days from contract date. The amount shall be paid to the seller against a conditional advance payment guarantee in favour of the buyer, issued by that bank.

'Ten (10) per cent of the contract value at delivery through letter of credit, payable at sight with and confirmed by (the agreed advising bank). The letter of credit shall be issued by (the agreed issuing bank) and shall have reached the advising bank in form and substance acceptable to the seller in accordance with the contract, not later than 45 days from the date of the contract. The letter of credit shall be valid for three months and be payable against the following documents:

- at sight bill of exchange, drawn on the advising bank;
- invoice in triplicate;
- packing list;
- certificate of origin, issued by ..., showing ...;
- insurance policy, issued by ..., blank endorsed, covering (risks, value, payable, etc);
- full set of clean-on-board marine bill of lading, blank endorsed and showing (shipping date, ports, etc).

'The letter of credit shall permit partial shipments but not transhipments.

'Eighty-five (85) per cent of the contract value after delivery through 10 bills of exchange, of the same amount and due half-yearly, drawn on and accepted by the buyer, avalized by ... (the issuing bank) and provided with a transfer guarantee by the central bank of .... The bills shall be placed in deposit with (the advising bank) at the same time as the letter of credit is issued. In each bill is to be included interest at x % pa calculated up to its final maturity.

'The bills shall be fully negotiable and payable in ..., and the letter of credit should contain irrevocable instructions that the bills are to be released to the seller when 90 per cent of the contract value has been disbursed. Before releasing the bills, the advising bank shall provide the bills with the seller's verified signature and blank endorsement but also with the respective date of maturity, the first bill maturing six months after the date when 90 per cent was disbursed under the letter of credit and the rest maturing successively semi-annually thereafter.

'All bank charges outside the seller's country are to be paid by the buyer.'

The final design of the terms of payment

The main purpose of the terms of payment is to establish the payment obligations of the buyer, including when and how they occur in relation to the seller's delivery obligations. This risk analysis has been thoroughly dealt with in earlier chapters, along with the function of the terms of payment and also the liquidity aspects and the capital requirements needed for the conclusion of the transaction. In reality there are, of course, many other factors that the seller must consider, not least the competition they can expect to face in winning the contract.

All these aspects will finally help the seller decide which terms of payment they should include in the offer or propose in the negotiations. Yet the terms of payments are only one aspect of the contract that has to be negotiated. Both parties will value all these parts differently and must be prepared to compromise on certain questions.

The final structure and design will, therefore, also depend on the seller's evaluation of the importance of the deal and its potential profitability in relation to the risks involved. When doing so, it will also test their ability to cover these risks through the terms of payment combined with available insurance and guarantees. The seller who has this knowledge will be able to make better, more profitable and more secure international business transactions.

Make use of the banks and trade organizations' experience

Previous experience is important when preparing risk assessments and deciding on the detailed terms of payment, but it is equally important to know the normal practice in different countries in order to strike the right balance in a competitive offer to the buyer.

Many banks have a comprehensive network of branches, subsidiaries, affiliates or correspondents in most countries, along with a constant flow of international payments and documentary transactions that pass through their businesses each day. That gives them a good picture of established business practice and of what payments methods are used, but also what experience other domestic exporters have had in different countries.

Surprisingly, very few sellers take the opportunity to make full use of this knowledge, and the final general advice is therefore:

Do not hesitate to ask for help or assistance from your bank or the domestic trade organization when it comes to detailed terms of payment; they have that expertise.

Terms of payment in the quotation

LAMJASSA MOHAMMED ED FILS
Attn: Mr Kihal Sherif
17 Rue Mekki Ali
ALGER
Algeria

Quotation for Alarm Systems

Dear Mr Sherif,

We refer to your letter of 10 June 2012 and want to make you the following offer for our Alarm Systems, type Soundstrong 1300, subject to detailed contract documentation.

You will find a complete technical description in enclosure No. 1, which is the same as the one given to Mr Ali El-Bakr when he visited us this spring.

Quantity:	300 units Soundstrong 1300 with standard equipment according to enclosure No. 1.
Price:	USD 175 per unit, including standard equipment.
General terms:	See enclosure No. 2.
Delivery terms:	CIF Alger, Incoterms 2010
Delivery:	Shipment from Singapore within 1 month from receipt of approved letter of credit.
Terms of payment:	**Payment through letter of credit at sight in USD, issued by Banque Extérieure d'Algerie, Alger within 30 days from order, to be advised, payable and confirmed by the Commercial Bank Ltd, Singapore. The letter of credit shall be valid for two months after our acceptance of the L/C terms. All bank charges outside Singapore are to be paid by the buyer.**
Packing:	The goods are packed for export with 10 units per carton and 10 cartons per wooden case.

This quotation is valid until 18 July 2012. We hope it will be of interest to you and look forward to receiving your order.

Yours faithfully,
SUNDALE ALARMS LTD

Roger B Staines   Stephen Sayers

GLOSSARY OF TERMS AND ABBREVIATIONS

This glossary contains most of the trade finance words and expressions used in this handbook or directly related to its contents. To make the content less complicated and more precise, the comments are made from the point of view of the seller unless stated otherwise.

Most of the words and expressions below can also be found in the index for reference to a particular page in the book.

acceptance   Time draft accepted by the drawee, thereby creating an unconditional obligation to pay at maturity.

acceptance letter of credit   A letter of credit, which requires the seller to draw a term draft to be accepted by the nominated bank upon presentation of documents, whereby the seller receives a banker's draft instead of payment.

advance payment   Trading method where the seller receives payment before delivery, either as part of an agreed composite payment structure or due to low or unknown creditworthiness of the buyer.

advance payment guarantee   Undertaking on behalf of the seller's bank to repay the buyer in case of non-fulfilment of the seller's contractual obligations.

adverse business risks   Negative, corrupt and unlawful business practices related to international trade, ie bribes and money laundering.

advising bank   A bank, usually in the seller's country, which authenticates the letter of credit and advises it to the seller. The expression is also used when a bank authenticates a bank guarantee in favour of the beneficiary.

air waybill (AWB)   Transport document in airfreight as a receipt of goods and evidence of the freight agreement. An AWB is not a document of title and is not needed to claim the goods.

all risk insurance   Formerly a common insurance clause in policies to be presented under collections and L/Cs, now commonly replaced by Institute Cargo Clauses; *see* that term.

amendments   Alterations to instructions in a collection, or of the original terms and conditions in a letter of credit. The seller has the right to refuse such L/C amendments.

annuities   Lease payments, based on a combination of interest and amortizations of the underlying financial costs.

applicant   The party at whose request a bank issues a letter of credit. Sometimes also called account party; *see also* principal.

assignment   A method where the seller transfers the rights of proceeds, often under a letter of credit, to a third party.

at sight   A notation on a draft (bill of exchange), indicating that it should not be accepted but paid upon presentation. Often used in collections and letters of credit.

availability   A letter of credit may be available (or payable or honoured) for presentation of documents against payment at sight, deferred payment or acceptance; *see* these terms.

avalize (aval)   Where a guarantor, often a bank, issues its guarantee directly on an accepted bill of exchange or other financial instrument, thereby undertaking the payment obligations of the drawee on a joint and several basis. Other terms are bill guarantee and guaranteed acceptance.

back-to-back letter of credit   An arrangement where the seller offers an existing letter of credit as security to their bank for the issuance of a secondary L/C in favour of their supplier(s).

balance exposure   An often unrealized currency risk exposure within the company, reflecting different methods of calculating assets and debts for accounting purposes.

bank cheque   Cheque issued by a bank and sent directly by the buyer to the seller as a method of payment. Also often referred to as a banker's draft.

bank guarantee   An undertaking by a bank, on behalf of the principal to pay a certain amount in money to the beneficiary under certain conditions.

bank identifier code (BIC)   The same as the SWIFT address (often also called SWIFTBIC), used as identification of accounts, often in connection with bank payments or messages.

bank remittance   *See* bank transfer.

bank-to-bank credit   A buyer credit given by a third party (often the seller's bank) to the buyer's bank for on-lending to the buyer to pay cash to the seller for goods delivered.

bank-to-buyer credit   A buyer credit given by a third party (often the seller's bank) directly to the buyer to pay cash to the seller for goods delivered. Such credits normally demand a corresponding guarantee from the buyer's bank, covering the obligations of the buyer.

bank transfer   The most common method of payment where the role of the banks is to transfer funds according to payment instructions by the buyer. Also called bank remittance.

banker's acceptance   A time draft drawn on and accepted by a bank, often in connection with a letter of credit; *see also* acceptance letter of credit.

banker's draft   *See* bank cheque.

barter trade   Trade of goods and services with settlement in other goods or dependent on other trades being performed.

bid bond   *See* tender guarantee.

bill guarantee   *See* avalize (aval).

bill of exchange   Commonly used trade financial instrument, drawn up by the seller and, after acceptance by the buyer, being an unconditional payment obligation to pay at a specified future date. A bill is often referred to as a 'draft' until it has been accepted.

bill of lading   Transport document issued by the carrier for shipment by sea. The bill of lading is a document of title, which means that the goods will not be released to the buyer (the consignee) other than against this original document.

B/L   *See* bill of lading.

blank endorsement   A transfer of rights without specifying the new party, making the document, often a bill of exchange, a bill of lading or an insurance policy, a freely negotiable document.

bond   In the context of international trade, a guarantee instrument mostly issued by an insurance company, similar to a bank guarantee – which is the term generally used in this book for these instruments.

bond (guarantee or insurance) indemnity   The general term for an insurance cover against the risk for 'unfair calling' under a Demand Guarantee.

break-even price   The currency price needed at maturity to make the currency option profitable – calculated on strike price, premium and commission, if any.

buyer credit   Any arrangement where a third party, usually a bank, in agreement with the seller, refinances the transaction, giving the credit directly to the buyer or their bank for direct cash payment to the seller.

call option   One part of a dual put and call currency option, where a seller purchases a call option in their domestic currency to hedge the incoming foreign currency. The opposite is a put option – *see* that term; *see also* currency options.

cap and floor   A currency hedge technique, whereby the currency risk is restricted to an upper and lower limit.

capital goods   Industrial durable goods used for production of other goods for consumption, a distinction important in connection with available credit terms or with credit risk insurance.

cash cover   A term used when the applicant of a letter of credit is required to deposit money in favour of the issuing bank as collateral.

certificate of origin   Verifies the origin of the goods delivered. Often issued by a chamber of commerce in the seller's country.

charter party bill of lading   A special form of a bill of lading issued by the vessel owner, which may restrict its nature as a document of title (not normally allowed under a letter of credit).

CIS countries (Commonwealth of Independent States)   A regional grouping of some former Soviet republics, used in this book in relation to programmes of support from the European Development bank.

claim document   The document giving evidence for a claim to be presented under a bank guarantee.

clean bill of lading   A bill of lading without indication that goods are damaged and/or in unsatisfactory order at the time of loading.

clean collection   Collection in which only a financial instrument is included, often the bill of exchange.

clean payments   Payments to be made without a corresponding and simultaneous receipt of documents (bank remittance and cheques), contrary to documentary payments, *see* that term.

co-joint financing   A form of leveraged finance between development banks, commercial banks and export credit agencies that increases the scope for additional amounts put into projects and investments.

collection accounts   Accounts held by the seller in banks in other countries to be used for incoming payments from buyers in that country.

collection bank   Bank in the drawee's country, which is instructed to release documents to the buyer (the drawee) against payment or acceptance. Also called presenting bank.

combined transport document   *See* multimodal transport document. Such a document is normally not a document of title.

commercial documents   A general term for documents produced in connection with the delivery of goods or services, as compared to financial documents; *see* that term.

commercial interest reference rates (CIRR)   The minimum level for state-supported fixed interest rates according to the OECD Consensus rules; *see* Consensus.

commercial risks   Also called purchaser risks, covering not only the possibility of non-payment by the buyer, but also the risk for non-fulfilment of other contractual obligations, including those necessary for the seller's own performance.

commitment   In connection with letters of credit, banks undertaking in advance to the seller to confirm L/Cs, which may be issued by certain banks during a specified period of time, usually against a fee.

compensation trade   The sale of goods and services with payment often in a combination of money and other goods.

compliant documents   Documents presented which fully comply with the terms and conditions of the letter of credit.

composite terms of payment   An expression used in this book when payment is to be effected in separate tranches related to the underlying structure of the commercial transaction.

conditional guarantee   Guarantee becoming payable only if and when it is verified that the principal has defaulted in their obligations under the guarantee. The opposite is unconditional or demand guarantee; *see* these terms.

confidential factoring   Financing of invoices by the bank, of which the buyer is not aware – in this book called invoice discounting or invoice finance as opposed to notified factoring; *see* that term.

confirmation   A procedure whereby a confirming bank, normally upon the request of the issuing bank, guarantees the liabilities of that bank towards the seller.

confirming bank   The bank confirming the letter of credit to the seller; *see* confirmation.

Consensus   Guidelines issued by OECD establishing a common practice for restricting the use of state-supported export credits.

consignee   The party to whom goods are to be delivered, usually the buyer, the collecting bank or the forwarding agent.

consignor   The party who delivers the goods to the consignee according to a freight agreement.

contract CIRR   A form of state-supported interest rates; *see* Consensus.

contract frustration policy   *See* contract repudiation indemnity.

contract guarantees   Guarantees directly linked to the course of events in an underlying commercial contract.

contract repudiation indemnity   Credit insurance covering the political risks of changed or revoked approvals by an authority in the buyer's country, preventing the transaction from being correctly performed. Also called contract frustration policy.

convertible currencies   Currencies that can easily be exchanged against the main international currencies on a free and unrestricted market.

corporate cheque   A cheque issued by the buyer and, in the context of this book, sent to the seller as a method of payment; *see also* bank cheque.

correspondent bank   Banks in other countries with which domestic banks have account relationships or arrangements to verify signatures or authentication.

counter trade   The sale of goods where the transaction is dependent on a corresponding purchase of other goods within a common framework.

credit guarantee   Undertaking by a bank to guarantee any credit, loan or other obligation assumed by a subsidiary or affiliate of the principal or any third party, not capable of entering into the obligations on their own merits.

credit insurance (credit risk insurance)   Insurance against loss due to the inability or unwillingness of the buyer to pay for goods delivered. Credit risk insurance may cover a variety of risks, both commercial and political; *see also* these terms.

cross-border leasing   An expression used in lease transactions, when the lessor and the lessee are located in separate countries. Also a general expression for larger, more complicated leasing transactions using tax rules advantages in different countries.

cross rate   The price of one currency in terms of another as calculated from their respective value against another major traded currency.

currency accounts   Accounts held in foreign currency in banks, which could be used to balance currency flows/transactions without unnecessary currency exchange.

currency clauses   The use of special agreements between buyer and seller to cap or split the currency risk between the parties.

currency exposure   The real currency risk affecting the liquidity position, to which the company is exposed at any period of time; *see also* balance exposure and payment exposure.

currency hedges   Methods of minimizing currency risks and/or currency exposure.

currency options   A currency hedge different from a forward contract since the currency option is a right, not an obligation, to buy/sell one currency against another at a fixed rate within a specified period of time.

currency pegging   Officially or unofficially determined or controlled currency rates for an individual country against another currency, often the USD.

currency position schedule   The comprehensive schedule over the company's total currency risk exposure, containing both fixed and anticipated currency flows.

currency risk   The risk connected to invoicing in a foreign currency which, for example, when payment is received, may result in a lower amount in the seller's own currency than anticipated.

currency spread   The difference between the bid and offered rate quoted by banks in a freely traded foreign exchange market.

D/A   Abbreviation for 'documents against acceptance'.

D/C   Abbreviation for documentary credit or just credit, synonym for letter of credit (which is the expression used in this book).

default   Failure to pay an accepted financial instrument on maturity date or to perform any agreed contractual business obligation.

deferred payment   Payment made to the seller at a specified date after shipment or presentation of documents under a letter of credit, but without the use of a draft accepted by a bank; *see also* acceptance letter of credit.

demand guarantee   Undertaking by a bank to pay to the beneficiary the amount on first demand without their proving the right to the claim and without the consent of the principal.

development banks   Regional and mostly well-capitalized banks, owned by the participating countries, which support projects vital for the economic development of that region.

development funds   Regional and mostly well-capitalized funds, subsidiaries of the development banks, lending on 'soft terms' to projects of special importance for regional development.

direct export factoring   An arrangement where the seller's factoring company (the factor) has direct contact with the buyer in another country without the use of a local correspondent.

direct guarantee   A guarantee issued directly to the beneficiary by the seller's bank without using a local advising or issuing bank.

discounting   The purchase (with or without recourse) of an accepted term (usance) bill of exchange against an amount less than its face value.

discrepancies (in documents)   Non-presentation, non-consistency or other reasons why documents may not be approved under a letter of credit.

documents against acceptance (D/A)   When the buyer is requested by the collection bank to accept a term bill of exchange that accompanies the documents instead of payment at sight.

document against payment (D/P)   When the collection bank notifies the buyer about the documents for collection and requests them to pay the amount at sight as instructed by the seller's bank.

documentary collection   Where banks, acting on behalf of the seller, present documents for collection to the buyer against cash payment or acceptance.

documentary credit   *See* letter of credit.

documentary payments   A general reference to the two main documentary methods of payment, documentary (bank) collections and letters of credit. The opposite is clean payments; *see* that term.

document of title Transport document where the carrier undertakes not to release the goods other than against this original document; *see also* bill of lading.

D/P Abbreviation for 'documents against payment'.

draft Synonym for bill of exchange, but often used before acceptance of the bill; *see also* bill of exchange.

drawee Party on whom the bill of exchange is drawn and who is required to pay at sight or at maturity.

due date Maturity date for payment.

duty-exempt guarantee Undertaking by a bank, on behalf of the principal, to pay any customs duty for goods intended to be only temporarily brought into the country, but not brought out within the specified period.

EES countries (European Economic Space) A definition of both EU and non-EU European countries.

endorsement Transfer of rights on a trade or financial instrument, mostly made on the back of the document, either in blank or to a specific party; *see also* blank endorsement.

EU payments Bank transfers between most European countries, made in a specific format and according to rules stipulated by the EU.

European Bank for Reconstruction and Development (EBRD) A major development bank, supporting countries from central Europe to central Asia, including many former Soviet republics.

exercise price *See* strike price.

expiry clause A clause in a bank guarantee, limiting its duration.

expiry date The expiry date under a letter of credit which is the last date at which the seller can present documents to the nominated bank.

export credit agencies (ECAs) Government owned or supported insurance institutions, focusing on export risk cover for sellers/suppliers from that country.

export credits Credits that the exporter offers the buyer in connection with the sale of goods or services or credit given by third party to finance such transactions.

export factoring A method of short-form refinancing where the factoring company (the factor) purchases the seller's receivables and assumes the credit risk, either with or without recourse to the seller.

export insurance policy A standard export credit insurance issued to the seller, covering for example commercial and political risks.

export leasing Medium-term export finance facility for machinery, vehicles and equipment in particular, with the legal right for the lessee to use the goods for a defined period of time but without owning or having title to them.

export loans Advance payments by banks, based on the security of a letter of credit, up to a certain percentage of the L/C amount.

export risks Risks that may affect the individual export transaction and which the seller must evaluate and cover prior to the execution of the contract.

express payments Urgent payments through the SWIFT system, making the transfer available to the seller quicker than normal payments, but at a higher fee.

extend or pay Where the beneficiary threatens to claim under a demand guarantee unless it is prolonged.

facilitation payments A form of corrupt practice in international trade where payments are made to officials or employees in the buyer's country or elsewhere to smooth, hasten or facilitate the contract.

factor Synonym for factoring company; *see* export factoring.

financial documents Documents related to the financial aspect of the transaction and its payment (ie a bill of exchange) as compared to commercial documents.

financial lease An arrangement where the practical risk of ownership rests with the lessee and where the lessor, from the outset of the lease, expects to recover from the lessee both the capital cost of the investment as well as interest and profit during the period of the lease. The opposite is operating lease; *see* that term.

financial risks An expression for increased financial, liquidity and cash management impacts as a consequence of entering into a new commercial transaction.

first demand guarantee *See* demand guarantee.

force majeure Various specified conditions, including 'acts of God', which cannot be avoided through due care by the commercial parties and therefore may excuse them from performance.

forfaiting purchase of negotiable trade financial instruments, mostly avalized bills of exchange, without recourse to the seller; *see also* avalize (aval).

forward currency contract A contract between the seller and the bank, in one currency expressed in terms of another currency at a rate fixed at contract date, but with execution at a future date.

forward currency market The market for currency exchange transactions with delivery at a future date, but with the rate determined at transaction date.

forward discount rate   An expression often used when the forward exchange rate of a currency is lower than its spot value (the opposite is a premium rate).

forward option contracts   Forward exchange contracts that can be settled within a period of time instead of at a fixed date. Not to be mistaken for a currency option; *see* that term.

forward points   The trading technique in the interbank forward exchange market, where rates are expressed and quoted as differences in points from the spot rates as opposed to real currency rates, so called outright forward rates; *see* that term.

forward premium rate   An expression often used when the forward exchange rate of a currency is higher than its spot value (the opposite is a discount rate).

forwarding agent's certificate of receipt (FCR)   Transport document indicating receipt of goods from the seller and the arrangement of transportation according to instructions. It is not a document of title.

freely negotiable   A statement, often in a letter of credit, giving the seller the right to present the documents for negotiation at any bank.

full payout lease   *See* financial lease.

full set   Documents (often the bill of lading) with more than one original, where all originals have the same legal rights. A full set is therefore often required under a letter of credit or documentary collection.

guarantee   *See* bank guarantee.

guaranteed acceptance (aval)   The undertaking of a bank, on behalf of the buyer (the drawee), to guarantee an accepted Bill of Exchange or Promissory Note, either directly on the bill or note (aval) or through a separate guarantee.

hard currency   The currency of a nation with economic strength and a long-term reputation for currency stability, which results in a high acceptability in international trade and currency markets.

hedge   An expression used for reducing outstanding currency or interest risks or fluctuations through compensating transactions.

honouring documents   A term in the new L/C rules (UCP 600) specifying three possibilities for honouring documents at presentation, at sight, by acceptance or by deferred payment.

IDA   The International Development Association (IDA), part of the World Bank, provides long-term interest-free loans and grants to the poorest developing countries.

IFC   The IFC, International Finance Corporation, a member of the World Bank Group, is the largest multilateral source of loan and equity financing for private sector projects in the developing world.

import licence   Document issued by authorities in the buyer's country to control or restrict the importation of goods.

Incoterms   International accepted trade delivery terms (Incoterms 2010) issued by the International Chamber of Commerce (ICC).

indirect guarantee   A guarantee issued to the beneficiary (often the buyer) by a local issuing bank based on a counter guarantee from an instructing bank, as opposed to the direct guarantee issued directly by that bank towards the beneficiary.

inspection certificate   Frequently used document where an independent third party verifies the quality, quantity or other aspects of the goods prior to shipment, in most cases upon instruction from the buyer.

Institute Cargo Clauses   Nowadays mostly used standard cargo or marine cargo clauses in international trade.

instructing bank   The bank forwarding instructions on behalf of the principal to a local bank (the issuing bank) to issue a guarantee in favour of the beneficiary.

interbank currency market   The market(s) established between major commercial and international banks for dealing in currencies (spot and forward), thereby also establishing interbank currency market rates.

interbank money market   The market(s) established between major commercial and international banks for dealing in short deposits in most trade currencies, thereby also establishing interbank money market rates.

interest contingency insurance   Where the seller takes a subsidiary transport insurance, should the buyer not fulfil their contractual obligation to insure the goods.

interest swap   An arrangement with a third party, usually a bank, where a commercial party wanting to hedge the interest rate agrees to exchange (swap) floating into fixed interest rate, or vice versa, during a fixed period.

International Bank Account Numbers (IBAN)   A fixed bank account numbering standard used within Europe, according to EU rules.

International Chamber of Commerce (ICC)   The world's only truly global business organization, based in Paris. They are also the issuing institution of generally accepted rules governing guarantees, documentary collections and letters of credit.

international leasing   *See* cross-border leasing.

intrinsic value   Term used in connection with currency options and describes the amount, if any, which could be realized if the option was to be sold before maturity.

investment insurance   A form of insurance covering long-term political risks, potentially affecting the value or performance of an overseas investment.

invoice discounting   Arrangements for provision of finance against the security of trade receivables, with recourse to the seller; *see also* confidential factoring.

irrevocable letter of credit   Under the new ICC rules (UCP 600) all letters of credit are by definition irrevocable, and therefore it is no longer necessary to state this term in an L/C.

ISP 98   International Standby Practices, rules covering standby letters of credit, issued by the International Chamber of Commerce.

issuing bank   The bank issuing a letter of credit on behalf of the applicant (the buyer). Also called the opening bank. The expression is also used when issuing a bank guarantee on behalf of the principal.

joint and several guarantees   The normal form of bank guarantee, where the beneficiary, at their discretion, can claim either the guarantor or the principal.

joint ventures   In this book, arrangements in primarily many developing and/or emerging countries, where the seller participates as co-owner in a project or in a larger export scheme to and within the local country.

jurisdiction   The place agreed on in contracts and financial instruments where disputes, if any, should be settled legally.

key customer risk insurance   Insurance policies covering and capping the outstanding risk on certain key risks in the seller's export ledger.

L/C   Abbreviation for letter of credit.

legalization   Certification of documents, normally done by an official or appointed representative of the buyer's country.

lessee   The contractual end-user of the machinery/equipment in a lease contract.

lessor   The owner and contractual counterpart to the lessee in a lease transaction.

letter of credit (L/C)   A method of payment whereby an issuing bank, upon instruction from the buyer, guarantees the seller to pay a specified amount of money against the presentation of compliant documents within a specified time period. Often also called documentary credit or just credit.

letter of indemnity   A bank guarantee issued on behalf of the buyer in favour of the shipping company against their delivering of the goods without presentation of the original bill of lading.

letter of support, letter of comfort or **letter of awareness**   Different forms of undertakings, but not in the form of a guarantee, normally issued by a parent or group company, indirectly supporting credit or other obligations assumed by subsidiaries or affiliate companies.

London Interbank Offered Rates (LIBOR)   The interbank money market in London for short-term deposits in most currencies, thereby establishing this market's lending interest rates.

lines of credit   Arrangements of credit lines between banks in some larger exporting countries and local banks in mostly developing countries, to be used for financing of small- and medium-sized export transactions.

master letter of credit   The term for the original letter of credit, based on the security of which a second letter of credit is issued; *see also* back-to-back letter of credit and transferable letter of credit.

matching   The offering of government-supported credit risk insurance cover to suppliers in one country on the same terms as offered by other government agencies to their exporters.

maturity   Due date for a term bill of exchange or other financial instrument.

method of payment   The agreed form of payment to be used by the buyer, either open account payments through bank cheque or bank transfer, or by documentary collection or a letter of credit.

money laundering   A process, also carried out in connection with international trade, through which the proceeds of criminal activity are disguised to conceal their actual origins.

multimodal transport document   Transport document evidencing shipment of goods by more than one means of transportation.

negotiable document or instrument   A document or financial instrument where rights and obligations are freely transferable to another party.

nominated bank   An expression used in connection with L/Cs when a bank is authorized by the issuing bank not only to negotiate but also to pay or to accept drafts as the case may be.

non-compliant documents   Where the documents presented, or their details, are not in accordance with the terms and conditions of the letter of credit.

non-convertible currencies   Currencies not traded freely on an international currency market, often restricted by internal regulations and currency controls.

non-negotiable documents/instruments   Documents or financial instruments where their rights and obligations are not freely transferable to another party.

non-recourse financing   *See* project finance.

non-tariff barriers   A general phrase describing non-regulated and often disguised barriers to international trade, mostly practised by individual countries to protect their own trade or industry.

notified factoring   Financing of invoices of which the buyer is informed, normally through an assignment on each invoice. In this book also called factoring only.

notify party   The party who is to be informed by the carrier about the arrival of goods at the destination.

noting   The first stage in protest of a dishonoured bill of exchange.

ocean/marine bill of lading   *See* bill of lading.

on-board bill of lading   Notation on the bill of lading that the goods have been loaded on board the ship. Often a requirement in a letter of credit.

on-demand guarantee   *See* demand guarantee.

on their face   An important expression when dealing with documents and letters of credit, indicating that banks examine the presented documents with reasonable care, but without responsibility for their accuracy or genuineness.

open account (payment terms)   Payment terms, often including a short-term supplier credit, extended to the buyer at shipment without any written evidence of indebtedness.

opening bank   Expression sometimes used instead of (letter of credit) issuing bank.

operating lease   An arrangement where the lessee is using the equipment on a less than full payout basis and where the risk of ownership rests with the lessor who thereby also retains a financial risk in the arrangement.

Organization for Economic Cooperation and Development (OECD)   An international organization of member states helping governments to implement common economic and social solutions globally, including establishing common rules for government support of trade and industry.

outright forward rates   Forward exchange rates normally quoted towards customers as compared to the forward points quotations between banks; *see* that term.

parallel financing   *See* co-joint financing.

(The) Paris Club   An informal group of official creditors from the larger economies whose role it is to find coordinated and sustainable solutions to payment difficulties experienced by debtor countries.

payment exposure   The currency exposure resulting from in- and outgoing flows in foreign currency within the company, often reflecting the potential and real currency risk. The opposite is balance exposure; *see* that term.

payment guarantee   Undertaking, normally in the form of a bank guarantee, on behalf of the buyer, to pay for the seller's contractual delivery of goods or services.

performance guarantee   A very common contract guarantee, covering the seller's delivery and performance obligations according to the contract.

points   The spread in the interbank currency market between the buying and selling rate; *see also* forward points.

political risks   The risk for a commercial transaction not being duly performed due to measures emanating from the government or authority of the buyer's own country, but also from any other foreign country.

postal risks   The risk of cheques or documents not being received by the counterpart, with risk for non-performance and/or payment disputes and delays.

pour aval   *See* avalize.

pre-contract CIRR;   A form of state-supported interest rates to be applied for before the signing of the sales contract; *see* Consensus.

premium   The up-front fee that the buyer of a currency option pays to their counterpart, usually a bank, similar to an insurance premium.

presenting bank   The bank presenting the documentary collection to the buyer and collect payment. Also named collecting bank.

pre-shipping finance   Finance earmarked for manufacturing or other costs for an export transaction before shipment.

principal   The same as applicant, the party instructing a bank to process a documentary collection or to issue a guarantee; *see also* applicant.

product risks   Risks, including manufacturing and shipping risks, which are related to the product itself, and which the seller has to evaluate and cover in order to be able to fulfil their contractual obligations.

progress payment guarantee   Undertaking on behalf of the seller to repay payments made by the buyer during the contract phases, but where the buyer, because of the seller's non-fulfilment, cannot make use of the delivery until completion.

project finance   Finance arrangements for larger projects, generally based on the revenues of the project, mostly secured on its assets and less on the creditworthiness of the buyer. Often called non-recourse financing.

promissory note   A form of financial instrument in international trade and more detailed than a bill of exchange, where the buyer irrevocably promises to pay to the seller according to a fixed schedule.

protest The formal procedure after noting of a dishonoured bill, where the notary public issues a formal protest, which can be used in legal proceedings.

purchaser risks *See* commercial risks.

put option One part of a dual put and call currency option, where an exporter sells a put option to hedge a scheduled payment in foreign currency. The opposite is a call option; *see also* currency options and call options.

rail waybill (RWB) Rail transport document as receipt for goods and evidence of freight agreement. A RWB is not a document of title and is not needed to claim the goods.

recourse The provision whereby a refinancing party reserves the right against the seller to reclaim any amount not paid by the buyer/drawee on maturity date of the refinanced instrument.

red clause letter of credit A letter of credit containing a clause that authorizes the advising or nominated bank to make an advance payment to the seller prior to delivery of conforming documents.

reduction clause A clause that automatically reduces the undertaking under a bank guarantee in line with the successive fulfilment of the obligations by the principal or in any other way, stated in the guarantee.

reference banks Banks selected in a loan agreement to be used as quoting banks to establish the reference interest rates.

reference interest rates The recognized money market rates for most trade currencies, established on an interbank market at a specific time during the day, or established in any other way as specified in a loan agreement.

repurchase agreements (A) Trade in which payment is made through products, generated by the equipment or goods being delivered by the seller.

repurchase agreements (B) Arrangements used in leasing transactions as additional security for the lessor, where the manufacturer or original supplier agrees to repurchase or arrange in some other way for the equipment in case of default of the lessee.

retention money guarantee Undertaking on behalf of the seller to comply with any obligation after delivery such as installation, start-up, etc, but where the buyer has already made payment.

revocable letter of credit Formerly a form of letter of credit, which could be cancelled or amended during its validity. Under the new ICC UCP 600 this is no longer a defined term, since all L/Cs are by definition irrevocable.

revolving letter of credit A letter of credit that is automatically reinstated after each drawing, but with some restrictions on total amount or number of reinstatements.

sight bill *See* at sight.

silent confirmation A confirmation of a letter of credit towards the seller made by the advising bank or some other party, but without the instructions to do so from the issuing bank.

Society for Worldwide Interbank Financial Telecommunication (SWIFT) An international cooperative bank network for payments and messages.

soft currencies The opposite of hard currencies; *see* that term.

spot exchange rate The fluctuating market price of one currency expressed in terms of another currency, for immediate delivery.

spot market The market for currency exchange transactions with immediate delivery or typically within two banking days.

standby letter of credit As opposed to an ordinary commercial letter of credit, the standby letter of credit is usually drawn on only in cases where the applicant fails to perform a specified obligation. The standby letter of credit is often used as an alternative to a bank guarantee.

strike price Also known as the exercise price, which is the stated price at which the holder of a currency option has the right to exercise the option at maturity.

structured leasing *See* cross-border leasing.

structured trade finance In this book a reference to ad hoc trade finance techniques, often arranged by or through specialized financial institutions.

subsidiary insurance *See* interest contingency insurance.

supplier credit Arrangements where the seller is extending a fixed credit period to the buyer, either for shorter periods in connection with open account trading terms or for longer periods through some form of a financial instrument.

surety bond An undertaking from a third party, often an insurance or a surety company, to pay a certain sum of money or under certain conditions with the alternative obligation to fulfil or arrange for the completion of the underlying commercial contract, should the principal default in their obligations.

SWIFTBIC *See* bank identifier code (BIC).

tender exchange rate insurance The use of insurance for the seller to cover the outstanding currency risk between the period of a firm offer until acceptance, if any, from the buyer.

tender guarantee Undertaking on behalf of the seller to stand by the offer/tender, should it be accepted. Often also called bid bond.

term bill Bill of exchange to be paid at a later due date.

terms of delivery   The detailed terms and conditions agreed between the parties to govern the delivery of goods. The rules set by ICC, Incoterms 2010, are by far the most commonly used in international trade.

terms of payment   The complete terms and condition agreed between the commercial parties, related to the buyer's payment obligations, including the chosen method of payment.

third-party documents   Documents under letters of credit (and collections) issued by other parties where the seller must be certain these can be correctly issued for presentation under the L/C (or be included in the agreed collection documents).

trade practices   Established trade rules in a country either by common practice or by rules set by ICC, which are by far the most commonly used in international trade.

trade refinancing   Any arrangement where the seller is using receivables or separate finance instruments to offload a trade credit given to the buyer.

transfer guarantee   A separate undertaking issued by a central bank or authorized commercial bank, guaranteeing both the allocation and the transfer of foreign exchange out of the country.

transfer risk   Restrictions caused by government authorities, preventing the buyer from purchasing the foreign exchange for local currency and/or transferring the currency out of the country.

transferable letter of credit   Permits the seller to transfer under certain conditions the rights and obligations under the letter of credit to one or several of their suppliers.

two-factor export factoring   An arrangement where the seller's factoring company (the factor) makes use of a local factoring company for the contract arrangements with the foreign buyer; *see also* direct export factoring.

UCP   UCP 600, Uniform Customs and Practice for Documentary Credits. ICC rules for letters of credit.

unconditional guarantee   *See* demand guarantee.

unconfirmed letter of credit   The issuing bank always guarantees a letter of credit, but if unconfirmed, no other bank has the obligation to honour compliant documents when presented by the seller.

undertaking to provide guarantee   Undertaking to have the relevant guarantee issued if the offer is successful. Often issued by a parent or group company in support of a subsidiary.

unfair calling   Claim by the beneficiary under a demand guarantee without having any contractual reason to do so.

URC   URC 522, Uniform Rules for Collection, issued by the ICC.

URCG   Uniform Rules for Contract Guarantees, issued by the ICC.

URDG   Uniform Rules for Demand Guarantees, issued by ICC.

usance bill (or usance letter of credit)   An expression sometimes used for a term bill of exchange or letter of credit with a future payment date, thereby extending the buyer a specified period of credit.

validity period   The period under which a guarantee, a letter of credit or any other similar undertaking will be honoured by the issuing bank.

value date   The execution date for foreign exchange contracts.

warranty guarantee   Undertaking on behalf of the seller, covering any contractual maintenance or performance obligations during a period of time after delivery or installation.

with/without recourse   *See* recourse.

(The) World Bank   A global 'bank' consisting of five different organizations, of which the best known are the International Bank for Reconstruction and Development (IBRD) and the International Development Association (IDA).

INDEX

NB: page numbers in *italic* indicate figures or tables

Accounting Standards Board   170
advance payment guarantee *see* repayment
      guarantee
advance payment standby *see* standby L/C
adverse business risks   21–24
   anti-corruption policies   23–24
   bribery   22
   definition of   21
   and export credit agencies (ECAs)   135
   harm caused by practices   23
   money laundering   22–23
African Development Bank (AfDB)   182
African Development Fund (AfDF)   182
air waybill   50
American Institute of Marine Underwriters
      17
Arrangement on Officially Supported Export
      Credits ('Consensus')   132, 133,
      163, 164, 175
Asian Development Bank (ADB)   182
Asian Development Fund (ADF)   182
Association of African Development Finance
      Institutions (AADFI)   179
Association of Development Financing
      Institutions in Asia and the Pacific
      (ADFIAP)   179
Association of European Development
      Finance Institutions (EDFI)   179
Association of National Development
      Finance Institutions in Member
      Countries of the Islamic
      Development Bank (ADFIMI)
      179
Asuransi Ekspor Indonesia (ASEI)   130
Atradius   21, 131
aval *see* guaranteed acceptance

balance exposure   107
Banco Nacional de Comercio Exterior SNC
      (BANCOMEXT)   131
bank letter of credit policy   136
bank transfer   36–45, *37*
   'clean payments'   37
   collection accounts   40–41
   delays in   41–44
      financial problems   43–44
      interest charges   43

      reasons for   42
      supervision and follow-up   43
      terms of payment   42
   e-commerce   44–45
      OECD B2C e-commerce guidelines
         44
   in the EU   41
   payment before delivery   40
   payment structure and trade pattern
      37–38
   SWIFT (Society for Worldwide Interbank
      Financial Telecommunication)
      system   38–39, 45, 82, 188
      Business Identifier Codes (BICs)   39
      express payments   38
      SWIFTNet   39, 144
barter trades   74
Berne Union   129
bid bond *see* tender guarantee
bid bond standby *see* standby L/C
bill discounting   117
bond insurance policy   137
bribery   22
Business Identifier Codes (BICs)   39
buyer credits   160–65
   buyer credit insurance policy   136
   definition of   160
   terms and conditions   163–65
   vs supplier credits   *161*

cargo insurance   17–19
   brokers   18
   exclusions   18
   Institute Cargo Clauses   17
   international insurer networks   19
   open cover   18
   person responsible for arranging   17
   seller's interest contingency insurance
      17, 18
carriage and insurance paid (CIP)   13
carriage paid to (CPT)   13
cash management   5, 185–86
CFR *see* cost and freight (CFR)
cheque payments   45–47, *46*
   corporate cheques   45
   postal risk   47
   sample bank cheque   *47*

China Export & Credit Insurance
Corporation (SINOSURE)   130
CIF *see* cost, insurance and freight (CIF)
CIP *see* carriage and insurance paid (CIP)
'clean payments'   37, 190
Coface   21, 25, 130
commercial risks   19–21
    credit report providers   21
    definition of   19
    outside the OECD   20
    sources of help   20
commercial standby *see* standby L/C
commitment fee   59
commodity profiles, international   4
Companhia de Seguro de Créditos, SA
(COSEC)   131
Compania Espanola de Seguros de Credito
a la Exportacion (CESCE)   131
compensation trades   74
composite terms   194–96
Consensus *see* Arrangement on Officially
Supported Export Credits
('Consensus')
contract guarantees
    performance guarantee   86
    progress payment guarantee   86
    repayment guarantee   86
    retention money guarantee   86
    tender guarantee   85
    warranty guarantee   87
contract repudiation indemnity   128–29
convertible currencies   101
corporate cheques   45
cost and freight (CFR)   13
cost, insurance and freight (CIF)   13
counter-trade   74–76
    barter trades   74
    compensation trades   74
    example of   75–76
    offset counter-trades   74
    reasons to use   74
    repurchase agreements   74
    summary of   76
CPT *see* carriage paid to (CPT)
credit guarantee   88–89
credit report providers   21
currency derivates   116
currency exposure   106–08
    balance exposure   107
    currency position schedule   108, *109*
    managing   108–09
    payment exposure   107
currency markets   102
currency risk   27–29, 99–120
    convertible currencies   101
    currency abbreviations   28

currency derivates   116
currency development   29
currency exposure   106–08
    balance exposure   107
    currency position schedule   108, *109*
    managing   108–09
    payment exposure   107
currency markets   102
definition of   27
euro, the   100
    bill discounting   117
    choice of invoicing currency   110–11
    currency clauses   117
    currency options   114–15
    currency steering   111, *112*
    forward currency contracts   113–14
    payments brought forward   111–13
    short-term currency loans   116–17
    tender exchange rate insurance
        117–18
    internal currency management   118–20
    rates, calculating   119–20, *120*
non-convertible currencies   101
pegging   99–100
spot market   102
spot trade   102–06
    buy and sell rates   103
    currency information, getting   104
    forward transactions   104–06
    spread   103
    strong vs weak currencies   28
currency steering   111, *112*

D&B   21
DAP *see* delivered at place (DAP)
DAT *see* delivered at terminal (DAT)
DDP *see* delivered duty paid (DDP)
delivered at place (DAP)   13
delivered at terminal (DAT)   13
delivered duty paid (DDP)   13
demand guarantees   79, 90–92
    bond insurance policies   92
    example   90
    unfair calling, risk of   91
development finance institutions (DFIs)
        178–79
documentary collection   47–53, *49*
    bill of exchange   51, *52*
    bill of lading   50
    credit risk insurance   51
    documents against acceptance (D/A)   48
    documents against payment (D/P)   48
    documents involved   51
    inspecting the goods   50–51
    licences   53
    role of banks   48

Uniform Rules for Collection (URC 522) 53

documentary credit (DC) *see* letter of credit (L/C)

duty-exempt guarantee 89

e-commerce 44–45
 OECD B2C e-commerce guidelines 44
Eksport Kredit Fonden (EKF) 130
electronic L/Cs 63, 65
Euler Hermes Kreditversicherungs-AG (EH) 130
Euro Interbank Offered Rate (EURIBOR) 166
European Bank for Reconstruction and Development (EBRD) 182
European Investment Bank (EIB) 182
European Investment Fund (EIF) 182
'exercise price' 114
EXIM Bank Malaysia 131
Experian 21
Export Credit Bank of Turkey (TURK EXIMBANK) 131
Export Credit Guarantee Corporation of India Ltd (ECGC) 130
export credit insurance 121–40
 applying for 138–39
 export credit agencies (ECAs) 122, 129–35, *130–31*
  Berne Union 129
  commercial matching 133
  guidelines and coverage 133–35
  tied aid 133
 forms of 135, *136–37*
 invalidating cover 124
 private sector 124–29
  bond/guarantee indemnity insurance 129
  contract repudiation indemnity 128–29
  investment insurance 129, 139–40
  market sector cover 127
  tailor-made policies 128
 risks not covered 123
 standard policy 127–28, 138
 summary of 140
Export Credit Insurance Corporation (Poland) (KUKE) 131
Export Credit Insurance Corporation (Sri Lanka) (SLECIC) 131
Export Credit Insurance of South Africa Ltd (ECIC) 131
Export Credits Guarantee Department (ECGD) 131
Export Development Canada (EDC) 130
export factoring 156–59, *158*

Export Guarantee and Insurance Corporation (EGAP) 130
export leasing insurance 173–74
exporters, leading *3*
Export–Import Bank of Thailand (THAI EXIMBANK) 131
Export–Import Bank of the Slovak Republic (SLOVAK EXIM) 131
Export–Import Bank of the United States (EXIMBANK) 131, 134
Exportkreditnämnden (EKN) 131
EXW *see* ex works (EXW)
ex works (EXW) 13

FAS *see* free alongside ship (FAS)
FCA *see* free carrier (FCA)
financial leases 169–70
financial risks 29–31
 bureaucracy and banking delays 30
 definition of 29
 reasons for payment delays 29–30
 terms of payment 30
Finnvera plc 130
FOB *see* free on board (FOB)
foreign currency insurance policy 137
forfaiting 159–60
forward currency contracts 113–14
forwarding agent certificate of receipt (FCR) 50
free alongside ship (FAS) 13
free carrier (FCA) 13
free on board (FOB) 13
frustration of contract 26–27
 insurance for 129–29

GarantiInstituttet for Eksportkreditt (GIEK) 131
guaranteed acceptance 87
guarantees 77–98, *83*
 contractual disputes 78–79
 cost of 84–85
 definition of 77–78
 demand guarantees 79, 90–92
  bond insurance policies 92
  example 90
  unfair calling, risk of 91
 example guarantee 80
 guarantee types
  credit guarantee 88–89
  duty-exempt guarantee 89
  guaranteed acceptance 87
  letter of indemnity 89
  payment guarantee 87
  performance guarantee *80*, 86
  progress payment guarantee 86
  repayment guarantee 86

retention money guarantee 86
tender guarantee 85
transfer guarantee 87
warranty guarantee 87
International Standby Practices (ISP 78)
    88, 95
open account trading 82, 84
    commercial L/Cs 82
    commercial standby L/Cs 84
    conditional payment guarantees
        84
    demand payment guarantees 84
parties involved 79–80, 82
standby L/C 78, 80, 92–95
    advantages of 94
    commencement and expiry dates
        96–97
    jurisdiction 96
    structure and design *81, 95*
    summary of 98
    surety bonds 78
    terminology 79
    Uniform Customs and Practice for
        Documentary Credits (UCP 600)
        88, 95
    Uniform Rules for Contract Guarantees
        (URCG 325) 88
    Uniform Rules for Demand Guarantees
        (URDG 758) 88
    User's Handbook to the URDG 92

Hong Kong Export Credit Insurance
    Corporation (HKEC) 130
Hungarian Export Credit Insurance Ltd
    (MEHIB) 130

importers, leading 3
Incoterms® 12–13
    terms 13
Institute Cargo Clauses 17
Institute of London Underwriters 17
Inter-American Development Bank
    (IDB/BID) 182
International Bank Account Number (IBAN)
    41
International Bank for Reconstruction and
    Development (IBRD) 180, 182
International Chamber of Commerce (ICC)
    13–14
    bookshop 14
    core services and activities 13
    Incoterms® 12–13
        terms 13
    membership of 14
    publications 9
        Incoterms (715) 12, 13

International Standard Banking
    Practice (ISBP) 68, 70
International Standby Practices
    (ISP 78) 88, 95
Uniform Customs and Practice for
    Documentary Credits (UCP 600)
    54, 68, 70, 88, 95, 193
Uniform Rules for Collection
    (URC 522) 53
Uniform Rules for Collection
    commentary (550) 53
Uniform Rules for Contract
    Guarantees (URCG 325) 88
Uniform Rules for Demand
    Guarantees (URDG 758) 88
User's Handbook to the URDG 92
International Development Association
    (IDA) 180, 182
International Finance Corporation (IFC)
    176, 178, 180, 182
International Forfaiting Association (IFA)
    160
International Organization for
    Standardization (ISO) 28
    Business Identifier Codes (BICs) 39
International Standard Banking Practice
    (ISBP) 68, 70
International Standby Practices (ISP 78)
    88, 95
International Union of Credit Insurers 129
invoice discounting 154–56
Islamic Corp for the Insurance of Investment
    & Export Credit (ICEIC) 131
Islamic Development Bank 182
Israel Export Insurance Corp. Ltd (ASHRA)
    130
Istituto per i Servizi Assicurativi del Credito
    all'Esportazione (SACE) 130

joint ventures 177

Korea Trade Insurance Corporation
    (KSURE) 131

leasing 169–74, *171*
    cross-border leasing 171–73
    export leasing insurance 173–74
    financial leases 169–70
    leasing insurance policy 137
    operating leases 169
letter of credit (L/C) 54–73, *61–62*
    advantages for buyer 55–56
    advantages for seller 55
    and complex business transactions
        71–72
    'complying presentation' 54

definition of   54
discrepancies   69–71
electronic L/Cs   63, 65
example   64
and fraud   55
'honouring'   54
inspecting the goods   68–69
International Standard Banking Practice
    (ISBP)   68, 70
key aspects   60
period of validity   56
place of presentation of documents
    57–58
in pre-financing   72
presentation of documents   63
security   58–59
    confirmation   59
    'silent confirmation'   59
third-party documents   67
time for payment   56–57
transferable L/Cs   60, 73
Uniform Customs and Practice for
    Documentary Credits (UCP 600)
    54, 68, 70, 88, 95, 193
letter of indemnity   89
lines of credit   174–75
local currency finance   175–76
London Interbank Offered Rates (LIBOR)
    165

money laundering   22–23
multi-buyer export insurance policy   136
multilateral development banks   180–83
European Bank for Reconstruction and
    Development (EBRD)   182–83
International Bank for Reconstruction
    and Development (IBRD)   180,
    182
International Development Association
    (IDA)   180, 182
International Finance Corporation (IFC)
    176, 178, 180, 182
Multinational Investment Guarantee
    Agency (MIGA)   180, 182
Multinational Investment Guarantee Agency
    (MIGA)   180, 182

National Export-Import Bank of Jamaica Ltd
    (EXIMBANK JAMAICA)   130
Nippon Export and Investment Insurance
    (NEXI)   130
non-convertible currencies   101
Nordic Investment Bank   182

Oesterreichische Kontrollbank (OeKB)   130
Office National du Ducroire (ONDD)   130

offset counter-trades   74
open account trading   82, 84
    commercial L/Cs   82
    commercial standby L/Cs   84
    conditional payment guarantees   84
    demand payment guarantees   84
operating leases   169
Organization for Economic Cooperation and
    Development (OECD)   19, 23
    Arrangement on Officially Supported
        Export Credits ('Consensus')
        132, 133, 163, 164, 175
    B2C e-commerce guidelines   44
Organization of Petroleum Exporting
    Countries (OPEC)   164
overseas investment insurance   137

packing finance see pre-shipment finance
Paris Club of Official Creditors   132
payment exposure   107
payment guarantee   87
payment methods   33–76
    bank transfer   36–45, 37
        'clean payments'   37
        collection accounts   40–41
        delays in   41–44
        e-commerce   44–45
        in the EU   41
        payment before delivery   40
        payment structure and trade pattern
            37–38
        SWIFT (Society for Worldwide
            Interbank Financial
            Telecommunication) system
            38–39, 45, 82, 188
    charges and costs   34–36
        fees   36
        handling charges   36
        payment charges   36
        risk commissions   36
    cheque payments   45–47, 46
        corporate cheques   45
        postal risk   47
        sample bank cheque   47
    counter-trade   74–76
        barter trades   74
        compensation trades   74
        example of   75–76
        offset counter-trades   74
        reasons to use   74
        repurchase agreements   74
        summary of   76
    documentary collection   47–53, 49
        bill of exchange   51, 52
        bill of lading   50
        credit risk insurance   51

documents against acceptance (D/A) 48
documents against payment (D/P) 48
documents involved 51
inspecting the goods 50–51
licences 53
role of banks 48
Uniform Rules for Collection (URC 522) 53
four basic methods 34, *35*
letter of credit (L/C) 54–73, *61–62*
advantages for buyer 55–56
advantages for seller 55
and complex business transactions 71–72
'complying presentation' 54
definition of 54
discrepancies 69–71
electronic L/Cs 63, *65*
example *64*
and fraud 55
'honouring' 54
inspecting the goods 68–69
International Standard Banking Practice (ISBP) 68, 70
key aspects *60*
period of validity 56
place of presentation of documents 57–58
in pre-financing 72
presentation of documents 63
security 58–59
third-party documents 67
time for payment 56–57
transferable L/Cs 60, 73
Uniform Customs and Practice for Documentary Credits (UCP 600) 54, 68, 70, 88, 95, 193
security of 33–34
vs terms of payment 33
pegging 99–100
per aval *see* guaranteed acceptance
performance guarantee 86
performance guarantee *80*, 86
performance standby *see* standby L/C
political risks 24–27
country information, getting 25
definition of 24
economic stability 26
frustration of contract 26–27
import restrictions 24
insurance for 128–29
labour market risks 26
non-tariff barriers 26

political stability 24–25
social stability 26
pre-shipment finance 143–46
and SWIFT 144
working capital guarantees 145–46
product risks 15–19
cargo insurance 17–19
brokers 18
exclusions 18
Institute Cargo Clauses 17
international insurer networks 19
open cover 18
person responsible for arranging 17
seller's interest contingency insurance 17, 18
contractual terms 16
manufacturing risks 16
transport risks 16–19
progress payment guarantee 86
project and structured finance guarantee 137
project finance 176–77
purchaser risks *see* commercial risks

rail waybill 50
repayment guarantee 86
repurchase agreements 74
retention money guarantee 86

Seguradora Brasileira de Crédito à Exportação S/A (SBCE) 130
seller's interest contingency insurance 17, 18
'silent confirmation' 59
simple demand guarantee *see* demand guarantee
single-buyer export insurance policy 136
Slovene Export Corporation Inc. (SID) 131
spot trade 102–06
buy and sell rates 103
currency information, getting 104
forward transactions 104–06
spread 103
spread 103
standby L/C 78, 80, 92–95
advantages of 94
commencement and expiry dates 96–97
jurisdiction 96
'strike price' 115
structured trade finance 169–83
development finance institutions (DFIs) 178–79
joint ventures 177
leasing 169–74, *171*
cross-border leasing 171–73
export leasing insurance 173–74

financial leases 169–70
operating leases 169
lines of credit 174–75
local currency finance 175–76
multilateral development banks
180–83
European Bank for Reconstruction
and Development (EBRD)
182–83
International Bank for Reconstruction
and Development (IBRD) 180,
182
International Development
Association (IDA) 180, 182
International Finance Corporation
(IFC) 176, 178, 180, 182
Multinational Investment Guarantee
Agency (MIGA) 180, 182
project finance 176–77
supplier credits 146–51
aspects to consider 147
medium- and long-term 149–51
refinancing of 151–60
bank loans 152–54
export factoring 156–59, 158
forfaiting 159–60
invoice discounting 154–56
short-term currency loans 148–49
supplier credit insurance policy 136
vs buyer credits 161
surety bonds 78
SWIFT (Society for Worldwide Interbank
Financial Telecommunication)
system 38–39, 45, 82, 188
Business Identifier Codes (BICs) 39
express payments 38
L/C issued through SWIFT 63, 65
SWIFTNet 39, 144
SWIFTBIC see Business Identifier Codes
(BICs)
Swiss Export Risk Insurance (SERV) 131

Taipei Export–Import Bank of China (TEBC)
130
tender bond standby see standby L/C
tender exchange rate insurance 117–18
tender guarantee 85
terms of payment 33, 42, 185–98
and cash management 185–86
common terms of payment 189
finalising the design 197
minimum requirements 186
method of payment 189–90
place of payment 187–89
time of payment 187

structure of
bank guarantee 191
bank transfer 190–91
composite terms 194–96
documentary collection 192
letters of credit 193–94
vs payment method 33
Tokyo Interbank Offered Rates (TIBOR)
166
trade finance 141–68, 143
buyer credits 160–65
buyer credit insurance policy 136
definition of 160
terms and conditions 163–65
vs supplier credits 161
and competitiveness 141
definition of 142
international money market 165–68
pre-shipment finance 143–46
and SWIFT 144
working capital guarantees 145–46
supplier credits 146–51
aspects to consider 147
medium- and long-term 149–51
refinancing of 151–60
short-term currency loans 148–49
supplier credit insurance policy
136
vs buyer credits 161
see also structured trade finance
trade risks 9–31
adverse business risks 21–24
anti-corruption policies 23–24
bribery 22
definition of 21
harm caused by practices 23
money laundering 22–23
commercial documentation 15
commercial risks 19–21
credit report providers 21
definition of 19
outside the OECD 20
sources of help 20
currency risks 27–29
currency abbreviations 28
currency development 29
definition of 27
strong vs weak currencies 28
financial risks 29–31
bureaucracy and banking delays
30
definition of 29
forms of 10–12, 11
reasons for payment delays 29–30
terms of payment 30

Incoterms® 12–13
  terms 13
insurance 10, 11
International Chamber of Commerce
    (ICC) 13–14
  bookshop 14
  core services and activities 13
  membership of 14
  publications 9
negotiation process 9–10
  local practices 10
official requirements 15
political risks 24–27
  country information, getting 25
  definition of 24
  economic stability 26
  frustration of contract 26–27
  import restrictions 24
  labour market risks 26
  non-tariff barriers 26
  political stability 24–25
  social stability 26
product risks 15–19
  cargo insurance 17–19
  contractual terms 16
  definition of 15
  manufacturing risks 16
  transport risks 16–19
risk assessment summary 31
terms of delivery 12–14
transfer guarantee 87
transferable L/Cs 60, 73
translation exposure *see* currency exposure

UK Trade & Investment 25
unconditional guarantee *see* demand
    guarantee
Understanding International Trade: an
    information guide for importers
    and exporters 55
unfair calling 91
Uniform Customs and Practice for
    Documentary Credits (UCP 600)
    54, 68, 70, 88, 95, 193
Uniform Rules for Collection (URC 522)
    53
  Uniform Rules for Collection
    commentary (550) 53
Uniform Rules for Contract Guarantees
    (URCG 325) 88
Uniform Rules for Demand Guarantees
    (URDG 758) 88
United Nations Trade Law Commission 12
User's Handbook to the URDG 92

warranty guarantee 87
working capital loan guarantee 136
World Bank, The 23, 164
  International Bank for Reconstruction
    and Development (IBRD) 180,
    182
  International Development Association
    (IDA) 180, 182
  International Finance Corporation (IFC)
    176, 178, 180, 182
  Multinational Investment Guarantee
    Agency (MIGA) 180, 182